KT-174-879

Join the Revolution

There's a revolution in healthcare today. We're taking more responsibility for our own wellness, and we're using complementary therapies designed to work along with modern medicine. Knowing that the physical, mental, emotional, and spiritual levels are all interconnected, we want to promote healing on all levels.

Author Jennifer Fraser believes the healing wisdom of our ancestors is within us all and, with training and practice, we can strengthen our natural abilities and become skilled healers. In *The Healer's Wisdom: Fundamentals of Whole Body Healing*, she teaches safe and effective healing techniques, including:

- Mind Power: visualizations and imagery, meditation, and affirmations

- Nutrition: specific healing foods and dietary supplements

- Bodywork: deep breathing, exercise, and hydrotherapy

- Massage Therapy: techniques and massage oils

- Herbal Healing: medicinal plants, essential oils, and aromatherapy

- Energy Treatments: healing touch and auras

- Chakra Work: the role of chakras in diagnosis and healing

- Crystal Healing: crystals and gemstones and their uses

- Color Therapy: specific colors for healing

- Emergency Care: first aid and how to recognize and handle emergencies

195 931

About the Author

Jennifer Fraser works as a practicing intuitive healer; she specializes in aromatherapy and energy treatments, which include chakra work, sound toning, color therapy, and crystals.

To Write to the Author

If you wish to contact the author or would like more information about this book, please write to the author in care of Llewellyn Worldwide and we will forward your request. Both the author and publisher appreciate hearing from you and learning of your enjoyment of this book and how it has helped you. Llewellyn Worldwide cannot guarantee that every letter written to the author can be answered, but all will be forwarded. Please write to:

Jennifer Fraser
℅ Llewellyn Worldwide
P.O. Box 64383, Dept. 0-7387-0182-3
St. Paul, MN 55164-0383, U.S.A.
Please enclose a self-addressed stamped envelope for reply,
or $1.00 to cover costs. If outside U.S.A., enclose
international postal reply coupon.

Many of Llewellyn's authors have websites with additional information and resources. For more information, please visit our website at
http://www.llewellyn.com

Jennifer Fraser

the
Healer's

crystal healing

Wisdom

NORWICH CITY COLLEGE LIBRARY		
Stock No.	195931	
Class	615.535 FRA	
Cat.	M	Proc. 3WKL

Fundamentals of Whole Body Healing

2002
Llewellyn Publications
St. Paul, Minnesota 55164-0383, U.S.A.

The Healer's Wisdom: Fundamentals of Whole Body Healing © 2002 by Jennifer Fraser. All rights reserved. No part of this book may be used or reproduced in any manner whatsoever, including Internet usage, without written permission from Llewellyn Publications except in the case of brief quotations embodied in critical articles and reviews.

First Edition
First Printing, 2002

Book design and editing by Karin Simoneau
Cover art © 2001 by Eyewire
Cover design by Kevin R. Brown
Interior illustrations by Jill Otto

Library of Congress Cataloging-in-Publication Data
Fraser, Jennifer, 1974-
    The healer's wisdom: fundamentals of whole body healing / Jennifer Fraser.
        p. cm.
    Includes index.
    ISBN 0-7387-0182-3
        1. Holistic medicine. 2. Naturopathy. 3. Healing. I. Title.

    R733 .F783 2002
    615.5'35—dc21   2001050636

Llewellyn Worldwide does not participate in, endorse, or have any authority or responsibility concerning private business transactions between our authors and the public.

All mail addressed to the author is forwarded but the publisher cannot, unless specifically instructed by the author, give out an address or phone number.

Any Internet references contained in this work are current at publication time, but the publisher cannot guarantee that a specific location will continue to be maintained. Please refer to the publisher's website for links to authors' websites and other sources.

Llewellyn Publications
A Division of Llewellyn Worldwide, Ltd.
P.O. Box 64383, Dept. 0-7387-0182-3
St. Paul, MN 55164-0383, U.S.A.
www.llewellyn.com

 Printed on recycled paper in the United States of America

For Doug,
whose love and support heals me completely

Contents

Acknowledgments

I would like to thank my editor, Karin Simoneau, and all the wonderful staff at Llewellyn for their dedication and encompassing vision.

Introduction

The Healing Path

Today our modern world is experiencing a dawning of accessible, practical, effective, and affordable healthcare in the form of complementary healing therapies. Many, many people are beginning to study ancient alternatives to standard medicine, as conventional medicine often does not adequately deal with the problems experienced by patients today. Complementary healing therapies encompass many of the oldest healing traditions on the planet. They are designed to focus on the whole body, gently and naturally promoting the body's own intrinsic healing processes to facilitate health and wellness. Complementary therapies work alongside of conventional medicine, blending the time-tested values of ancient healing therapies with the new techniques of modern alternative healing. They can be applied as healing therapies in themselves or can be used to ease the side effects of radical conventional treatments such as chemotherapy. A comprehensive system of alternative medicine incorporates a whole-body approach. These are natural treatments—not chemical manmade drugs and severe surgeries, but simple, pure therapies that gently facilitate the inner healing processes of the body. Applied properly, complementary therapies rebalance the body's functioning, enabling its systems to become stronger, healthier, and more efficient. These various treatments are not absolute cures, but instead are therapies that empower the body to heal itself.

The Healer's Wisdom is an instructional guide to complementary therapies. It was not written for those who want to seek patients; this type of professional healer needs certifications and doctorates. It is not a guide to help you to diagnose serious problems and illnesses; that kind of work is reserved for trained medical doctors. This book was written for the natural healers of our planet; the wise, gentle folk whose healing magic occurs when their patients find them. It is an instructional guide to safe and effective complementary therapies that can be administered to help relieve the pains from day-to-day ailments in yourself, your family, and those around you who may need your help.

As natural healers, our role is to be there when we are needed. We provide nourishment and support for a patient; present practical pain management techniques; administer safe, effective complementary therapies for diagnosed illnesses; deal with minor aggravating complaints; administer emergency first aid if necessary; and, most importantly, our task is to empower a patient to facilitate his body's own inner healing power. As natural healers, we do not replace regular physician care; rather, we work *with* medical doctors to give wisdom, love, and healing energies to a patient.

This book is a comprehensive and practical guide that covers the various components of health, including wellness maintenance, the nature of disease, safe and effective treatment of minor and chronic illnesses, pain management techniques, and disease prevention (by far the most important concept in healthcare is prevention). Specific treatments discussed in the book include the role of the mind in promoting health; diet and nutrition; herbal medicine; physical therapies like massage, hydrotherapy, deep breathing, and exercise; and healing in emergency situations. The text also encompasses energy field treatments such as aura and chakra therapy, crystal healing, and color therapy.

The Healer's Wisdom covers background information on the systems of the body, so you, the healer, have an understanding of its internal structure and functioning. It is extremely important that you spend the time to study and learn this information. It will allow you to gain a clear, concise picture of the inner workings of the body, a necessity in the knowledge base of a healer.

There are many complementary therapies that cannot be presented here— helpful therapies that require much more in-depth studies, including acupuncture, hypnosis, chiropractic treatment, and biofeedback training. Later in your healing quest you may want to look at some of these treatments and receive detailed instruction in them. You may also want to become certified and licensed in some of the healing therapies and techniques I have presented here, so you can perform these techniques professionally in a private practice.

Or, as a natural healer you may simply want to use your knowledge to heal yourself and others who may need your help. You do not need to heal others in order to be a healer; if all you ever do is apply the techniques from this book in order to maintain your own personal wellness, then you are a genuine healer. In any healing work, transformation must always begin with the self. A healer is only as good as the healing she has done on herself. The symbol of the natural healer is the spiral—a pattern of cycling wholeness, a circle that never repeats but moves outward and upward, encompassing all. But before you can reach out to help others, the center of your own healing spiral must be true.

I believe that anybody can learn to be a healer. Some people may possess better honed healing instincts than others, but with training and practice, anybody can strengthen their natural abilities and become a skilled healer. We all hold in our collective unconsciousness the ancient healing wisdom of our ancestors, and through exploration we can tap into this energy and apply it to aid our healing skills today.

And contrary to public opinion, it is not just women who are interested in complementary healing. The healing archetype is open to all who want to study it. Woman are more naturally drawn to healing, but men, too, are able to connect with their healing energy within, bringing love, nourishment, caring, compassion, and the desire to create wholeness to the healing profession. I hope that you will use this book as a guide to inspire your own healing energy.

This book is set up so you can learn the information and the various therapeutic techniques in small steps, building little by little, until you can create an encompassing knowledge base. Each chapter builds on the knowledge of the last, working to increase your healing wisdom. It is a course in self-healing that will facilitate personal development and transformation. Be prepared for your perceptions and beliefs to change as you progress through the course, for as we learn to heal others, we also experience a healing of the self.

The text can be used alone or in a study group with others. It is also an excellent reference guide. Work through the various therapies that you have an interest in, applying them to heal yourself and others. Some therapies may come naturally, and others may not feel right at all. You do not have to show a liking for every therapy.

For the book to be truly successful, you will need to do some practical healing work with the scope of the course. I can present you with the information, but it is the experiences that truly define a healer. Try to do a physical practicum in any area that interests you: take a class on crystals, get a basic first-aid ticket, book a massage lesson, explore energy healing through receiving a treatment yourself. Application of the techniques takes the healing energy that the mind has gathered in study and seats it into the body. We learn by doing; we become by being.

Your healing path will take you many places. The planet we live on is alive, and she yearns to teach us her ancient mysteries of health and wellness, happiness and wholeness. Tree, plant, rock, light, even animals hold healing wisdom inside, and when we learn to listen to her and her creatures we can perceive these profound energies of life. The healing power of nature is strong; spend the time to listen to her, for she will point out the way to restore balance and help aid the natural healing process.

As a healer, you will need to draw upon your own intuitive powers, your inner wisdom. For when we learn to listen, we also hear the wisdom of ourselves. The path of the healer was one that was wandered by our ancient grandmothers and grandfathers, and today their healing knowledge lies embedded deep within the inner recesses of the modern mind. Through enhanced awareness we can tap into this healing wisdom and use it to aid in our practice. Over the course of this book you will learn to do just this—to awaken the healer within. Through practice we learn to listen to the inner wisdom of the self, to trust that the power within will manifest the appropriate path.

By far the most important skill a healer can possess is the ability to listen. Listening supports and nourishes a patient. It is a simple gesture that heals through being consciously aware and attentive of a person and taking in what he has to share. Many problems can be helped by listening. So often we travel through life alone. As humans we need love and attention, and when we do not receive these needs, problems can manifest.

Illness does not happen out of the blue. It takes a long time coming, building slowly, cell by cell. Thus, it takes time to change patterns and cure problems. A specific symptom may manifest in one body part, but it is connected to the entire bodily system. All parts of the body are related, and all problems affect the whole. Therefore, it is essential that as a healer you focus on treating the whole person, and do not use an approach that only eliminates the symptom.

As natural healers we have a holistic approach to wellness. We are from the school of thought that says the whole is more than the sum of its parts. The physical, mental, emotional, and spiritual levels of a person are all interconnected, woven together to make a powerful whole. If one organ has a problem, then the entire body, the mind, the emotions, and the spirit all have problems as well. As a healer you need to strive to facilitate healing and balance on all levels of a person.

We treat each cell as special, encouraging and loving each tiny piece. In this way, the whole will flourish and be well. We look toward wholeness and love in order to help others live longer, healthier lives. Subtle energies pass from healer to patient; we are all connected in the healing process of life. And death is a part of healing as surely as life is. Every experience is integrated in a giant web of connections. For as we learn to heal each other, we also heal the self and the planet, for all are interconnected, all are related as one. Natural healing encompasses both the mind and the body and gives from the heart with nourishing and loving energy. It is complete.

I

Components of the Body

The system that we call the body is composed of a complex assemblage of cells, tubes, tissues, organs, glands, sensors, and nerves all working together to sustain existence. The body is truly a miraculous feat of engineering that demands our respect and our admiration.

It is necessary for healers to have an understanding of the essential systems of the body. This chapter includes information on the body's cells, structural system, respiratory system, circulatory system, digestive system, nervous system, the brain and the senses, hormonal control, defense mechanisms, energy field, and vibrational layers. Although this chapter is divided into separate sections covering the various systems, it is essential to remember that each system is innately linked to the next, as all components of the body work together to maintain the balance of life. The body is a complex assemblage of parts that function in a miraculous cooperative endeavor to sustain the whole.

As a healer it is important that you spend time studying this information. It provides essential groundwork for the start of your healing knowledge. It will allow you to understand the complex processes and needs of the body, presenting a firm foundation for your healing skills. It is one thing to learn the healing skills, but it is far better to know why you are applying them.

The Cells

We begin our exploration of the body with the cells, as they are the smallest living parts. Cells are the basic building blocks of life, with the body containing more than sixty million of them, all working together to form the individual systems. Cells perform all kinds of jobs, including manufacturing new chemicals, breaking down old ones, moving useful material through the body, excreting waste, dividing to create new cells, and many other essential tasks. Cells are constantly busy, and as they wear out they are continually replaced. A million new cells are formed every second. The liver is fully replaced in six weeks, the kidneys in one month, and the complete blood volume of the entire body is new in three weeks.

The complex structure of the body's cells allows them to perform their jobs. Each cell is driven by a nucleus, the brain center of the cell that contains the blueprint for the cell's purpose. Certain structures called *organelles* perform the actual work of the cells, creating chemicals and transporting them in and out of the cell. Each cell is surrounded by a membrane that holds the cell's contents in place and lets molecules pass through the cell. The cell is really like a living factory that networks with other factories to keep the body functioning at peak efficiency.

The Skeletal System

The skeleton is a complex framework of living material, containing over two hundred bones. The skeleton supports the body's tissues, protects internal organs, and provides anchor points for the muscles. Each bone is composed of active cells and has the marvelous property of being both flexible and rigid, as it is delicately formed from a mass of thin bone filaments.

Various joints permit a wide range of movement of the skeleton. Some joints are stiff and bracing, as they are filled with cartilage, like the supportive joints of the spine. Cartilage is very slippery and works to lower friction and absorb shock. Other joints are very flexible, as they are lubricated with synovial fluid; thus, they are called *synovial joints;* the knee joint is an example of a synovial joint.

Ligaments help to control the movement of joints. These tough fibrous cords attach to the bone casing on either side of the joint and hold it firmly in place, preventing it from twisting beyond its normal range of movement. Sometimes under heavy stress a ligament will tear and cause a painful injury, but ligaments really work to prevent more serious joint injuries.

Muscles

Movement of the body involves the coordination of the muscles. There are three types of muscles: striated muscles, which are composed of long fibrous cells bound tightly together; smooth muscles, which line the walls of the body's tubes and cavities, including the stomach, intestines, and blood vessels; and the cardiac muscle, which controls the heart beat. Smooth muscles and the cardiac muscle are known as involuntary muscles, as they work automatically without conscious effort, while striated muscles are anchored to bones and are primarily under the conscious control of the brain. There are over six hundred muscles in the body that we have conscious control over in order to facilitate movement.

Voluntary muscular action is really very simple: it works on the principle of contraction and relaxation. The brain sends a chemical nerve signal down to the muscle to send it into action. The muscle then physically reacts to the messenger. Most muscles function in pairs; one muscle contracts to move a bone or organ as another muscle relaxes. In order to reverse the movement and pull the bone back to its original position, the first muscle must relax and the second muscle then contracts. It takes the coordination of many muscles to produce the body's movements.

Muscles consume up to five times the amount of energy they produce, and their efficiency can be increased with exercise. Exercise is important—it supplies the body with higher oxygen levels, increases circulation, burns excess fat, and strengthens the muscles, heart, and lungs. Exercise is truly an essential first step in preventing many health problems.

The Respiratory System

The respiratory system brings life-giving air into the body. Oxygen is needed by the cells so they can burn food to fuel themselves in order to complete their various tasks. This process is called *cellular respiration,* and it begins when food arrives at the cell in the form of the simple sugar called *glucose.* Glucose is burned by the cell in order to release the energy contained in it. The hydrogen in glucose combines with oxygen to form water, while the carbon mixes with the oxygen to form carbon dioxide. Carbon dioxide must be expelled, as it is toxic to the body.

When we inhale, air is brought into the mouth and rushed down the larynx and into the windpipe, also known as the *trachea.* Inside the chest the trachea branches into two pieces, with each tube, or *bronchus,* leading into each lung. The tubes continue to redivide inside the lungs, becoming narrower and narrower until they are very tiny pipes called *bronchioles.* Around the end of each bronchiole hundreds of air sacs are clustered, much like a bunch of grapes. These tiny air sacs, called *alveoli,* are wrapped with webs of blood vessels that pick up the oxygen that flows through the thin walls of the alveoli. Unwanted carbon dioxide traveling in the blood stream passes into the alveoli to be expelled out of the body when we exhale.

There are miles of passages in the lungs. The lungs are an important elimination organ of the body, as they expel toxic carbon dioxide from the system and replace it with life-supporting oxygen. The lungs are like elastic bags that expand and draw air in when we inhale. Chest muscles pull the ribcage upward, while another domed layer of muscles (the diaphragm) flattens, expanding the lungs by pulling them downward. Air rushes in, filling the vacuum. The exhale is a no-effort movement, as the lungs collapse naturally when air is exhaled.

We need clean fresh air for normal body functioning, and yet most of us are shallow breathers and do not use all of our lung capacity. If we do not breathe fully, toxic residues are not fully removed from the body. There are several breathing techniques included in this book that promote deep breathing.

Ailments that infect the respiratory system include hay fever, asthma, bronchitis, pneumonia, sinusitis, and lung cancer.

The Circulatory System

Once oxygen is infused in the blood it must be delivered to the cells. The blood of the body works like a transport fluid that carries oxygen and food to the cells and removes waste products, taking them to the kidneys, liver, and lungs for filtering and disposal. It also works to help the guard the body against disease.

Blood is composed of three types of cells: circular shaped red blood cells that contain the substance hemoglobin, which carries oxygen; large white blood cells, called *leukocytes,* which fight infections; and tiny irregular-shaped cells, called *platelets,* which are responsible for the clotting factor of blood. Most of the blood's essential cells are formed in the marrow of the spinal bones, the ribs, and the breastbone of the body.

The heart is a powerful structure that pumps the blood throughout the body in an intricate system of blood vessels. This unique organ is like an automatic pump that works entirely on its own, functioning without an electrical activation. Most other muscles of the body need nerve stimulation to work, but the heart functions without conscious stimulation, even if removed from the body. As long as there is blood to pump, the heart will pump it. The heart is really composed of two pumps, a small one on the right side that controls the pulmonary circulatory system, and a larger, more powerful pump on the left that controls the systemic circulatory system. Both systems are part of the complete circulatory system and will be discussed later.

As the heart beats faster it supplies the body with more blood, increasing the oxygen flow to the body, and when it slows down it pumps less blood and, therefore, less oxygen. It speeds when we are physically active, as the body's cells are working harder to burn fuel and need more oxygen than at a resting rate.

The blood traveling through the body's vessels is controlled by muscular waves produced by the vessels, and they work to help maintain a constant blood pressure in the body. Too little blood and the cells may not get the oxygen they need, too much blood and the vessels and cells may be adversely affected. Blood pressure normally remains relatively steady and can be measured to determine the health of the circulatory system. Abnormally high blood pressure is a condition called *hypertension,* and it is connected to heart attacks and disease.

There are sixty thousand miles of blood vessels in the human body, and through them blood flows constantly, delivering oxygen to the cells and removing waste products like carbon dioxide. There are two distinct circulation systems in the body: a small system called the *pulmonary system* that feeds blood to and from the lungs in order to replenish the oxygen supply, and a larger system, the *systemic circulation system,* that supplies the oxygenated blood to the rest of the body. Both systems are controlled by the heart, with the pulmonary flow being controlled by the pump on the right side of the heart, and the systemic flow being controlled by the left side of the heart.

The pulmonary system only supplies blood to and from the lungs. It is the system that is responsible for replenishing the blood with the much-needed oxygen. The right side of the heart pumps deoxygenated blood away through a wide artery that feeds the blood into branches of small arterioles that lead to each lung. The arterioles further divide into minute capillaries that wrap around the alveoli, the tiny air sacs of the lungs. As the blood travels over the lungs, hemoglobin molecules in the red blood cells pick up oxygen from the alveoli and hold it. Here unwanted carbon dioxide molecules are removed from the blood and passed into the alveoli for the lungs to expel. The oxygenated blood flow is then fed back to the heart to be pumped through the systemic system.

In the systemic system, the now oxygen-rich blood is cycled throughout the whole body. The left side of the heart pumps the blood away through the arteries and down into branched arterioles. Just like the arterioles that lead to the lungs, the arterioles of the rest of the body divide into tiny capillaries that lead to the tissues of the body. When the blood flow reaches the capillaries, the hemoglobin of each red blood cell releases the oxygen molecule it was carrying so the needed oxygen can be absorbed by the individual cells. The hemoglobin then picks up any unwanted carbon dioxide and carries it back to the heart, where the blood is pumped into the pulmonary system so the carbon dioxide can be exchanged for fresh oxygen in the lungs.

The return system of blood vessels that carries the carbon dioxide-filled blood to the heart is like the system of vessels that carry oxygenated blood from the heart, but the main tubes and their branches are called *veins* and *venules* rather than arteries and arterioles.

Inside the body oxygenated blood traveling in the arteries is a deep scarlet color, while deoxygenated blood traveling in the veins is a dark, bluish-red color. For this reason, diagrams of the circulatory system will show the fresh oxygen-rich blood as red, and the deoxygenated carbon dioxide-filled blood as blue.

The heart and the circulatory system is very susceptible to disease. Heart disease accounts for half of all the deaths in the United States. The consequences of modern living are contributing to the increase of heart disease. Excess fat and low nourishment from processed foods clogs blood vessels and robs the body of nutrients; high stress levels increase blood pressure and oxidize cholesterol; too little exercise forces the systems to work harder and wear down; and cigarette smoking immensely contributes to coronary heart disease. One in every two smokers dies from smoking.

But heart disease is one of the most preventable chronic diseases. Through proper eating, exercise, stress reduction, and nutritional supplementation, the body can reverse damage and prevent future injury from happening. Heart disease can be prevented, which is good news for the millions of people who are at risk for developing the disease.

The Digestive System

The body breaks down the large molecules of food that we eat into tiny pieces that can be carried by the blood and absorbed by the cells. It is important that we eat a well-balanced diet of fresh foods that are high in nutrients, such as vegetables, fruits, fish, low-fat meats and dairy, seeds, and nuts, in order to ensure that our bodies are receiving the correct amounts of nutrients required for proper growth and maintained wellness.

The process of digestion begins in the mouth, where the jaw muscles snap the teeth together, grinding food particles into a pulp. An enzyme in saliva called *amylase* starts to break down starch molecules into simple sugars, and it also lubricates the food pulp so it can easily pass down the throat and into the esophagus. The food ball, called a *bolus,* is propelled downward by a process called *peristalsis.* In this process powerful waves of muscle contraction and relaxation pulse down the esophagus, pushing the bolus into the stomach.

Once in the stomach, the bolus is subject to both chemical and physical digestion. Glands in the stomach wall secrete gastric juices made of acid and enzymes that break down the food, while the peristaltic action of the stomach further churns the particles. The stomach walls are lined with a thick coating of mucus that works to protect it from the strong chemical juices. An ulcer is a painful condition that occurs when the mucus breaks down and the gastric juices start to eat at the tissues. The stomach acts like a bag that holds the partially digested food, allowing it to slowly pass by peristalsis into the small intestine.

When the food enters into the small intestine, it is a semifluid mash that is called *chyme.* In an area of the small intestine called the *duodenum,* the nutrients from the chyme are further broken down and then absorbed into the bloodstream. Bile that is manufactured in the liver is excreted into the intestine to help break down fat globules, while special enzymes break down amino acid chains of protein, and even more enzymes break down carbohydrates into tiny simple sugar molecules like glucose. The nutrients are absorbed through the millions of minuscule folds in the small intestine called *villi.* Each fold is covered in tiny capillaries that carry the precious food nutrients to the liver. The food particles that cannot be absorbed, like cellulose, are pushed into the large intestine and expelled out of the body through the anus.

The colon is the name for the last part of the large intestine. Its health is extremely necessary for proper digestion. We must have consistent bowel movements or the buildup of toxins and waste in the intestines creates blockages that can manifest as disease. To help the health of the intestines we need to eat high-fiber foods such as whole legumes, grains, vegetables, and fruit.

The role of the liver is to purify the blood of old cells and waste material. It is located in the lower part of right rib cage. The liver manufactures bile, and it also acts as a sort of dispatch center, sending food to the area where it is needed. It primarily controls the dispatch of glucose to cells, as glucose is the main energy source of the body's cells. The liver also keeps the useful amino acids from digested protein and sends what it cannot use to the kidneys for disposal. This waste fluid is called *urea,* and is a major component of urine.

The kidneys are an intricate filtration system of tubes that absorb all useful nutrients from the blood and allow water and wastes to flow onward into a collecting duct. Urine is about 96 percent water and 4 percent toxic wastes. The more water you drink, the lighter your urine will be. A dark-colored urine can indicate a urinary infection.

The urine drains through two pipes, one projecting from each kidney, called the *ureter;* it then passes into the bladder, an expandable holding sac. The bladder opens into two rings of muscles called *sphincter muscles.* The first one is an automatic muscle that relaxes when the bladder is full, and the second one we control. Urine passes out of the body through the rings of muscle when we relax our muscles and open the second sphincter.

The Nervous System

The nervous system works to coordinate the systems of the body. Nerves are like messengers of the body—they carry information to the organs and muscles, allowing us to formulate instant responses to the stimuli we are encountering. The nervous system is really composed of three structural systems: the central nervous system, the peripheral nervous system, and the automatic nervous system.

The central nervous system, or CNS, is comprised of the brain and the bundle of nerves running down the spine known as the *spinal cord.* The brain and spinal cord are encased in protective structures of bone and layers of supporting fluid and tissues. The brain resides inside the skull, and the spinal cord lies inside the spine bones.

Thousands of little nerves spread out from the CNS and connect to all areas of the body, forming what we call the *peripheral nervous system.* The peripheral nervous system has two types of nerves: sensory nerves that carry messages to the CNS from the body's sense receptors, and motor nerves that send instructions from the CNS to tissues and willfully controlled muscles. The automatic nervous system regulates internal involuntary operations like heart rate, digestion, and glandular function.

A nerve is like an electrical wire that transmits messages. The electrical impulses travel around the body through strings of interconnected cells called *neurons.* The neurons are not directly connected, but are separated by a tiny gap called a *synapse.* Electrical impulses leap across the gap while chemical transmissions involve the use of a special chemical called *neurotransmitters* to carry the message across the gap. To prevent the muscles from being overwhelmed by nerve signals, the synapses have receiving cells that can either pass the message or block it from being transmitted. It takes a fine balance between passing a nerve signal and inhibiting it in order to prevent the body from being overstimulated.

The Senses

Our five senses—sight, hearing, smell, taste, and touch—are important internal systems that allow us to perceive the world around us. The organs of the senses contain extremely sensitive receptors that transmit nerve messages to the brain for identification. The brain then deals appropriately with the messages, giving response orders to the body. The senses are essential survival tools, feeding us constant information about the world and allowing us to respond to dangerous situations.

Sight

The eyes allow us to perceive the world through the miraculous process of sight. No camera can equal the optical performance of the eye, with its sharpness and tremendous focusing range. It can automatically adjust its sensitivity to the amount of light present in the environment. Light is very important to the body; it enters the eyes and is absorbed by the cells.

The eye is really best looked at in two parts: the front part, which contains the lens needed to form the image, and the back part, which has the retina that registers the image. The transparent front cover of the lens is called the *cornea,* and it is the part that actually focuses the light rays from the environment on to the retina. The pupil is the dark spot in the middle of the eye. Controlled by the colored iris, the pupil is actually a circular window that helps improve the focusing of the image. When the amount of light in the environment is low, the pupil opens wide to let a maximum amount of light in, but when the light is ample, it narrows to create the sharpest image possible.

The retina is where the image is focused on the back of the eye. It contains a great deal of light sensitive receptors, over 130 million of them! The receptors record the light pattern created by the image and then transmit image signals to the brain via the optic nerve. The eye contains two types of receptors: rods that pick up images in both bright and dim lighting, and cones that distinguish color. Color is really just different lengths of light waves that the brain distinguishes through the stimulation of the individual cones. Cones only work with light, so at night they cease working and we only see with rods; thus, we do not see colors at night. There are three different types of cones; each reacts to a specific color—red, blue, or green—but the cone receptors overlap greatly.

Sound

The ears are valuable to us as a warning system, communication device, and pleasure mechanism. Sounds are really waves of vibration traveling through the air, and the complex organ of the ear is able to miraculously transform these vibrations into the enormous variety of sounds we hear in our world.

The ear is designed to collect sound waves from the air and funnel them into its passageway where they can be identified. The ear contains three parts: the outer ear, the middle ear, and the inner ear. The outer ear is the large flap we can see on the head, and its main job is to collect and funnel the sound waves into the middle ear. The passageway leading to the middle ear is coated with wax and lined with tiny hairs in order to keep out dirt and other irritants.

Inside the middle ear, the sound waves strike a membrane that is stretched over the passageway. This membrane is called the *eardrum,* and it passes the vibrations onto three tiny bones inside the ear, called the *hammer,* the *anvil,* and the *stirrup.* The three bones are linked together, and they work to amplify the sound waves, with each bone striking the next and transferring the sound along the inside of the ear. The last bone, the stirrup, knocks against the oval window, a thin membrane that is stretched over the entrance to the inner ear. The sound vibration is compressed and amplified here as it passes through the membrane into the inner ear.

Inside the inner ear, the pressure waves enter the *cochlea,* a fluid-filled passageway that is coiled up inside the ear like a snail shell. The cochlea is lined with small hairs that are called the *organ of Corti,* and it is these hairs that are really responsible for us being able to hear. As the sound waves run through the cochlea causing the hairs to wave back and forth, the hair cells transmit nerve signals to the brain to identify. The specific sound that is heard by the brain depends on which hairs are triggered to send signals.

Touch

The receptors for the sense of touch are spread out all over the body; there is not one square inch of skin that does not contain a touch receptor. The body's receptors are very sensitive and respond to a wide variety of sensations, from the gentlest touch to a pain sensation. They even determine hot and cold temperatures. When a skin receptor is stimulated, it sends a nerve signal directly to the brain for identification. The speed of the nerve signals tells the brain how heavy the touch is and the temperature of the touch. The receptors do not constantly send off signals though, as they adapt quickly to the stimulus. Once the brain has been notified of the touch there is no need to constantly send signals. This is why we cease to feel clothes and watches after we have been wearing them for a while.

Taste

The taste receptors of the body are found on the pores of the tongue in the form of little bumps called *taste buds*. The ten thousand taste buds on the tongue pick up distinct food flavors: the buds at the tip of the tongue respond to sweetness, the receptors at the sides detect salty foods, the taste buds near the back of the tongue identify sour foods, and the taste receptors at the very back of the tongue recognize bitter flavors. The saliva-dissolved food particles travel over the taste buds, and the receptors activate nerves that carry taste signals directly to the brain. The taste signals are processed in the brain, along with other signals such as food texture, smell, and temperature, in order to give us the full flavor of the food we are eating.

Smell

The sense of smell is a miraculous sense, as the human nose can distinguish over three thousand different chemicals. The ability to smell is an excellent survival mechanism of the body, as it can detect rotten food and poisonous substances. Inside the top of the nose there is a small area that contains about five million tiny olfactory receptors. These receptors are connected to nerve fibers that lead to the brain. The smell signals are transmitted through the nerve fibers to the olfactory lobe of the brain for analysis.

The Brain

The complex control center of the body, the brain is like a computer that is divided into several distinct regions, each with its own purpose. There are several billion neurons in the brain, with each one connected to thousands of tiny nerve fibers, creating billions of pathways for nerve signals to travel along. The brain requires an enormous amount of food and oxygen to function. The blood stream carries needed food and oxygen, and the brain uses almost one-quarter of the body's total blood supply.

There are three main parts to the brain: the brain stem, the cerebellum, and the cerebrum. The top of the spinal cord is called the brain stem, and this is where the nerve bundles widen to form the *medulla* and *pons*. The medulla and the pons (the place where all the nerves cross to enter the brain) are responsible for basic involuntary bodily functions like heart rate, blood pressure, breathing, circulation, and digestion.

At the back of the medulla lies the cerebellum. It coordinates body movements and facilitates the voluntary muscles to work in the right order. It further controls our sense of balance.

In the center of the forebrain lies a small ball called the *hypothalamus*. It coordinates the actions of the automatic nervous system; these actions include body temperature, thirst, hunger, sleeping, and waking. It also plays a role in influencing our emotions. Beside the hypothalamus is the *thalamus,* which is responsible for relaying all nerve signals from the senses into the cerebral hemispheres, known as the cerebrum.

The cerebrum is covered in the cortex, a layer of gray matter that is convoluted into dense folds that receive and interpret the messages from the thalamus. The brain grew outward from the brain stem during the course of evolution and so as our abilities advanced, the outer areas of the brain grew to control more sophisticated conscious activities like speech, movement, and critical thinking. The cerebral hemispheres are huge and wrinkled and densely packed with nerve fibers. They receive all conscious sensations such as sight and hearing, and this is also where we make decisions on our actions. Thoughts and intelligence are contained here as well.

Sleep

Humans spend over one-third of their lives sleeping. Body functions like brain activity, heart rate, breathing, and digestion all slow down during sleep. Throughout the night we experience phases of deep sleep that alternate with rapid eye movement sleep, or REM. REM sleep brings on vivid dreams. While no one knows for sure why we dream, many people think that dreams allow the mind to reflect on the day's experiences and relay messages from the subconscious mind to the conscious mind.

We all need different amounts of sleep, anywhere from four hours to ten hours a night. But when we find that we need over ten hours every night, this is a signal to consider lifestyle, diet, exercise, and emotional concerns to see what is causing the excess need for sleep. Problems relating to sleep include insomnia, sleepwalking, and overtiredness.

Hormones

Hormones are chemical messengers that work in conjunction with the nervous system to regulate the body. Hormones carry signals like nerves, but instead of split-second transmission, hormones deliver messages through the bloodstream at a much slower pace; however, their results are more widespread throughout the body and last longer.

Most hormones are made in specific glands that lie next to major blood vessels, called *endocrine glands.* Endocrine glands include the hypothalamus, which controls body temperature, thirst, hunger, sex drive, and secretions from the pituitary gland; the pituitary gland in the front of the brain, which controls bone growth and regulates the activity of the other glands; the pineal gland, which helps regulate the body's circadian rhythms and plays a role in the process of reproduction; the thyroids at the throat, which control the use of fuel and body development; the parathyroid, which sits behind the thyroids and controls the level of calcium in the blood; the thymus, which controls the production of infection-fighting white blood cells; the adrenals, which sit on top of the kidneys and control the salt and water balance in the body and help the body deal with emergencies; the pancreas, which controls the level of sugar in the blood; and the ovaries in women or the testes in men, which control sexual development and the production of eggs and sperm.

The endocrine glands produce various types of hormones. There are hormones that equalize certain systems of the body, such as insulin, which maintains blood sugar levels. When the pancreas does not produce the proper amount of insulin, the body's cells cannot absorb glucose and its level in the blood rises, producing a disease known as diabetes. There are also hormones that regulate development, such as growth and sex hormones. Adrenaline and noradrenaline are yet other types of hormones; their job is to prepare the body for peak performance when needed. In dangerous situations we experience an adrenaline rush, a condition during which the adrenal glands react on an alarm signal from the brain and release a flood of adrenaline and noradrenaline into the body to boost the heart beat and energy level in order to fight or flee from the danger.

The Defense System

The immune system is a very complex system designed to protect the body from harmful microbes. The amount of potential invaders in our world is enormous, with microbes living in the air, soil, water, in food, and on objects.

The skin is our first line of defense, as it prevents disease microbes from directly penetrating the body. If the skin becomes punctured, special chemicals in blood cause the formation of protective clots and scabs in order to seal the wound against further infection and blood loss. The skin also acts as an elimination organ, as it allows sweat to pass out of the body, carrying away internal toxins and working to cool the body through the process of evaporation.

If bacteria does get into the body, as in the case of a puncture wound, defense cells go to work attacking the foreign entity. As the bacteria damages and kills the cells around the wound, the cells release chemical messages into the surrounding tissue. These chemical messages are like cries for help. One of these chemicals, histamine, causes an inflammation of the area. It widens the blood vessels around the injury in order to increase the blood supply to the area, and it also increases the permeability of the blood vessel walls so that white blood defense cells can enter the tissue to attack the bacteria. Inflammation is a sign that the body is beginning to heal itself in a defense response to the attacking bacteria.

The white blood defense cells are called by the *chemical messages,* and they rush in to attack the bacteria. A type of granular leukocytes, called *neutrophils,* swallow and digest the foreign bacteria in a process called "cell eating," or *phagocytosis.* The neutrophils die in the process, and, thus, much of the pus that surrounds a wound is really dead white blood cells. Other nongranular types of white blood cells also travel to the infected area and engulf bacteria. They further provide instructions to help other defense cells identify and attack the intruding bacteria.

If the bacteria gets past the defense cells, it will be attacked by the body's lymphatic system. The lymphatic system is composed of tiny capillaries that function as drainage pipes for any excess tissue fluid, or lymph. The pipes gather the lymph from the spaces between body cells and direct it back into the blood stream. The lymph is filtered in lymph nodes and any invading microbes are removed by defense cells that are concentrated within the node.

But bacteria does not just enter the body through the skin. It can come from other sources like inhalation, eating, or drinking. Antibodies are cells that are specifically created to guard the body against particular infections, giving the defense system another level of protection. A germ that provokes an antibody response is called an *antigen,* while the specific response is called the *immune response.*

While a baby grows in the womb, it receives antibodies from its mother. But during the few weeks after birth a baby starts to make its own antibodies. Lymphocytes in the lymph nodes aid in this process. B lymphocytes create antibodies to fight disease microbes, while T lymphocytes fight microbes that hide inside cells and cannot be reached by antibodies.

As part of our society's medical treatment, we get regular vaccines to protect us from infectious diseases. A vaccine for a specific ailment is actually made from a harmless minute amount of the infectious microbes. The microbes stimulate the immune system to produce antibodies so the body can build a defense against the disease.

The Energy System

The human body is composed of cells, tissue, blood, and bone, but it also has a vast energy component. Quantum physics tells us that we, along with every molecule of the universe, are composed of dynamic waves of energy and space. The body is infused with an electromagnetic field that completely surrounds the physical form. This personal energy field is called the *aura,* and it holds traces of every experience that a person has been through. Psychic healers can detect these experiences; they can feel old breaks of the bone, perceive healed cancers, and even detect past incidences of physical abuse.

The aura is maintained by an anatomical alignment of energy concentrations called the *chakras.* Seven major chakras run in a line down the middle of the body and act as openings to the auric field. Through them the aura can give and receive all forms of energy. The auric field interacts with the universal energy field of the environment and also the fields of other living things.

When the field is functioning normally, it acts as a protective system for the body, defending the physical form from the full force of psychic vibrations and molecules of disease and negativity. However, the aura can become imbalanced and cease to function efficiently. Through stress, anxiety, improper diet, illness, lack of exercise, extreme emotions, or simply neglect, the flow of personal energy can become blocked or even deficient in areas. These conditions can eventually manifest as disease and injuries. Energy healers can detect and correct the field's problems, facilitating proper flow by removing blockages and filling in areas of deficiencies. Work on the energy field promotes physical healing of the body's tissues. Healing therapies for the energy system include aura therapy, chakra healings, and the application of the energy of crystals and colors.

Spiritual, Mental, Emotional, and Physical Layers

As human beings we exist on four vibrational levels: spiritual, mental, emotional, and physical. The levels progress from the highest and fastest vibrations of the spirit to the densest and slowest vibrations of the physical. The spiritual layer is the place of light and pure energy of the soul; the mental layer is where we hold intellect and make judgments and decisions; the emotional layer contains our feelings and passions; and the physical layer is the dense matter of the body.

Each level is an essential component of the self and is innately linked to the next. A problem on one level affects all. A disease in the physical layer is really the last sign of imbalance, as the problem first manifests in the spiritual, mental, and emotional layers. When working with healing energies it is important to consider the interrelationship of all the levels.

I would like to tell you everything about the cell, the bone, the blood, the brain, the intricate network formed by the activity of each tiny piece of the body working together to sustain life. But we cannot learn it all here. I ask you to please get a biology textbook and read about the specifics of the processes—the complexity of each cell, how the kidney uses its intricate filtration tubes to create urine, the marvelous job done by the liver to cleanse the body, the role of the glands and hormones to promote change in the body. I would like to discuss each cell that manufactures a life-giving substance, each tiny tube that transports something somewhere, each complex and fascinating process has a purpose and a name. But there is simply not enough space. Read, learn all you can, and then absorb it. This knowledge is a must in the study of the healer and will benefit your healing skills greatly.

2

Understanding the Healing Process

The body possesses an innate ability to heal itself. Here we will look at the healing process of the body in more depth, and discuss the role and responsibilities of the healer.

*M*ost of us live our day-to-day lives not sick with debilitating diseases but rather suffering from minor irritants—conditions such as asthma, anemia, headaches, fatigue, lack of energy, allergies, digestive problems, emotional upsets, and immune system deficiencies. These aliments can cause small daily annoyances, insignificant problems that are not usually enough to substantially disable us. Many times we do not even consider ourselves sick because these conditions have become a normal part of our lives.

But we do not have to suffer from these minor ailments; they are not supposed to be normal conditions for the body. The body is meant to function at optimum performance. It needs—in fact, craves—wholeness and health. What testifies to this need for peak equilibrium is the amazing fact that the body can heal and repair itself, reverse seemingly permanent damage from blindness, paralysis, cancer, diabetes, and other severely debilitating situations.

However, most of us let small irritants wear us down over time. Daily stresses create blockages in the physical channels of the body, weakening veins and arteries, inhibiting nerve circuitry, stagnating the body's energy flow, and hindering respiration pathways. The delicate balance of the systems are disturbed, and the body struggles constantly to reharmonize them. Minor conditions are like slow attacks on the body, degenerative assaults that gradually wear down equilibrium and wellness, and this can lead to severe disease.

Studies show that 30 percent of us will die between the ages of forty-five and seventy (Louria 1989). And yet a lot of the illnesses and conditions that precede premature death, such as debilitating physical decline, memory loss, adult diabetes, heart disease, and cancer, can actually be prevented. These illnesses do not have to be a part of aging. Through proper health maintenance, degenerative conditions can be avoided or even cured in the earliest stages.

Healthy living profits a person spiritually, physically, emotionally, and mentally. The more energy you invest into taking care of yourself in your younger years, the more it benefits you in later years. Many studies have proven that it is never too late to start making changes in your life, and it is important that you understand this. Even at age eighty, it is still not too late to begin a modified exercise program, stop smoking, or make improvements in diet. Simple preventative measures can make an enormous difference in health.

We have seen that the physical body is the densest level and, thus, is the last level to manifest the signs of an illness. It is a mirror of all the other levels. The condition of a physical disease can be seen in the actual word "disease"—a state of unease and unbalance in the body. Diseases and problems are like guides of the body, signs that show us the path to transformation and wellness. They alert us to the fact that change is needed and point out the way to balance, to easement. Symptoms are part of a complex warning system that can reveal many things about a person's health. They are really the natural attempts of the body to balance and heal itself. A fever is a symptom of an infection that is produced by the body in an attempt to fight the infection.

If we can learn to listen to the messages behind our illnesses, we can become aware of new strategies for healthier living. Too often we overcomplicate and confound problems, expounding their negatives and refusing to stop and explore the inner wisdom they hold. Illnesses are signposts that point out the way to change. Pain, too, is a survival signal, alerting the conscious mind to internal problems so we can make changes to prevent worse damage from occurring. It is a beacon for transformation, but we only become aware of it when we examine its signals and ask ourselves how we can correct the imbalance.

Conventional modern medicine is considered to be allopathic. This means that treatment is designed to eliminate the body's symptoms and does not deal with the originating cause. Modern medicine often does not look deeper into signals, but uses procedures like surgery to cut and remove bothersome problems: antibiotics to purge the body of all bacteria, killing both good and bad; tranquilizers to sedate and numb; the use of impersonal and often painful high-tech equipment to obtain information; and powerful drugs that have severe and devastating side effects. While these extreme methods work for some situations, they fail for others.

If we only focus on eliminating the symptoms of the disease, it can manifest permanently in the body. As natural healers we need to look beyond the symptoms to find the root causes of problems. If I have recurring digestive problems, I can take medicine to alleviate my pain, but I need to ask myself what is causing the problem. I need to look at my entire lifestyle, including diet, habits, exercise, stress, mental patterns, emotional states, and spiritual inclinations to find the originating causes. Often the physical layer is not the source of the issue; it frequently goes deeper into the emotional and mental layers. A natural healer's approach is more than body orientated; it takes into account all layers. A holistic approach allows us to reach deeper levels of healing and break through the barriers often missed by conventional medicine.

Whether we recognize it or not, we create our own worlds through our thoughts, actions, and words. We are usually unaware of our role as creator of our own worlds, but the more we come to realize this, the more we can make conscious choices to change our worlds for the better. Most of us are born healthy, and the problems we experience are mainly self-created.

Disease can often be a karmic issue as well. Many of us carry health issues from our past lives. It is important to examine illness patterns in our present lives, as they are often health problems we have dealt with in other lives.

Recognizing and striving to stop harmful patterns now can eliminate the cycle of these problems.

It is important to realize that there can be many complicated causes for illness, and we will not always know why a problem has manifested. But it is not always essential that we know. Conditions are caused by an imbalance somewhere, and sometimes all that is needed to heal them is a willingness to rebalance the body. The paths we travel are individually created by ourselves, shaped and altered by our life patterns.

Thus, if we create our conditions from within, then true healing can only come from within. We are completely responsible for our own health; only we can make the decisions to create changes in lifestyle, diet, attitudes, habits, and exercise levels. Everybody has the potential to heal themselves, and as healers we can help others release this potential in themselves. We do not heal patients . . . they heal themselves. We may give them healing vibrations, but it is truly up to the patients to decide how they will use those energies. Sometimes a body will get well; other times it will not. The only person who can cure is the person who owns the disease. We just help people connect with their own healing wisdom.

Often patients want the healer to do the work, but this is not going to happen. We cannot rely on doctors to maintain our health; healing is always much more effective and quicker if the person takes primary responsibility and is actively involved in the process. Problems provide us with wonderful opportunities for growth and self-improvement.

It is important to realize that people need time and gentleness to come to an understanding, to find the truth in situations. It may take several healing sessions for enlightenment to occur. Healing is a constant dynamic process of refinement and modification of ideas and concepts. Illness is formed from many causes, and the gifts it brings are multilayered as well.

But the body is our ally in the healing process. It is a self-regulating system, programmed to heal. Look at the immune system; it reacts when we have a cut, clotting to stop blood loss and sending defense cells to the area to kill bacteria and repair tissues. Deep in the cellular layer we hold the essential energies of good health, and deep within the brain we hold ancient ancestral energies of healing. These energies were crucial to our survival as early humans, and in our healing work we will use techniques to tap into these potent energies to apply them in modern healing situations.

As human beings one of our highest needs is the daily influx of healing energies. We all lug around the wounds of life. Each of us holds pain from past experiences and deals daily with feelings of guilt and fear. Through experience we can learn how to deal with this energy, but it is a struggle. Healing vibrations can help soothe personal agitation, as they wash through the systems of the body and cleanse the excess energy from the corners of the mind and receptors of the soul.

Individuals who maintain close social relationships experience loving, healing vibrations on a day-to-day to basis and, thus, they live longer and are healthier. Many studies have shown that people who have strong social supports experience lower stress levels, have a healthier level of blood pressure, and suffer from less depression, cancers, and cases of heart attacks and heart disease than people who are isolated (Campbell 1993, Louria 1989). Laughter is known to boost the immune system. When we connect with others we have people with whom we can share smiles, laughter, and love. Healers gives love to their patients as well as healing energies. I will tell you that unconditional love is the most powerful thing in the universe; it can cure cancer, end wars, and heal the planet.

General Guidelines for Healers

To be a healer is to be in a position of trust and responsibility. It demands that we adhere to an ethical code when working with the energies of another person. In this section we will discuss some of the fundamental guidelines that are needed in the study of the healer.

Complementary therapies can be used to treat minor problems that you know are not serious, such as insect bites and stings (in those patients who are not experiencing allergic reactions), colds, occasional diarrhea and constipation, digestive upsets, minor gas, occasional insomnia, minor headaches and stomachaches, motion sickness, minor sprains and bruises, symptoms caused by moments of stress and tension, earaches, minor skin irritations, and very minor burns.

But you must insist that someone with a serious problem see a licensed doctor before you offer any healing suggestions. We do not diagnose problems unless we are specifically trained to do so. Many people who seek treatment from you may be doing so because they are frightened of what a doctor may say. You would not want to temporally alleviate a patient's symptoms and prevent detection of a serious condition. Complementary therapies always work best within the context of conventional medicine.

Serious problems that require professional medical attention include persistent and recurring ailments like chronic constipation and diarrhea, internal pain with no apparent cause, continual fatigue, skin rashes, recurring headaches or earaches, breathing problems, serious depression, and chronic insomnia. Individuals experiencing severe conditions like fever, flu, violent nausea, hallucination, fainting, dizziness, pain, or heart problems must seek the immediate advice of a licensed doctor. Also, any condition that does not improve, worsens, or lasts over three days should be brought to the attention of the patient's physician.

With a diagnosed illness it is possible to use complementary therapies for treatment, but a patient needs to discuss the proposed treatments with her doctor first. Never ignore the advice of medical doctors. As natural healers we work beside doctors and conventional medicine, never in opposition with them. Please do not oppose a patient's choice of a doctor, either. As a healer, patients trust you immensely, allowing you access into their lives and their health concerns, and you need to be mindful and respectful of their choices.

Generally, meditation and positive visualization treatments, nutritional recommendations, energy techniques such as aura and chakra manipulation, color and crystal healing, and properly administered treatments of massage, hydrotherapy, and aromatherapy are safe and effective regimens for most problems. But each treatment has certain contraindications, which are specific conditions under which you should not administer the treatments.

The care of cancer patients is an example of a contraindication for the healing treatment of massage. Massage is thought by some to be harmful to cancer patients, as the movements may spread the cancer cells through the body. New research has discovered that gentle massage can be beneficial for cancer patients, but any massage treatment should be okayed by a cancer patient's doctor first. The contraindications of each healing treatment are discussed thoroughly in the appropriate sections of this book. As a responsible healer, it is essential that you learn about and respect the contraindications of each treatment. And we never, ever heal someone without their permission, except in an emergency situation. And if you do not have first-aid certification, in emergency situations it is often best to call 911 and follow the advice of the operator. To heal someone without his permission violates his free will and, ethically, is a karmic error. So, for example, do not slip herbs into a person's food or schedule treatments for problems when it is clear that he does not want your help. At times you may be approached by well meaning relatives or friends of an ill person and asked about treatment for that person. As a healer you need to always ask whether or not the person wants treatment or healing advice. Generally, if a person wanted advice or treatment, he would have sought it for himself.

This concept is so important to adhere to because even when you think that you are helping someone, you may actually be harming her. Some people need to hold on to their problems. Prolonging an illness can grant a person many beneficial circumstances: comfort, attention, respect, pity, sympathy, suspension from fear, opportunities to rest, vent, withdraw, or it can even give a person an opportunity to think about the course of her life. Illness is a teacher of many things, and it is not the healer's job to decide when a person has learned enough and is ready for change. It must always be the responsibility of an individual to seek treatment when she is ready to accept the difficult work of transformation. For some people, this may be never.

I know that it can be frustrating to watch a person, especially a loved one, struggle with a situation when you know you could help, but if you have offered your skills and the person refuses to accept them, then you must accept that he has chosen to deal with the situation without you. This does not mean that you cannot offer your help again; if you truly feel that you can help him, then by all means, offer once more, but it does mean that you must respect his decision and not interfere with the situation behind his back. This can be a very difficult concept for some healers to understand and accept, and so it is important that you think about it now and make a conscious decision to avoid interfering before there comes a time when you are emotionally involved in a personal situation of this nature.

It is essential that you practice the skills of healing on yourself first. Learning to work with the self can be a new and frightening concept to some, but it is a necessity. The center of your healing spiral must be true in order for it encompass others. So practice the therapies in your daily life: fill your diet with healing foods; study the properties of the various herbs and make some herbal teas to treat your own minor symptoms of everyday living; purchase a few essential oils and experiment with the soothing and stimulating powers of aromatherapy; practice the bodywork techniques of massage, deep breathing, and hydrotherapy on yourself; learn to detect and strengthen your body's own energy field, explore the effects of crystal healing, and try out the various energies of color to heal complaints. There are many practical exercises included in this book, and you need to make a genuine effort to work through them and apply the various techniques to your own situations of healing.

Learn as much as you can, as education is the key to your power. In all the aspects of your studies, read the recommended books. Therapies evolve as new information about the body is discovered, and it is important that you make an effort to keep up to date on the therapies you are interested in applying to your healing practice. Read new books as they are published. Realize that your understanding of disease and healing will change over time and through experiences.

Study the information, and then take the time to apply it to practical situations. Practice your healing skills as much as you can. People love to get massage treatments and energy healings. Perfect your techniques on your friends and family, and ask for their feedback in order to see how you are doing.

The studies of the healer can be quite consuming. It is important that you remember to take time to heal yourself. In their quest to help others, many healers often neglect the messages of their own bodies. If you ignore the conditions of your body, you can become seriously ill through association with others who are ill. Your immune system must be strengthened so it can resist the daily bombardment of germs. It also takes an enormous amount of personal energy output to heal others, and if you are not in maximum health, the extra energy outlay can be harmful to your own body. If you are not well, then you must focus on healing yourself before you begin to heal others.

You need to learn how to recognize the times when you should not heal. As humans we cannot exist in a state of positive vibration all the time; we are emotional creatures who do not always give out loving, healing vibrations. Sometimes we can project harm, either by will or by ignorance. It is the responsibility of the healer to strive to understand the cycles of the self and learn how to properly use healing power. If you are ill, tired, stressed, in a bad mood, experiencing an altered state of mind, suffering from depression, or are otherwise preoccupied, then you need to realize that these are not appropriate times for you to heal another. Under these circumstances your energy must be focused on healing your own mind and body before you offer to take on the responsibility of another person's health. Your credibility as a healer demands it. Being responsible also takes into account the ability to recognize when a healing situation is beyond your skills and when it is appropriate for you to recommend that an individual see a licensed medical practitioner.

In the text I often refer to a person in need of healing energies as your "partner," for truly this is how I feel. A healer does not hold a position that is superior to the person with the difficulty; rather, a healer and a patient are partners in the healing process. As a healer, it is important that you work on fostering a nonjudgmental attitude. There is no room for smugness or conceit in a healer's demeanor, as all people need to be treated with respect and sincerity. The healer acts as a guide, introducing the patient to her own inner healing power. It is the complete responsibility of the patient to take control of her own healing. Sometimes in life we shy away from accepting personal responsibility, and you must realize that it is not the job of the healer to take on this responsibility. Our primary task is to empower a patient to shine in her own power. The healer provides a map of the journey, but the actual traveling has to be done by the patient. It is important that you stress to your patients their responsibility to implement positive behaviors for the healing process to be effective.

As a healer you also need to keep detailed notes of your healing research, applied treatments, and the results. Create a healer's notebook with two sections: one for your treatment studies and personal research, and the other for documenting specific treatments. Be very thorough about recording the day, the patient, his allergies and other important personal information, the problem, and the specific treatment. You should also judge your performance, and create a written evaluation of the steps you took. This will help you to learn the skills you have mastered and the skills you may need to practice more.

I realize that most of your healing situations will be informal, impromptu circumstances such as administering a shoulder rub to a coworker or recommending an herb to a neighbor for a cold, but it is important that you take the time to record the specifics of the situation in your notebook. Any healing situation, no matter how small, should be noted. You should especially record your own personal healing situations and treatments. This record is a physical chart of your healing experience and should be taken very seriously. It gives you a basis with which you can consult in the future for effective treatment suggestions, and it is also a permanent record of your accumulating skills and abilities.

Specific Steps of a Healing Treatment

There are three parts to a healing treatment: the initial assessment, the work of the treatment, and the aftercare. The initial assessment is a consultation period for you and the client during which you will figure out together the exact healing energies the patient may need. This is not a medical diagnosis, as we are not trained to make those types of decisions. Rather, an assessment is an information-gathering session that will allow you to formulate a specific healing plan for the individual.

What is the client looking for in a treatment? What treatments has he tried before? Has he seen a licensed physician for a medical diagnosis of his condition? As a responsible healer you need to encourage your patients to consult with a licensed doctor for a proper diagnosis of problems. We cannot treat people who have serious problems if they have not first seen a doctor. Encourage your clients to have annual medical tests such as general physicals, breast examinations, pap smears, blood tests, and prostate checks.

In your assessment, decide as a healer what you think the client needs. Ask the client to explain what she thinks she needs, and carefully listen to what she has to say. It can be useful to jot down a few notes while she talks. Often a patient will consciously withhold pertinent information from you. Pay attention to detail, closely observe the patient and try to see her as she really is. Ask the patient if she is taking any medicines or has any problems that you should know about, like injuries, allergies, cancers, or emotional difficulties. Ask women about pregnancies. Encourage your patients to discuss their lives with you, and then listen and look carefully at their responses.

Gather as much information as you can, and then you and the client should decide on a course of action. Be sure that you thoroughly discuss the steps of any proposed treatment with him. Sometimes clients may be apprehensive about the suggested treatment, and if they are not receptive to one treatment, suggest another. If a person does not believe in the ability of "rocks" to heal, then he will not benefit from even the most intensive crystal healing treatment. You know that belief is very important in healing success. By watching the reactions of your clients, you will be able to tell during the initial consultation which techniques the client is open to receiving at this time.

Flexibility in your practice is also very important. A valued skill of the healer, flexibility allows you to flow with the changes of life, to modify your approach to fit a new situation. Not every healing approach is appropriate for every person. What works for one person may not work for another, as each body is different and reacts individually to a situation. Specific healing treatments need to tailored to accommodate a person's biochemical uniqueness. Some healers have a tendency to rush into administering a treatment to a patient because it worked successfully for someone else. You need to slow down and spend time considering the best treatment for the individual person. Learn to use a variety of techniques in your work, as there are many effective healing approaches available to healers today. Over the course of the book you will learn various techniques to tap into your inner healing sense in order to look for underlying causes of situations and to determine the best course of treatment to follow for the individual.

Be sure to discuss any proposed treatment with the patient thoroughly. Do not withhold information from patients, as they trust you to be honest with them. And do not be afraid to admit that you do not know something, or that you need to research a topic. A patient will respect your honesty.

Do not give a prognosis or tell a patient that a therapy will cure a condition. A prognosis is only to be given by licensed doctors. We never know when the healing will occur, or even whether it will occur at all. We simply transfer healing energy to the body, and the body uses it as it needs in its own time. Complementary therapies work to balance the body, allowing it to heal itself; they do not cure ailments or illnesses. Again, only a person who holds the energies of the problem can transform the problem. We do not cure; we simply help individuals cure themselves. We also do not want to give false hope. There is always hope, and patients need to believe this, but as a healer you do not want to be overzealous and promote false hope. I tell my clients that after the treatment is administered, we need to wait and see how their bodies respond.

What you can do is empower your patients to look for the gift of their problems; every difficulty has a truth to teach, every illness leads us to answers about what the body needs. Even in pain there is a gift, as it allows us to understand pleasure and points out a path back to happiness and enjoyment. As we explore deeper into our distresses, we push past limitations and blockages.

Through imbalance we are lead to discover insights and find new possibilities. Anything really worth learning is hard and often painful. But when we learn to listen to the messages of our bodies, when we learn to seek the deeper wisdom within, then health and vitality become available to us. Cell by cell we can then replenish the body, harmonize it, and heal it.

Be careful that you do not blame a person for his pain or problems. We may create our own conditions, but we build them in order to learn from them, not to be criticized or blamed for them. Try to open a person's awareness, and see if he can come to a realization about the positives or the lessons of his problems. You can gently guide patients through any unhelpful patterns in their lives that you may observe, but be careful not to judge or accuse. Our role as healers is to inspire a person's life force, to promote and activate it, and to allow it to heal its owner.

In the second part of a healing treatment, we begin administering the actual work of the treatment. With any treatment you need to remember that human beings are extremely fragile. Be careful with your clients; do not get so close to them that they feel uncomfortable. A healer needs to possess an understanding of personal limits and boundaries. Sense when a partner has reached her boundaries, and at that moment, do not pry. People give up what they need to, when they need to. It is a very intimate situation to be involved in a person's healing process, and you want to be able to help a person without invading. Too many doctors are already cold and intruding.

In bodywork and energy treatments, the best healers are those who are invisible, as they allow patients to completely enjoy the experience, unaware of their presence. Some people are innately shy and sensitive, and you don't want to make them feel uncomfortable by assaulting their personal space. Also, ensure that you never touch a person inappropriately. Over time and through practice you will learn how to tailor your healing treatments so you will put people at ease and only help to a level that they can comfortably accept.

Respecting limits also takes into account client confidentially. Anything that clients tell you as their healer is a strict confidential matter between the two of you. It is not to be repeated with others. You should also learn the valuable technique of forgetting what is said outside of treatment, for if you do not, you will be carrying these things around with you. It is one thing to empathize with an individual's pain, but it is completely another to embody it.

You need to remember that this is your partner's pain, her gift to learn from, her own experience from which to gain perspective. This is not your pain. Your pain is different, distinct, tailored to you and your gifts. Do not take in other's pain. You do not need external energy of this form. As a healer, your first responsibility is to take care of your own health and emotions. Love, laugh, support, share, nurture, guide, teach, give, but do not embody.

Have the courage and wisdom to stop and think objectively. How can you help this person to open? How can you ensure that you are safe? Pay close attention to your natural instincts, follow your feelings, and let your own healing guides lead you to the right answers. If someone makes you feel uncomfortable, you do not have to heal him. Realize it is not your responsibility to heal the world.

In all your studies and practice, it is imperative that you take proper precautions for your own safety. Do not handle herbs or essential oils that you are allergic to; do not massage with an oil that irritates your skin or annoys your sense of smell; do not massage or touch open sores, rashes, or broken skin on a patient; be very careful to avoid coming in contact with the bodily fluids of a patient; do not try to help patients with severely contagious illnesses; avoid contact with children who have measles, mumps, or chicken pox if you have not had these childhood illnesses; always strengthen your own energy shield before working with another person's energy; and be sure to eat something after expending your own energy. These are simple guidelines, but they must be adhered to in order to protect your own health.

It's also essential that you make a commitment to thoroughly wash your hands before and after any healing treatment and even before and after handling herbs and essential oils. Many illnesses, including the common cold, are spread through hand-to-hand contact. You should be washing your hands several times a day, anyway. You would not want to get a massage from someone who has dirt under her fingernails, and neither does your client.

Washing your hands is not only sanitary and works to prevent the spread of disease, but it also has psychological effects as well. Through repeated usage it will signify to your mind that healing work is about to be performed. It acts as a trigger, facilitating your conscious mind to tap into the innate healing energy held within the unconscious and bring it up to your conscious awareness. In this way your work can be empowered with healing energy. In order for this technique to be effective, you need to make it a strict habit to wash your hands before and after all healing work.

I want to talk for a moment about the hands. The hands are miraculous creations of blood and bone and tissue. We are as advanced as we are in our evolutionary path because of the power of the hands. They pushed the course of evolution to unlimited heights, possessing the incredible ability to create what the mind desires. The hand is a marvelous invention with a complex assemblage of parts that enable it to perform work, to pick up and hold things, to create new manifestations, and to contain such grace, delicacy, and possibility.

As a healer, your hands are the most essential tool you own. They reveal everything about you. Through your hands you will learn how to touch someone, how to handle their body so you create feelings of pleasure and wellness in their form. In your work, practice adapting your fingers to the form of a person's body, tracing down the curves and contours, sensing the energy field, and perceiving the subtle lines of the person's physical and energy boundaries. As you work with your hands they will develop acute sensitivity, and you will become conscious of every muscle movement and every bend of the fingers. A healer's hands are a valuable, natural tool.

When you are administering healing treatments it is important that you are properly prepared. Accurate knowledge of what you are doing and self-protection are essential, but there are subtler guidelines to follow as well. Be sure that you are working in a place where you feel comfortable. Being comfortable in your surroundings puts you in a state of ease and enables you to do your job to the best of your abilities. I charge my healing room with positive energy and place a large quartz crystal in each corner to create a protected, healing center. If you are performing a healing in an unfamiliar environment, then I suggest you place quartz crystals in each corner of the room to create an energy field that will balance the energy of the room.

You should also avoid wearing strong perfume, as the scent can be bothersome to some people and will interfere with their experience. Before you perform any healing treatment, spend some time in meditation, breathing and mentally centering yourself for the work you are about to do. In chapter 3 there are several healer's exercises for mental preparation. Perform them before undertaking any type of treatment. And always try to be prepared in your practice, to have all the resource material and tools that you need available with you whenever possible.

It must be said that you are completely responsible for the comfort of a person while they are in your care. The more relaxed and open you can make a patient feel, the more successful your healing treatment will be. The healer needs to be approachable and possess a manner that embodies sensitivity, warmth, caring, and openness. If a person is comfortable, he can be led to understand, to see new approaches, to find the roots of imbalance and disease, and to see how to weed them out of the body.

Give time to each patient. Do not rush through a massage because you need to pick the kids up from school. Schedule treatments when you have ample time to spend with each person. Some bodywork treatments, like massage and energy healing, can evolve into a whole afternoon session. Bodywork treatments and energy work can drastically alter a person's sense of time, so it can be wise to set a time limit beforehand so both you and the patient understand when the session is over.

There is a strong meditative aspect to healing. When we focus the mind and draw upon the consciousness within, we are intuitively guided. The truth bubbles forth, the correct answers just come. In all your healing work, strive to focus on what you are doing; push mundane thoughts aside and stay aware of what is going on with you and the patient. Watch for physical changes in her demeanor, like changes in breathing patterns, skin color and texture, and auric field colors and boundaries. These shifts will let you know how a person is responding to treatment.

It is such an intimate thing to open the heart of another, to guide him to his own tides of personal healing power. We keep our power so tightly bottled up, so compressed from fear inside of our self-constructed shields, it's no one wonder we get cancers. There is too much energy concentrated in one core; power is meant to flow, to cycle, to give out and get back. Only in flow is the soul at peace and does love manifest freely.

When we start to realize this flow, there is a release that occurs on all levels. The soul sings, the mind races, the body pulses, and the emotions flow. Be aware of the sensitivities of your patients. As their bodies begin to heal, they will pass through the detoxification process and will need your support. Detoxification has been called a healing crisis because as the body cleanses itself, old symptoms and emotions rise to the surface and enter into the conscious mind on their way to expulsion. Mental, emotional, physical, and spiritual levels all give off energies during the purging process, and bathing, crying, and exercise can all be useful for speeding up the process. Detoxification is an important part of healing, as it can prevent the progression of a problem from the acute phase into a chronic condition. As a healer you need to support a person through the detoxification process.

Emotional release can come at many points of a healing treatment, and you need to be loving and supportive when it happens. Focus your partner on deep breathing and feeling secure in her mental safe place, have tissues ready, and give a hug if asked for. You do not have to have a solution; it is enough to simply listen and be there. Often there is no need to say anything at all. The power of silence can be very great, indeed.

The third part of a healing treatment is the aftercare discussion. At this point you and the client should discuss the treatment. What did he get out of it? Is he feeling better, looking better? Explore any insights that you or the client may have had during the treatment. Discuss with him any aftercare particulars of the specific treatment, and any other healing recommendations you may want him to consider, such as diet and nutritional changes, suggestions about how to stop smoking, exercise regimens, daily meditation and positive thinking, and professional help.

You also need to perform a personal analysis of each session. Trace the steps you took, pinpointing which ones were easy and which you may have had difficulties with and need more practice. Write down your results in a notebook. Be honest. At any point did you lose centering? How can you prevent this for next time? What did you and the client accomplish during the treatment? Was there a visual difference in her body after the treatment? Was there more that you could have done? What do you think are some of the originating causes of the illness? What else did you suggest to help the client? What do you need to work on in your personal life as a healer? Remember that you should not exhausted by a healing, but rather infused and energized with healing energy from the universe, and if you are fatigued, then you need to look at ways to protect yourself.

Realize that it may take a long time for healing to occur. You must be respectful of flow and timing in your practice. Some problems have more to teach the person and this instruction cannot be rushed. As healers, we are here to gently guide others to the path of personal healing empowerment; we are not here to push them. Things change when they are ready, and not one second before.

After administering a healing treatment, you need to take personal time for yourself to replenish your energy and soothe your spirit. Enjoy an herbal tea, eat some nourishing food, soak in a healing bath, gently exercise, nap, meditate, or curl up with a good book. You need these simple, spiritual moments of solitude to rejuvenate your body and soul. It takes a lot of energy and love to heal another, and it is important that you give this love and attention back to yourself.

I think it is important to discuss the issue of payment. If you are not certified in any of these treatments, then I do not feel that it is right to ask for payment, and, indeed, many state laws prohibit an unlicensed bodywork practitioner to operate professionally. I generally do not ask for payment; I help people because I want to. People often give me gifts of food, bodywork, or friendship in return for my healing skills, and, for me, that is payment enough. And, of course, by far the greatest gift that a healer can receive is a patient's wellness.

3

Healing and the Mind

Complementary healing is a comprehensive approach to wellness that not only focuses on treating the body, but encompasses the mind as well. New revelations in science bring us overwhelming evidence demonstrating the incredible power of the mind's ability to heal the physical body.

The mind has an enormous influence on the self; it ultimately regulates every part of us and every part of our lives. It alone holds the power to heal or to harm, as the mind's thoughts are potent energy streams, direct allies that can help us or foes that can hurt us, depending on how we use them. If an individual does not believe he will be well, then he will not be. We all know we can think ourselves sick, but few of us really know that we can think ourselves well. The inner strength of the mind can be directed for healing just as easily as it can be focused on harm. The mind is probably the most important element in wellness, and attending to it is vital in promoting recovery.

Thoughts are simply charged energy packets that can produce drastic changes in the body. External stimuli from outside sources hits our personal energy fields and is either absorbed or deflected. We have a choice about whether we want to keep the external thought energy and take it into the mind or let it slide off of us; in other words, we choose how we want to think according to perceptions of past experiences that condition the mind to either assimilate or reject the new energy. As we accept external energy it further influences our personal thoughts because the subtle mind energy draws other like-minded thoughts to it just like a magnet, building a pattern of energy. Positive thoughts collect more positive thoughts, but dwell on the negative and all you will see will be more negativity.

The pictures we create are molded in the mind, but their energy stream's projections get stuck in the auric field around the body. Thus, we manifest what we think, as we live in those pictures constantly; we live in the aura. When we focus on something we give it life, so it is important that we create positive pictures and keep them positive. Putting good thoughts in the mind is like filling the body with fresh nutritious food. If we fill the mind with negative, self-defeating thoughts, it is like eating a steady diet of candy bars and soda pop. What you feed your mind is just as important as what you feed your body.

There is also a strong connection between the emotions and health. Between the brain and the immune system there are direct neurological pathways. Unexpressed feelings such as fear, guilt, anger, or jealousy act as neurochemicals in the body, stimulating the nervous system and triggering uncontrollable reactions like acceleration of heart rate, intensified breathing, tightening of the stomach, and repeated bouts of wear on the organs. They keep the systems of the body constantly active, stressing the tissues and decreasing the strength of the immune system and the individual organs. Repressed emotions can literally burn out the body and leave it susceptible to disease. They can cause weight gain, cancer, ulcers, baldness, poor circulation, stomach pain, constipation, diarrhea, and other illnesses.

Stress also greatly aggravates existing conditions and contributes immensely to the progression of disease. It provokes physiological changes as it raises blood pressure, affects metabolism rate and heart rate, and can trigger skin outbreaks. Chronic stress causes the brain to release hormones that inhibit the immune system and reduce the number of lymphocytes and other defense cells in the body. Studies have shown that people under constant stress have increased rates of cancer, arthritis, infections, and other ailments (Campbell 1993, Kabat-Zinn 1990, Louria 1989). Conscious worrying does the same thing. Worrying prevents the full experience and happiness of the moment because we are too consumed with what might happen. We could better use that energy to focus on more positive outcomes instead. Here is an example of how stress and emotions can physically harm the body.

While waiting for the results of a cancer biopsy, you really have two streams of thought that you could follow. You could assume that the tumor is benign, which most of them are, or you could create the image that the tumor is cancerous in your mind. This visualization produces strong emotions, such as fear, anger, and pain, which literally flood the body. The body then physically reacts to the emotions and becomes stressed, constantly tense, and overworked as it tries to handle these extreme feelings. All this negative stimulation increases the possibility that cancer could form in the body. We need to create positive mental images, our own movies that are uplifting and not filled with negative possibilities, as the body reacts in such a powerful way to the images of the mind.

The more effort you put into understanding the power of the mind, the greater you can tap into the healing power within. Healing begins with consciousness, an awareness, a realization, an understanding of the situation. If a person is unwilling to see the patterns behind her condition, to sit and really examine the mental blockages and biases she holds, treatment may temporarily alleviate the pains and problems of the body, but it will not cure her; for what manifests in the body always starts in the mind. Exploration of the mind can reveal unconscious motives for the illness and provide a place from which to start healing. Without this mental exploration, the problem will repeat itself.

But if we make a true effort to strive to identify and transform negative patterns, then healing can take place in small everyday ways. The stresses and hassles of normal life can be diffused before they build up and manifest as negative energy patterns, causing serious personal crises and illnesses. Through understanding we can change in subtle ways: we can release negative thoughts, stop harmful mind energy patterns, conquer fears, and dissolve strong repressed emotions. A small change in the mind can have an enormous effect on the body.

This chapter discusses various techniques you can use to tap into the powers of the mind in order to aid the healing process. It contains a meditation for healers to connect to the ancient wisdom held within, and also valuable methods to use with clients to allow them to activate their own inner healing energies. Techniques presented include relaxation, meditation, and visualization, also known as guided imagery. Through application of these techniques, patients can learn to change their mental approach to health, find new ways to handle stress, resist the detrimental effects of illness, and inspire healing creativity to promote health and maintain wellness.

Visualization

Visualization is defined as seeing with the mind. In healing, visualization is used to manifest results, as we create a picture within the mind that gives personal energy a clear and focused form. The skill of visualization is one of the most important to learn in order to work successful healing. So that you can practice and perfect the skill of visualization, I have included some basic visualization exercises. Try to work through them all. In this day of technology, some people find it easier to think of the mind as a blank computer screen on which they can call up any image that they want. This concept may work for you.

Here is a beginning visualization exercise for you to attempt. Position a lit candle in front of you on a table. Look at the candle flame, paying close attention to all the details about the flame, then close your eyes, and try to visualize the flame in your mind. See how long you can concentrate on holding the image of the flame. If you lose it, open your eyes and have another look at it, and then try again. Use your mind to really see the flame. After you can hold the candle flame in your mind successfully, attempt to visualize changes in the flame. Make it larger, make it smaller, make it brighter, or change its color.

There is a theory that those who have trouble visualizing are using a sensory language other than sight. They may be using auditory or somatic learning styles. If you work on creating a visual learning style, your visualizations will improve. Visualization is one of the most important skills to perform in healing. It is the basis for shaping the mind to produce healing vibrations, and is vital in energywork. If you are having difficulty, begin to train your mind to think more visually. Closely observe your surroundings. Look for the details in all you see. Try to precisely describe objects that you see, like a shoe or a lamp. Spend some time drawing. Practice this basic visualization exercise until you can do it successfully before moving on to more complex exercises.

A more advanced technique is to look at a plant in front of you. Really study the details, the colors, the outline of the leaves, the texture, the overall shape and pattern of the plant. Close your eyes, and see it in your mind. Make the plant grow in your mind, bud and bloom, wither and die, then flourish and bloom again. Make it pass through the cycles of life.

Take a mind journey. Close your eyes and visualize a special place—a rocky beach, an ancient grove, a raging waterfall, a sacred place of peace and beauty that speaks to your spirit. What do you see there? Look at everything, and add the necessary details to your visualization to make it as real as you can. You will be surprised at how vivid and real you can make your image. A spoken-mind journey can also be an intense bonding experience to share with a partner. You can very quickly attune with the mind of another, and you will both be amazed at how you can share the same vision and even add the same elements to the vision at the same time.

The following visualization exercise is a more complicated technique and may require more practice. Recall the image of the candle flame in your mind. Now see if you can hold the flame with your eyes open. This is where the real power of visualization comes in. When you can hold an image in your mind with open eyes, then you can manifest anything. When we experiment later with energy, you will need to visualize energy with open eyes. Practice this technique. Put the candle back in front of you if you need it to create the initial image in your mind.

The Healer's Meditation

The Healer's Meditation is a powerful guided visualization that allows you to tap into the wisdom of your inner healer. For at least two million years humans have been practicing the techniques of natural healing, as our evolutionary survival depended on our ability to heal and care for each other. The healing wisdom of our ancestors is ingrained in the dark recesses of the modern mind, and each of us has the ability to connect with this potent energy and apply it to enhance our healing skills. Humans only consciously use about 10 percent of the mind, leaving an enormous amount of untapped mental energy. As natural healers we connect into that unused energy and combine our modern healing knowledge with the ancient memories and wisdom of our evolutionary ancestors to enhance our skills. Through meditation and guided imagery, the healer can travel deep within the psyche and seize the power held within. This inner knowledge will guide you as a healer, enabling you to guide your patients to connect themselves to their own healing power.

The following meditation is a useful exercise for connecting to the healing power of the mind. It can be performed before administering a healing to awaken to the power within, or it can used when you are unsure of an appropriate treatment and are looking for answers. It may take several attempts for the meditation to be successful. Be patient and try it at different times of the day for maximum results. Record the meditation on a tape, as it is more effective when it is read in your own voice.

Lie down in a comfortable position and close your eyes. Breathe deeply, slowly, in and out, and begin to turn your attention down into the wisdom of your mind. Go deep into your mind, down into the dark ancient energies. Walk down into the ancestral cave of your mind, past tissue and bone, past conscious thought, down into the deepest parts of your mind. As you are walking you see a light inside of your mind; it is the spiritual light of your soul, your connection to all who have walked before you. As you walk toward it, you see it is a fire—a life-giving fire in the darkness of the cave. There is an old ancient person, loving and wise, who tends the fire. This is your inner healer. This person holds all the wisdom that has been gathered over the course of your evolution—all the knowledge, all the power, all the secrets of life, and now this ancient person will share them with you. Lean in close to this person; linger beside this person and the warmth of the fire . . . what does the ancient one say to you? What does this person have to share? Listen very carefully. This ancient one has a special message just for you; a message from deep within your spirit.

Now when you are done talking to your inner healer, thank this person for the gift given to you. Turn and begin to walk back through the cave, back to your conscious mind, back to everyday existence. When you are ready, open your eyes.

Once you have established contact with your inner healer, expect to receive messages and insights pertaining to all parts of your life, and not just when you are performing a healing treatment, either. When you open to inner knowledge, you increase your psychic ability, and you will begin to perceive new wisdom about the world. Often my inner healer will enlighten me with insights long before I need them, and I will wander around perplexed by some pertinent piece of information for days or even weeks until I finally find myself in the situation where it needs to be applied. If you take the time to listen to your inner healer and appreciate the wisdom of the ancients, your skills as a healer will be greatly enhanced.

Mental Scanning

Mental scanning is an exploratory technique that the patient can use to examine her body from a cerebral perspective in order to investigate the reasons behind her problems. Many problems are rooted in the mind, and as we think in metaphors, mind scanning can reveal symbolic insights about the physical layer. Deep down a person knows why she is experiencing the illness or the ndition, and mind scanning allows her to tap into her body's wisdom and ιcover the truth about the situation. Healing cannot take place until a person comes to terms with the root causes of the problem, acknowledging and claiming the imbalance, and mental scanning can bring about this symbolic acknowledgment and open the door to healing possibility.

The steps of the technique are outlined in the pages that follow, with the portions that are to be asked to the client presented in italics. Later in the book we will apply the mental scanning technique to enhance other healing therapies.

To begin, you need to discuss the treatment with your patient. Inform him that you will be using symbolic exploration of his problem to discover the root causes behind the ailment. Voice dialogue allows us to question why and to open the mind to listen for answers. It is important that you teach your patients to question, to search beyond the surface for the truth. Gently ask them about the situation and have them reflect on why they think the problem is occurring and what they can do to rebalance the systems of the body.

When guiding patients through body exploration, have them sit or lie down in a comfortable position. Be sure to guide them through the meditation slowly, allowing them time to progress at their own speed through the steps. I like to write down clients' responses to the questions so they can have them to reflect on later. It is important to realize that this is a time for gathering information, not interpreting it. Leave judgments and deciphering for later. Be sure to let clients know that they should not worry if the responses seem strange, as the mind works in symbols and all will become clear in the proper time.

Close your eyes and focus on your breath. Breathe in and out slowly, as your mind focuses down, down into deeper consciousness. Look deep into your body, deep into your tissues and your bones, your blood and your cells. What do you see in your body? What do you feel? Where do you feel pain or problems? Let your attention relax into the pain. I know it may feel unpleasant, but if we wish to understand it, then we must fully experience it.

Ask the client to fully describe the problem.

> *How does the condition really feel? What words would you use to describe it? Is it a color, a sensation, a pulse? What does it look like in your mind? How do you see it?*

After fully exploring what the problem looks like to the client, turn the focus of the exercise to what insight the client can obtain. Encourage your patients to take their time and really explore all aspects of their condition. Look for key words and images that can be explored fully to give metaphorical insight to a problem.

> *What gifts of insight can be gained about the situation? Look for impressions, signals, insights, and images from your body. Do you see any pictures in your mind? What do you think the symbols mean?*

Use symbolic connections to explore the problem further. For example, a person with a constant leg pain may be guided to ask the following questions to herself:

> *Is there something that is paining me in my life? Do I not have a leg to stand on in my work, relationships, family life, recreational time? Am I pulling my own weight in all that I do? Am I supporting others too much? Is there enough support in my life for me? Am I being pained or influenced by others? How do others contribute to the situation?*

Have the client ask her body to help with the problem and look for ways to improve the situation.

> *Ask your body to help you. Ask it what the necessary course of treatment should be. What insight can you gain from it? What steps can you take to heal or help yourself?*

.s with any bodywork treatment, this can be a very emotional time for a person. If the client experiences an emotional response, encourage her to remain calm. Speak comforting words, reassuring her that she is loved. Have her breathe in healing energy—energies of forgiveness, love, comfort. Rose quartz is a strong healing stone that emits soothing, loving vibrations, and giving an emotional client a piece to hold on to can help her to relax and feel safe.

When you and the client feel that the situation has been explored to its full potential, have her return her focus to her breathing and bring her mind back to conscious awareness. Guided imagery techniques are presented on the pages that follow. These techniques can be used to further explore the aspects of the problem or the injury.

Guided Imagery

Guided imagery is one of the best forms of communication with the body. This technique uses the complex electoral power of the mind to tap into the nervous system and generate an authentic response. We actually fool the body into thinking a mental image is the same as a real experience. The body reflects the belief system of the mind. Imagery can invoke physical responses in the nervous system, including sexual arousal, changes in breathing and heart rate, variations in brain waves, and levels of hormones present in the blood, and it can also affect the strength of the immune system.

If you think that you are in danger, your body reacts as if the danger is real, manifesting intense physical reactions like increased heart rate, sweat production, rapid breathing, and flooding your system with feelings of fear, anger, and anxiety. We have all experienced goose bumps while listening to a scary story. But visualize a soothing environment and your body responds in the opposite manner, filling your system with relaxed feelings, deepening breathing, and lowering stress and blood pressure.

When applied in a healing treatment, guided imagery has been shown to slow down respiratory functioning, lower blood pressure, and strengthen the immune system by raising the level of lymphocytes and immune cells in the blood. It also can relieve chronic pain and stress, strengthen the organs, and is applied to fight illness and disease.

At the beginning of this chapter we used the scenario of a person waiting for biopsy results to illustrate how emotions can effect the body. Under a healing treatment, guided imagery can be used to treat such a condition. We use the mind to flood the body with images of the tumor shrinking and fading away. The body's cells then react in a positive manner to the mind's image, increasing the possibility of healing.

The steps of the treatment follow. The visualization technique is used to correct imbalances and alleviate pain in the body, and should be tailored to a patient's specific healing needs. It is very effective when added to the end of a mental scanning session. When performing the technique, again, be sure the patient is comfortable and relaxed, and do not rush the treatment. You want to progress at your partner's own speed.

> *Close your eyes. Relax and breathe deeply. Turn your attention inward, focus your mind, and look deeply into your body. See the place on your body that pains you. See the problems, the blockage in the tissue, the broken bone, the diseased cells.* (Use an image appropriate to the patient's need.)

> *What does it look like? Feel the illness, the pain. Experience it fully. Now begin to see the bad particles smoothed away, carried away, to be eliminated out of the body. As you breathe out, release the problem, the pain. Your breath carries it out of your body. See the illness leaving your body, the tissues becoming healthy and pure.*

> *As you breathe in, you take in life-giving oxygen that nourishes your body. The oxygen is little golden drops of pure goodness that repair your cells. See these little helpers knit back together tissues, harmonizing the body, soothing pain and inflammation. If there is any pain or tightness in an area, think warmth and healing into it. Fill it with healing drops of oxygen and love.*

The body is becoming balanced and functioning smoothly; the tissues are strengthening, becoming pink and healthy, and are filled with little drops of golden light. Now send joy through your body—gratitude for all your organs, health for all cells, love for each tiny piece.

Allow your partner time to visualize the images, and when he is ready, ask him to return his attention to his breathing and slowly open his eyes.

A client can use this visualization at home to continue on with the treatment and promote self-healing.

A Healing Visualization

The following exercise is another common visualization technique that is useful for relieving pain, both physical and mental. It employs the imagery of water to cleanse the mind and body. It can be used with clients during treatment, and they can also apply it at home to encourage health and relaxation.

Imagine a beautiful place outdoors where you feel safe, warm, loved. It is a peaceful place, filled with sunshine and greenery. Walk through your place; walk down to a beautiful healing pool in the center of the greenery. The waters sparkle with love and positive energy, and you know they have healing powers. Slowly enter the healing waters. Be washed by them, enveloped in their love; feel the water flow over you, and all your hurts and pains are simply washed away. The waters carry away pain, emotional and physical. Release your feelings of pain, hurt, guilt, fear, and anger to them. You are being cleansed by these healing waters. They are nourishing, soothing, healing, purifying. You are healed in their warmth. When you are ready and filled with the love from the healing waters, gently leave the pool and walk back to the greenery, feeling refreshed and renewed with health. Now allow the visualization to fade, bringing your awareness back to this room and this time. Open your eyes when you are ready.

A Guided Relaxation Exercise

This exercise encourages relaxation in the whole body and can be performed in the mind, or it can be recorded on an audiotape and played back as needed. Try it before going to bed as a cure for insomnia. Take your time with the exercise; it should take about fifteen minutes to completely relax the whole body.

To begin, lie down comfortably on your back and close your eyes. Regulate your breathing so it is slow and focused. Turn your attention to your feet; feel them becoming warm and relaxed. They are heavy, sinking into the bed, sleeping. Now feel the ankles getting heavy and warm. They, too, are relaxed and sleeping. Move up the body to the calves and turn them off, feeling them get heavy and warm. And now your thighs are sleeping, also. Continue to move up the body, turning off the hips, the buttocks, the stomach, the chest, and the arms, feeling the parts of your body become heavy and warm, relaxed. Turn off your neck, jaw, face, tongue, eyes, and forehead. When your whole body is fully relaxed, lie there and feel the stillness, the warmth, the security, and the healing energy of your body.

Affirmations

Affirmations are positive messages that are used in repetition in order to program the mind and cleanse the self on both energy and cellular levels. They allow us to deflect external energy instead of assimilating it by keeping the mind focused on beneficial energy thoughts. Affirmations fill the void spaces where negative ideas might creep in and poison the mind. Used correctly, these simple and creative phrases can alter the mental perspectives, emotional attitudes, and physical habits that are causing the disease and illness. Affirmations are truly valuable tools of transformation.

Our role as healer is to show our partners how to bring out their own strength and healing energies, so an affirmation should be tailored for an individual's specific situation and needs. It should be phrased in the first person and focused on the positive work being done in the present in order to direct the mind into believing that change is happening. For as we know, the body responds to what the mind believes. Affirmations do not need to be complex; indeed, simple and straightforward images are often most effective. It is wise to have your clients devise their own affirmations so they have personal meaning to the client and, thus, will be more effective in promoting healing.

Proper affirmations should sound something like the following:

For general healing: *I am healthy and well, strong and powerful.*

To repair a broken bone: *My bone is healthy and fit; it is regrowing strong.*

I like to have the patient softly repeat an appropriate affirmation while I am administering a treatment such as massage or energy work. But not every person feels comfortable with affirmations and it is important to realize this. It is good to have clients write out the affirmations, as this can help them feel more secure about using them; it also allows them to form connections to the phrases, and they will be more likely to apply them in moments of daily meditation. Clients can also create an audiotape of their affirmations to listen to, and post reminder notes around the house, car, and office.

4

The Healing Power of Food and Vitamins

Next to air, food is the most important substance we put into our bodies, yet it is often overlooked as a healing treatment. But, indeed, health and wellness starts with the food we feed ourselves, and it can be maintained by a steady diet of fresh, nutrient-rich food, and a regular supplementation program.

Hippocrates wrote, "Let food be your medicine and medicine your food." He understood the vast importance of food as fuel and medicine for the body. If you put garbage into the fuel tank, the engine will not perform to maximum efficiency, but fill the tank with fresh nutrient-rich fuel and the engine will thrive. The old maxim is true: you are what you eat. Countless research studies have proven that healthy eating prevents cancers, heart and liver disease, diabetes, stroke, obesity, vision problems, birth defects, immune system problems, allergies, and many other debilitating ailments (Haas 1992, Louria 1989). Food is really the most important and simplest way to promote wellness and maintain personal health.

Our daily replenishment of energy is the key to the survival and balance of the body's systems. We want to strive for good eating habits, fueling the body with a diet that is rich in fresh plant foods including whole grains, seeds, nuts, vegetables, fruits, and lentils, and moderate in low-fat portions of meat, fish, and dairy.

A diet like this is called a macrobiotic diet, and it is a firsthand energy diet. Vegetables and fruits are considered to be the purest forms of nourishment, as plants have the ability to take in energy from the sun and use it to manufacture their own food. When we eat plants, we are receiving firsthand sun energy. Animals cannot make their own food; the only way they can get energy is to ingest plants or other animals. When we consume animal flesh, the nutrients we receive are diluted, as they are secondhand sun energy. As you can see, we lose vital energy and nutrients at each level of the food pyramid.

A macrobiotic diet keeps the body slim and lowers the chances of contracting cancer. We see lower rates of obesity and cancer in Asians, as their diet is primarily macrobiotic, and studies have shown that vegetarians have much lower incidences of cancer. This type of diet provides the body with maximum energy, eliminates fatigue, and increases endurance and strength. Problems like arthritis, obesity, diabetes, constipation, and high blood pressure are all diet related, and the chances of manifesting these problems can be reduced by eating a vegetarian diet.

Foods full of saturated fats, sugar, salt, white flour, red meat, and refined starches can be harmful to our bodies. In your diet, try to eat natural, raw foods instead of commercially prepared products, as processing also destroys valuable nutrients.

Even continually eating the same foods can be hurtful, because the repetition can upset the body's balance. The average person has a standard diet of the same seven foods, and this low variety of food choices contributes to allergies and hypersensitivity to foods. We need a variety in our diet, as more colorful foods equals more minerals. In our low-nutrient, fast-food culture we all need to look at changing our relationship with food to promote health and wellness. In the following sections we will discuss some of the various components of foods and their impact on our health.

Caffeine

Caffeine is a substance that stimulates chemicals in the brain to increase alertness, but it also speeds up the body's natural rhythms, raising insulin levels and causing nervousness, instability, anxiety, insomnia, and irritability. It is an addictive stimulant that is found in coffee, chocolate, tea, and sodas. With caffeine you need to decrease your intake gradually or you may experience withdrawal symptoms like headaches, fatigue, or depression. Replace a daily coffee intake with decaffeinated coffee, green teas, juices, water, or herbal teas.

Sugar

Sugar. We all love it—in our coffee, on our cereal, when sweetening our foods. Sugar is a tasty treat, but it can wreak havoc on the system. Refined sugar stresses the kidneys and drains the body of minerals, protein, and essential calcium. It rots the teeth, and also is a key factor in the development of adult diabetes and yeast imbalances in both men and women. Honey is a much better choice than sugar; it is composed of simple sugars that are more easily digested by the body. Dried fruit can also be used to sweeten foods.

Pesticides

Pesticides in our foods can be very dangerous. They cause birth defects, cancer, nerve damage, and immune system deficiencies. Many foods carry trace residues of pesticides, and the list of highly contaminated foods contains such favorites as strawberries, cherries, peaches, apples, celery, and peppers. It is important that we thoroughly wash all produce very carefully before eating and try to buy food grown locally, as food produced in North America contains lower levels of pesticides because regulations on the amounts farmers can use are stricter than regulations in third world countries. Try to eat safe foods that have husks to protect them, such as watermelons, coconuts, bananas, cauliflower, oranges, and pineapples. It is wise to peel potatoes and apples, as the pesticides can concentrate in the skin of these foods. This phenomena of pesticides accumulating in the skin of foods has been termed the Snow White Syndrome.

Additives

Chemical additives used in food products include preservatives, emulsifiers to prevent water and fat from separating, sugar and artificial sweeteners, salt and other flavorings, and dyes for color. The safety of additives is often questioned. A good approach is to buy fresh raw foods instead of processed products, and be sure to read labels. If there are more chemicals than natural substances listed, pass on the product.

Weight Loss

The key to weight loss through diet lies in low-fat portions, small helpings, minimal snacking, and balanced food choices. On a weight reduction diet the calories from fat should be less than 30 percent of total intake for the day. Choose reduced-fat foods such as low-fat milk, sherbet instead of ice cream, plant-based foods instead of artery-clogging fatty meats, and when you are eating meat, choose lean cuts, and lots of fish and skinless chicken. Beware of the hidden fat in foods like cheese, sauces, commercially prepared dishes, and restaurant meals.

Eat foods in moderation. Also, eat at meal time and avoid snacking so you don't spoil the next meal. If the food is good, you will not want to snack. Choose dense food such as carrots and apples, as the denser the food, the more chewing it needs, helping you feel satiated so you eat less. Try to plan social activities that do not center around eating. Allow yourself a yummy treat now and again, and if you go on an uncontrollable eating binge, just resume the diet where you left off.

Fiber

Fiber is a natural laxative that keeps the intestines healthy and works to prevent colon cancer. There are two types of fiber: insoluble and soluble. Insoluble fiber cannot be dissolved by the body and instead works as an internal cleanser, moving food wastes through the system and preventing them from accumulating and creating dangerous toxins. It is found in brown rice, vegetables, almonds, and fruit. Most animal products contain little or no fiber.

Soluble fiber can be digested by the body. It works to lower cholesterol and helps curb diabetes by controlling blood sugar levels. High levels are found in apples, oatmeal, carrots, lentils, beans, and peas. Sometimes fiber can cause digestive upsets, so you need to increase your fiber intake gradually and be sure to drink plenty of liquids to aid the digestion process.

Protein

Protein supplies the body with amino acids, chemical building-blocks used for growth and maintenance of tissues. Animal foods like eggs, meat, milk, poultry, and fish are considered to be complete sources of protein, as they contain all nine essential amino acids that the body cannot naturally produce. Plant foods like nuts, seeds, grains, and vegetables do not contain all the needed amino acids and are thus called incomplete proteins. Vegetarians must carefully combine their food choices to create complete proteins in order to ensure that they are receiving all the nutrients their bodies need.

Carbohydrates

A carbohydrate is a nutrient found in bread, cereal, grains, pasta, rice, potatoes, beans, honey, maple sap, and fruits. This substance can originate in either a simple form (sugar) or complex forms (starches and fiber), but during digestion the body breaks down all carbohydrates into a simple sugar called *glucose*. Glucose is burned by the cells in order to provide energy to fuel the systems of the body. Experts recommend that 55 to 60 percent of the diet should consist of carbohydrates, but the typical American diet contains far too much simple sugar and not enough complex carbohydrates to be healthy.

Fruits and Vegetables

Fruits and veggies are the staple of life, and the crunchier they are and the more color they have, the better they are for you. Colorful fruits and vegetables strengthen the immune system, fight disease, and prevent colon/rectal cancers and heart disease. They contain antioxidants, which are a type of phytochemical. Phytochemicals are disease-fighting substances found in plant foods that deactivate the damaging free radicals in the body; they work to prevent cancer and boost the immune system. There are hundreds of different phytochemicals, with vitamin C, E, and beta-carotene being the most common antioxidants.

Antioxidants are found in high levels in red peppers, yellow peppers, broccoli, carrots, pumpkin, squash, spinach, tomatoes, cantaloupe, and apples. The cancer-fighting beta-carotene is found in dark green, orange, and yellow fruits and vegetables. Oranges, peaches, broccoli, cantaloupe, grapefruit, and brussel sprouts are high in vitamin C, while sunflower seeds, wheat germ, almonds, pecans, and hazelnuts contain high levels of vitamin E.

Try to eat at least five half-cup servings of vegetables a day, and at least two fruits. Buy your vegetables fresh instead of frozen, and eat them raw, as they contain more nutrients and enzymes than cooked vegetables. If you do cook them, steam them instead of boiling them so they maintain their nutrient content.

Fats

Fats are essential to the body because they help it to absorb vitamins and supply it with linoleic and linolenic acids for proper growth. But the typical American diet contains far too much fat, and this is a major problem that is contributing to the rise of heart disease in the country.

There are four types of fats: saturated fatty acids, monounsaturated fatty acids, polyunsaturated fatty acids, and transfatty acids.

Saturated fats are fats that are generally solid in room temperature. These include butter, hard cheese, animal fats, and oils like coconut and palm. Higher levels of saturated fats are correlated with heart disease and high cholesterol levels.

Monounsaturated fats include products like canola oil, olive oil, nuts, seeds, and avocados. This type of fat is considered healthier than saturated fat, as it can lower bad cholesterol levels and raise the level of good cholesterol in the blood.

Polyunsaturated fats are found in other vegetable oils like corn oil, sunflower oil, flaxseed, and also fish oils and oily fish like salmon, tuna, herring, and sardines. They contain the essential omega-3 and omega-6 fatty acids. These acids are very beneficial for the body, as they lower blood cholesterol levels and protect against heart disease.

Artificially hydrogenated fats like margarine are known as transfatty acids. These fats create chaos in the hormonal system, alter DNA, and have been linked to contributing to the development of cancer. Use nonhydrogenated margarine or butter on your food instead.

When it comes to using oils, olive oil is the best to buy, as it has heart-strengthening properties and contains healthy monounsaturated fat. Beware of cottonseed oil. It is used in prepared foods such as candy, cookies, cake mixes, tortilla chips, and smoked oysters. Cotton is not a food crop, and because of this, farmers can use very high levels of pesticides during the growing process. After the cotton has been harvested, the seed oil is then sold for use in food products. The oil may still contain harmful levels of pesticide residue.

Water

Next to air, the most important thing our bodies need is pure unpolluted drinking water. Water flushes the toxins from our systems and helps the kidneys to function. It softens stool and makes bowl movements easier. Drink up to eight glasses a day. So much of our water supply around the world is becoming dangerously polluted, and we need to be very careful to ensure a high quality of drinking water. Do not drink water straight from the tap, as it is often highly chlorinated. Filter your drinking water or buy bottled water. If you can smell the chlorine in your water, then it is too much for your body to safely ingest. Let your tap water run for a few minutes to flush the pipe system before using the water, and never use water from the hot tap for cooking, as impurities from the hot water tank can leach into the water.

Vitamins and Minerals

Vitamins and minerals are elements that prevent various diseases. They are not drugs, but are natural substances that are found in living things and, as such, cannot be patented. With all the stresses we endure in today's world, in addition to the low nutritional value of food, I believe every person needs vitamins. A vitamin and mineral supplement is essential to enrich the nutrient value of the average diet. Be sure to choose a good multiple vitamin from a reputable company. Pick a product that is dye free, sugar free, wheat free, and yeast free.

There are many reasons why vitamin supplementation is necessary. The high stress of the modern lifestyle robs the body of vitamins, as does the overuse of antibiotics and medicines. Cigarettes, alcohol, and caffeine use further decrease the body's ability to receive nutrients. Most foods in the Western diet are loaded with nutritional-deficient white sugar and white flour. These two substances cause more harm to the body than good. The staple of the American diet, fast food, has often been referred to as filler, not food.

Even fresh foods can contain toxins and have low nutritional value. Pesticides, pollution in the air, soil, water, and radioactive wastes all leave residues in produce, while chemical additives like waxes, dyes, bleaches, preservatives, and artificial ingredients add no nutritional value and may be toxic in themselves. Soils are becoming nutrient depleted from overuse, and chemically fertilized food is a poor nutritional option. Most fruits and vegetables are picked before they are ripe—a negative thing because vine ripening is necessary for the food to develop the full nutrients it should have.

Vitamins are necessary for proper health, and the body can produce some vitamins on its own, but most, however, have to come from the diet. Levels from RDA (recommended daily allowance) are inconsequentially low. Most healers recommend a daily multivitamin. There is little chance of toxicity with vitamins if they are used appropriately and with common sense.

Fat Soluble Vitamins

Vitamin A: An antioxidant, vitamin A works to prevent cells from becoming oxidized. Needed for growth and cell development, vitamin A maintains healthy nails, hair, skin, bones, teeth, gums, and glands. It helps with ailments such as allergies, respiratory infections, eye problems, and skin problems such as acne, boils, and eczema. Best sources of vitamin A include liver, salmon, and other cold water fish, orange and yellow fruits and vegetables such as oranges, carrots, and squash, and also leafy green vegetables. A normal dosage of vitamin A is ten thousand IU a day, and it is recommended that you take zinc along with vitamin A, as zinc is needed by the body to assimilate the vitamin.

Vitamin D: Vitamin D is needed for calcium absorption, and it helps the body build strong bones and teeth. It is beneficial in bone and tooth diseases, as well as arthritis and epilepsy. It also prevents colds. Vitamin D is found in egg yolks and fish oils, and also in fortified milk and butter. It can also be produced by the body with sun exposure. Recommended amounts of vitamin D are about 800 IU a day.

Vitamin E: An important antioxidant, vitamin E maintains muscles and red blood cells. It also protects fatty acids. Good sources of vitamin E are found in eggs, vegetable oils, nuts and seeds, and leafy green veggies. The suggested amount is 800 IU a day. Take vitamin E supplements daily for about two weeks before and after surgery to promote recovery and speed healing. A potent skin healer, you can poke the end of a vitamin E capsule with a pin and apply the liquid to rashes, burns, cuts, wrinkles, cold sores, and liver spots in order to promote healing and alleviate scarring. It is an anticancer agent and helps to reduce high blood pressure and heart disease. For patients with heart disease, vitamin E usage should be discussed with their doctor, as dosages of over 150 IU a day are not recommended for those people suffering from heart problems, and any usage in this case should be monitored.

Vitamin K: Vitamin K is essential for proper blood clotting. It is found in green leafy vegetables like spinach and cabbage, green tea, liver, pork, alfalfa, and organic yogurt. Vitamin K is usually only available by prescription.

Water Soluble Vitamins

Vitamin C: Vitamin C is an important antitoxin and antioxidant that strengthens blood vessel walls, promotes absorption of iron, heals wounds, and helps control blood cholesterol. It can be used to boost the immune system in the cases of infections, colds, ear problems, gum disease, and eye diseases. It is also used to promote healing in cases of diabetes, ulcers, sinus problems, poor blood circulation, high cholesterol, gallstones, hepatitis, anemia, and joint disease. Good sources of vitamin C include citrus fruits and juices, berries, melons, peppers, broccoli, and potatoes.

Healers normally recommend about 1,000 to 2,000 mg of vitamin C a day, although higher dosages can be used in treatment of a condition or as a preventive measure. Vitamin C is nontoxic, but an excess may result in nausea or diarrhea for some people. If this happens, simply reduce the dosage. Taking a 1,000 mg dosage of vitamin C every two hours for one day at the first sign of a cold may prevent the cold. In taking higher dosages of vitamin C, you need to drink plenty of water, between six to eight glasses a day, to prevent the formation of kidney stones.

The B Vitamins

The B vitamins are a group of vitamins that function together. They should be taken together in a good quality B complex vitamin, as each needs the rest to promote optimum health. This water soluble vitamin should be taken with a meal for maximum absorbency. B complex is recommended for those suffering from stress, depression, migraines, PMS, yeast infections, allergies, nervous disorders, asthma, and epilepsy. Vegetarians in particular should take a daily B complex vitamin, as vitamin B_{12} is only obtained through animal meats. When purchasing a B complex, be sure to look for one that contains folic acid (vitamin B_9), biotin, and lecithin. Lecithin is composed of two B vitamins: choline and inositol. The following list is a description of each of the individual B vitamins and their primary food sources.

Thiamine: Thiamine, or vitamin B_1, is essential to energy metabolism, and it also helps the body maintain appetite, digestion, and proper nerve function. It is found in nuts and seeds, pork, legumes, and fortified grains and cereals.

Riboflavin: Necessary for adrenal function and energy metabolism, Riboflavin, or vitamin B_2, is found in meat and poultry, milk and dairy products, mushrooms, and fortified cereals and grains.

Niacin: Also known as vitamin B_3, Niacin is needed to metabolize energy and promote normal growth. It is found in meats, poultry, seafood, eggs, milk, and legumes. Breads and cereals are often fortified with niacin.

Pantothenic Acid: Pantothenic acid, or vitamin B_5, aids the body in metabolism, synthesizes substances like cholesterol, antibodies, hemoglobin, and certain hormones, and stabilizes blood sugar levels. It is found in virtually all foods.

Vitamin B_6: Vitamin B_6, or pyridoxine, promotes protein and carbohydrate metabolism, proper nerve function, and synthesis of red blood cells. It is found in meat, fish, poultry, grains and cereals, potatoes and soybeans, as well as in dark green leafy vegetables.

Folic Acid: Folic acid, or vitamin B_9, is used by the body to produce DNA, red blood cells, and certain amino acids. It is found in many raw vegetables, including broccoli and avocados, yeast, liver, and legumes. It is an important nutrient for pregnant and nursing women.

Vitamin B_{12}: Found in all animal products, vitamin B_{12} is needed to make red blood cells, DNA, RNA, and myelin to cover nerve fibers.

Biotin: Found in egg yolks, cereals, and yeast, biotin helps the body carry out the process of metabolism.

Minerals

Minerals cannot be made by the body and must come from the diet. They are essential in tissue formation, building strong bones and teeth, and they also help the body absorb vitamins. Most minerals are obtained from a balanced diet, although it is advisable to take a multivitamin and mineral supplement daily to ensure the body receives all the nutrients it needs to maintain wellness. Extra supplementation is sometimes necessary, especially with calcium to prevent many diseases and problems associated with aging, but beyond additional calcium, supplementation should be discussed with a physician, as side effects can often occur.

Calcium

Calcium is the most abundant mineral in the body. It builds strong bones and teeth, and it is vital to blood clotting, nerve function, muscle action, and metabolism. It is found in milk and dairy products, tofu, salmon, and dark green vegetables. Many individuals suffer from calcium deficiency and develop conditions like rickets, which affects children, soft brittle bones that easily fracture, and osteoporosis. Eight hundred mg of calcium a day are recommended, but many people, especially women, need extra calcium, up to 2,000 mg a day. Calcium is used to treat bone and tooth diseases, arthritis, stress, high cholesterol, menstrual problems, leg cramps, headaches and migraines, heart disease, multiple sclerosis, and problems associated with menopause.

Chromium

Chromium works with insulin to metabolize glucose in the body. Good sources include brewers yeast, whole-grain products, liver, cheese, and molasses. This mineral can help prevent diabetes and hyperglycemia. It also lowers cholesterol levels and blood pressure. It is a trace mineral, so very small amounts are needed by the body.

Copper

Copper composes many enzymes and is essential for iron absorption, skin pigment, red blood cell and connective tissue production, and nerve fibers. It is found in liver, shellfish, legumes, nuts, and prunes. Deficiencies of copper are rare and extra supplementation in not normally needed. In fact, doses over 15 mg a day can be harmful.

Fluoride

Added to drinking water, fluoride is a mineral that prevents cavities and other dental problems. The process of adding fluoride to water is an issue under heavy controversy. Opponents claim fluoride is a carcinogen that damages the liver, while the general prevailing scientific opinion is that it is a beneficial health measure. Fluoride is seldom included in mineral supplements.

Iodine

This mineral is used by the body to make thyroid hormones and is found in seaweed, kelp, fluoridated water, and iodized salt. A deficiency in iodine can lead to goiter or an overgrown thyroid gland, obesity, and lethargy. An iodine deficiency during pregnancy can result in mental retardation of the infant, a condition known as cretinism. Most people get enough iodine, but pregnant women sometimes need extra. A good multivitamin and mineral supplement should contain enough iodine for the average person.

Iron

Found in seafood, legumes, and meat, especially liver, iron is needed by the body for the transport and storage of oxygen. Symptoms of iron deficiency include weakness and fatigue, anemia, brittle nails, loss of hair, diarrhea, irritability, and low resistance to disease. The average Western diet is ample in iron, although menstruating and pregnant women may need more. The recommended dosage is about 10 mg a day. You should avoid taking iron supplements with certain types of antibiotics; check with your physician before taking any supplements if you are on medication.

Manganese

Manganese is necessary for bone and tendon formation, and also for metabolism. Good sources include coffee and tea (in small amounts), legumes, and bran. Manganese can be used to treat digestion problems, muscular sclerosis, epilepsy, diabetes, fatigue, and Alzheimer's disease. A deficiency of manganese is rare; symptoms include problems with muscle coordination, dizziness, hearing, and high levels of sugar in the blood. Pregnant and nursing women may need more of this mineral.

Molybdenum

Found in liver, dark green leafy vegetables, and whole grains, molybdenum is a mineral that composes the enzymes needed for metabolism and also helps the body store iron. A deficiency of this mineral is rare. More research into molybdenum is needed, but it seems to play a part in helping the body fight AIDS (acquired immune deficiency syndrome).

Magnesium

Magnesium stimulates bone growth, helps muscles function, and aids metabolism. It is found in leafy green vegetables, whole-grain cereals and breads, meats, poultry, fish, and eggs. Because it is in a wide range of foods, a magnesium deficiency is rare in the West, although alcoholism, kidney or liver disease, diabetes, persistent diarrhea, and pregnancy can deplete the mineral from the body. Deficiency symptoms include an irregular heartbeat, a quick pulse, cramps, and often mental disorientation and nervousness. Magnesium is combined with calcium in a supplement, as they need each other to work properly. Taking a magnesium supplement can help prevent kidney stones when using high amounts of vitamin C to treat problems.

Phosphorus

This mineral works with calcium and fluoride to help maintain strong bones and teeth. It is also essential for proper metabolism. Good sources of phosphorus include poultry, fish, egg yolks, legumes, and dairy products. A deficiency in phosphorus is rare; symptoms include teeth and bones problems, arthritis, and poor appetite.

Potassium

Potassium helps the body maintain fluid balance, proper metabolism, and muscle function. It is found in avocados, citrus fruits, bananas, legumes and other vegetables, as well as in whole-grain foods. A potassium deficiency can be caused by extreme stress, diarrhea, hypoglycemia, fasting, alcohol, caffeine, and diuretics used to treat high blood pressure. Symptoms include tiredness, extreme thirst, insomnia, heart problems, constipation, muscle weakness, and irritability. Potassium can be used to treat hypoglycemia, allergies, edema, and high blood pressure. Caution needs to be taken when using a potassium supplement, as an overdose can cause diarrhea, nausea, and dangerous cardiac problems. Discuss potassium use with a doctor, and eat natural foods for added supplementation.

Selenium

A powerful antioxidant, selenium works with vitamin E to prevent free radicals from harming the body. It is an antiaging and anticancer vitamin that is found in poultry, seafood, whole-grain foods, garlic, onions, and mushrooms. A deficiency of selenium may be a factor in the development of heart disease and strokes. Daily dosage requirements are between 50 to 80 mcg, with overdoses causing possible nausea, diarrhea, fatigue, skin damage, and loss of hair and nails.

Sodium

Found in table salt, seafood, dairy products, seasonings, and most processed foods, sodium regulates the body's fluid balance and helps promote proper muscle function. A sodium deficiency is very rare in the Western diet; most Americans suffer from an overdose. Excessive sodium is linked to high blood pressure, strokes, and edema. Do not add extra salt to meals and avoid high-sodium processed foods.

Sulfur

Sulfur is a component of amino acids and is found in every cell of the body. Good sources include protein foods; if you are eating protein you will be receiving an adequate amount of sulfur. Sulfur is used as a food preservative and can trigger allergies and asthma attacks in some individuals.

Zinc

Zinc aids the metabolic action of enzymes and is essential to growth and reproduction. Good sources of zinc include oysters, meat, yogurt, and fortified cereals and grains. Zinc loss occurs when the body sweats and during pregnancy and nursing. A deficiency of zinc can lead to fatigue, lethargy, loss of appetite, and increased susceptibility to infections. It can also cause Down's syndrome in a fetus. White spots on the fingernails is a telltale sign of a deficiency. Zinc can be used to treat dry and broken skin, acne, inflammation, poor vision, diabetes, infertility, irregular menstrual cycles, schizophrenia, hypoglycemia, Alzheimer's disease, and immune deficiency problems such as AIDS. The recommended daily dosage is 10 to 15 mg; an overdose can be dangerous, causing diarrhea, kidney failure, vomiting, heart problems, and bleeding, along with other various symptoms.

Specific Healing Foods

Apples

These fruits contain flavonoids, which are strong antioxidants that prevent cancer. In one Finnish study, regular apple-eaters had the lowest risk of developing lung cancer. Apples are a fantastic source of pectin, a soluble fiber that lowers blood cholesterol levels. They are an ideal food for a diabetic diet, as they contain fructose, a natural sugar that is absorbed into the bloodstream more slowly than table sugar (sucrose). Apples help reduce tooth decay, as the crunchiness of an apple stimulates the gums and the sweetness of the fruit draws saliva to the mouth, lowering the level of bacteria present there.

Bananas

Bananas are eaten to lower high blood pressure. They are very high in potassium, which causes the body to excrete sodium in the urine, helping to reduce blood pressure and the risk of heart disease. Potassium also decreases bloating and water retention. Woman can eat bananas to help combat menopausal fatigue.

Beans

Beans are a high-fiber food that lowers cholesterol. They also protect against colorectal cancer, and contain other anticancer compounds like isoflavones, sapons, and lignans. They are a good source of folic acid and vitamins A and C.

Bran

Bran is known as one of the richest sources of dietary fiber. It helps prevent constipation and can reduce the risk of certain cancers, including cancers of the prostate and colon. Bran promotes a feeling of fullness and can be helpful for those who tend to overeat.

Broccoli

Broccoli is an excellent source of vitamin C. It also contains high amounts of vitamin A and folic acid. It further contains significant anticancer compounds and has a high nutrient and fiber content. Broccoli boosts immunity and can protect against heart disease.

Carrots

Carrots harden and heal the gums. They contain very high amounts of vitamin A, which the body uses to build up a strong resistance against colds and harmful bacteria. Carrots are also known for improving the eyesight, especially night vision. They are also a good source of dietary fiber. They may help lower blood cholesterol levels and protect against cancer.

Cranberries

A good source of vitamin C, cranberries also contain bioflavonoids to help protect the body against cancer. They also help protect the eyesight. Cranberry extract can be taken to prevent or alleviate cystitis and urinary tract infections (the juice is too diluted and loaded with sugar to be effective; take cranberry extract in capsules to treat the urinary tract). If symptoms persist, see a physician for prescription antibiotics to treat an infection, as cranberry juice will not cure an established infection.

Garlic

The healing power of garlic is well documented. The pungent head of garlic is a powerful antibacterial, as it contains allicin, a substance that prevents and fights infections. It enhances the immune system, stimulating defense cells, and seems to play an important role in preventing and fighting cancer. Garlic is also used to treat asthma, arthritis, colds, headaches, and lowers blood pressure and cholesterol levels.

Ginger

Ginger is a plant that is an excellent source of minerals. The plant relaxes the stomach and intestinal tract, relieving nausea and vomiting. It works wonders on motion sickness. You can drink ginger ale, take it in pills, or eat candied ginger root.

Green Tea

A cancer-fighting beverage, green tea has been shown to help prevent cancer of the colon, rectum, and pancreas. It contains phenols, substances that cause death in human cancer cells. Green tea also plays a role in good dental hygiene—it contains fluoride and tannins that inhibit tooth decay.

Fish

Fish is also an excellent food to eat, as it contains omega-3 fatty acids. These are beneficial fats that lower blood pressure, reduce the risk of heart attack, and promote healing within the tissues of the body. The fatty acids are also beneficial to treat rheumatoid arthritis. Fish is a source of selenium, another nutrient recommended for people with rheumatoid arthritis.

Soy

Try to include some soy in your diet. There are many tasty soy products out there—soy burgers and sandwich fillers that actually look and taste like meat. It is low in calories and fat and is a good protein and iron source for vegetarians. Soy contains isoflavones, which are strong cancer-inhibiting substances. It reduces cholesterol and protects against heart disease.

Tomatoes

Tomatoes are a good source of vitamin A, vitamin C, and lycopene, an antioxidant that protects against cancers. Men who regularly eat tomatoes have been shown to have a lower risk of contracting prostate cancer.

Yogurt

Yogurt is a food that is eaten in most cultures throughout the world. It contains *Lactobacillus acidophilus,* friendly bacteria that closely resembles the bacteria in the human digestive tract. Strains of this bacteria in yogurt have been found to inhibit at least twenty-seven different kinds of harmful bacteria; thus, yogurt works to promote a healthy inner system (Bricklin 1982). Eaten daily, it also helps to cure yeast infections, aids in stopping chronic diarrhea, and adds essential calcium and protein to the body. Be sure to buy yogurt that contains "viable or living cultures."

5

Bodywork Therapies

Bodywork therapies are physical treatments that are applied to heal injuries and ailments. They include deep breathing, exercise, and hydrotherapy, which is the use of water in any of its three forms—liquid, solid, or steam.

The physical treatments of bodywork therapies can be very useful to the healer. In this chapter we will look at promoting wellness through controlled breathing, and using the power of breath to relax and ground a patient at the beginning of a healing session. The application of water can also be used in a healing treatment to alleviate pain and inspire calming energies. Through exercise, a patient learns to become aware of his body, and this awareness can bring healing insights to the mind. Beyond this, even minor exercise strengthens the body and promotes wellness.

Deep Breathing

The work of the body starts with breathing, for breath is the fuel of the soul. We consume twenty thousand liters of air a day and can only live for a few minutes without air. Breath is considered to be the movement of the spirit through matter. It fills the soul with life energy. On the inhale we receive energy, and we emit it on the exhale. Inhaled life energy activates the body's own energy, stimulating healing vibrations that flood the system. When we breathe, we also strengthen the link between the body and the mind, bringing knowledge from the mind to the body, and power from the body to the mind.

Most people are shallow breathers, and, hence, do not use their lungs and diaphragm to full capacity. When we do not breathe properly, we cut ourselves off from fully receiving life energy. Breathe in as deeply as you can through your nose. If you feel your insides move and pull up, then you know you have engaged your diaphragm.

Without the right amount of oxygen, our bodies cannot break down food properly. Deep breathing supplies us with the oxygen needed to correctly facilitate the digestion process. It also gives our brains extra oxygen that helps us to think more clearly and rationally. The brain works at a high rate of metabolism, so it consumes oxygen at an extremely fast pace. Deep breathing helps replenish this important oxygen supply. When we exhale, we release the toxic gas carbon dioxide, which is a by-product of metabolism that our bodies cannot use.

Through deep relaxed breathing and visualization, we can also give up pain, physical and emotional, that has been infused into the body and held throughout the course of our lives. Repressed pain causes blockages in the energy centers, and eventually disease and illness can occur. Breathing releases old emotions and hurts; it allows us to move on in our lives. It facilitates powerful healing.

You should practice slow deep breathing every day for at least five minutes at a time. The following is an effective deep breathing exercise. You can do the exercise sitting or lying down, whichever feels more comfortable to you. Close your eyes and inhale through your nose to a slow count of three, then exhale out your mouth to the same slow count. The point is to keep your breathing comfortably controlled. As you inhale, visualize taking in positive qualities, life and love, joy and vitality, sunshine and health. See these positive energies as a golden light. If you are sick, then see the energy you take in as a soothing, healing blue color.

As you breathe out, exhale all toxins and negative energies from your body. Visualize these negatives as black smoke leaving your mouth. Continue breathing like this for a few minutes. Pay close attention to the condition of your body, and breathe deeply into any area that feels pain, tightness, or needs healing. Really open up the lungs and send healing breath to that area.

It is a good idea to start every healing treatment with a breathing session. To bring a patient's mental focus to his breath, use a calm gentle voice and keep your words soft and light. Think soothing, as if you were talking to a frightened child. Talk slowly and tailor your words to the client's breathing patterns.

Close your eyes and breathe deeply. Inhale and bring your attention inward. Relax, give yourself over to your breath, and breathe deeply in and out. Take in clean fresh air with the inhale. Release any worries or tension, and breathe them out with your exhale.

When performing any type of healing treatment, you need to pay close attention to a person's breathing patterns. Shortening of breath is a clue that a person is going deep into self, experiencing strong emotions and images from past events. Use a gentle reminder to breathe in order to reestablish focus and rebalance the system with healing energies.

Hydrotherapy

Hydrotherapy is a safe and effective therapy that encompasses internal and external application of water. It includes hot and cold compress application, bathing, saunas, ice therapy, foot baths, and even drinking water. Water can soothe and relax the nervous system, or it can stimulate it. It promotes the circulation of blood and lymph fluid through the body, working to help the detoxification process through the movement and elimination of wastes and poisons. Water therapy can alleviate pain, aid the functioning of the urinary, bowel, and respiratory systems, and it also works wonders for the skin.

There are certain contraindications that you need to be careful of when using water therapy. Individuals with heart conditions or circulatory problems need to make sure that the water is not too hot. Watch for adverse reactions. The very young and old need to be cautious with hot water treatments as well. Those patients with circulatory disorders should not use cold water therapy.

Foot Baths

A foot bath in hot water can relieve swelling, as it diverts blood from other areas of the body. Foot baths relieve pressure from headaches, menstrual cramps, and, of course, sore feet. Soak the feet for fifteen minutes and then rinse them with cold water to finish the treatment.

Hot Baths

Hot baths can relieve pain and tension, promote sleep, and heal the skin. A hot bath can induce detoxification through perspiration. It also relieves stress, soothes aches and pains, and is very stimulating to the immune system. It can help heal injuries in muscles and joints and reduce swelling. It further works to ease internal congestion and blockages and helps improve circulation. A bath is a soothing, relaxing, physical and emotional healing experience.

Baths can be enhanced by the addition of several common household products such those listed below.

Apple Cider Vinegar: Vinegar helps relieve the itch of poison ivy, and aids the body in the detoxification process. Add .24 liters (1 cup) to the bath water.

Baking Soda: Add from .24 liters (1 cup) to 453.6 grams (1 pound) of baking soda to bath water to stop itching, skin irritation, and to facilitate healing of rashes.

Epsom Salts: These salts are especially useful in inducing perspiration, detoxifying the body, relieving soreness in muscles and joints, and bringing down swelling.

Sea Salt: You can pour some sea salt on a washcloth and add some essential oil like chamomile or rose to use as a scrub to exfoliate the skin.

Oatmeal: A natural product that relieves itchiness, sunburn, and hives, oatmeal is added to bath water to enhance the therapeutic effects on the skin. Purée .24 liters (1 cup) of uncooked oatmeal in a blender, and add it to running bath water.

Essential Oils: Essential oils can greatly enhance the therapeutic effects of a bath. Please refer to chapter 7, "Healing with Herbs," for beneficial oils. Fresh leaves and flowers can also be added to scent bath water for a relaxing, stress-relieving soak. Tie the plant material in cheesecloth and run the water stream over it, or steep the flowers in boiled water and then add the scented liquid to your bath.

Sitz Baths

A useful therapy for lower body problems is a sitz bath. Used to treat hemorrhoids, vaginal irritation, cramps, the pain from prostate problems, abdominal pain, and ovarian cysts, a sitz bath is a minibath where only the pelvis is submerged in water. Sit in the bathtub with your feet out of the tub and over the edge so only the pelvic area is submerged in the water. The water should be as hot as you can take it, and the treatment should last for at least five minutes but no longer than ten.

Cold Water Application

The application of cold water can be useful for treating lower body pain. Some healers recommend sitting in cold sitz bath, but I personally do not find the cold enjoyable and recommended a cold towel application instead. Submerge the towel in cold water, ring it out, and apply it to the appropriate area for a few minutes.

Ice Application

Ice applications are used to prevent skin injury and reduce swelling and pain from sprains, aches, and muscle problems. Ice works to narrow the blood vessels and limit inflammation and pain. Use ice therapy for headaches, nosebleeds, sprains, and swelling. Apply an ice pack for about twenty minutes directly on the injured area.

Hot and Cold Application

Alternating cold and hot application stimulates circulation, helps heal muscle problems, joint pain, and migraines. Apply the hot compress on the afflicted area for four minutes and then apply one minute of cold. Repeat the treatment five times, and always end with cold.

Cold Water Walking

One of the most potent ways to build up the body's immune system is to engage in periodic cold water walking. The cold water works to build up the body's resistance to infections. Fill a basin or bathtub with enough water to cover the feet, step in it, and march in place for up to five minutes. Be sure you have something to hold on to so you don't slip. After five minutes, step out of the water and dry your feet briskly with a towel. Rub the soles especially hard to stimulate them. Cold water walking can be done daily as a preventative action.

Exercise

Exercise delays bone loss, strengthens the heart, lungs, blood vessels, and muscles, increases energy levels, and relieves tension and stress. Cardiovascular and endurance training rids the body of excess fat and brings a larger supply of oxygen to the body, as it increases the strength of the circulatory system. Exercise truly promotes a well-functioning body.

Exercise includes any physical activity like swimming, biking, walking, jogging, dancing, aerobics, and sports. Stretching increases flexibility, loosens joints, and increases our range of motion, while weight training builds muscular strength and tone and increases endurance. Water exercise is the best way to strengthen the cardiovascular system; it benefits the heart and lungs without putting stress on the joints. It is effective for arthritis, pain management, and weight loss. If a patient is too sick or too elderly to exercise, a full body massage can stimulate the body and be just as good as exercise.

There is a difference between being big and fit and being big and unfit. No matter what size you are, if you are tired, worn out, and dragging yourself around, then you are unfit. Tiredness is a symptom that tells us change is needed. Listen to your body and make the necessary changes.

An easy way to add exercise to your life is to experiment with different sports and find one or two that you like. Or go for daily walks by yourself or with the dog. Take the stairs instead of the elevator, and try to park a few blocks from your destination. Engaging in regular exercise will strengthen and tone your body, and your muscles, heart, lungs, and mind will thank you greatly for it.

6

Massage Therapy

Massage is an ancient form of structured therapeutic touch that promotes healing through the application of precise pressure to the various muscles underlying the skin. It is considered to be an art form that, when performed correctly, facilitates a complete transformational healing experience for the patient.

From relieving headaches and muscular pains to soothing stress and tension, massage therapy is an effective treatment for a vast range of ailments. The gentle manipulation of tissue facilitates energy flow, aids circulation, increases the level of nutrients and oxygen that circulates through the cells, releases endorphins to kill pain, and helps aid the flow of lymph fluid to eliminate toxins in the system. Through massage, the mind is quieted and relieved, emotions are soothed, and the body yields, softens, and opens to undergo immense healing experiences.

We need touch in our lives. When we are deprived of touch we become unhappy, withdrawn, and even susceptible to disease, as isolation has been shown to lower the immune system. Countless studies have proven that babies and hospital patients develop and heal far faster when they are given regular periods of massage. In a time in our society when we are becoming increasingly afraid and wary of touch, therapeutic massage allows a strong level of communication and connection to form between people. It brings an awareness and a complete acceptance of the body, enabling a person to feel like a connected whole. And, most importantly, touch makes us feel loved. A massage is a sensory experience that one can fully enjoy unconditionally, without having to give back.

Therapeutic massage works through affecting the autonomic nervous system. It stimulates the sensory nerve endings in the skin, alleviating muscle pain and tension, stress, spinal curvatures, headaches, depression, and it also works to facilitate feelings of wellness and relaxation. It further helps promote the circulation of blood and lymph fluids through the body. Waste products from muscular activity, like carbon dioxide, lactic acid, and urea, can build up in the body's tissues, and massage aids the drainage of these toxins. Through the elimination of excess waste, stress and fatigue are also reduced. Massage also improves skin health. It is a powerful process that facilitates healing from illnesses and disease through promoting rebalancing of the body's natural systems.

Massage can be used as a relaxation therapy, as it slows the breathing cycle to calm and soothe an overstimulated patient, or it can be applied as a stimulation therapy to rev up a sluggish system. Try massage before or after exercise, to warm up the body or to cool it down to prevent injury and postexercise stiffness. With the addition of various essential oils to a basic massage carrier oil, the healing properties of a massage can be further enhanced, as the skin absorbs the therapeutic essences of the oils. Regular massage can be used as a preventative agent in a wellness maintenance program, or as a specific treatment for various ailments. A properly administered massage is a wonderful, soothing experience with vast healing benefits.

I think it is important for you to get a massage yourself so you can personally understand exactly how the treatment is supposed to feel and experience firsthand how relaxing and healing touch can be. Then begin your own work by practicing the various stroke techniques on yourself and your friends and family. Nobody ever turns down a volunteered massage.

The more you work with your hands to develop feeling in them and learn to sensitize them to the muscles of the body, the better masseuse you will be. Personal energy is used in physical manipulations as well as in massage, and through experimentation you will also learn how to control and direct your energy to enhance a massage. With practice anybody can learn to administer a good, healing massage.

The Skin

With any type of bodywork therapy you first want to consider the skin. The skin is the largest organ of the body, and it carries and reflects all the feelings and emotions of its owner. Skin problems can be created by stress, anger, guilt, and fear, and these emotional difficulties can manifest in many ways, including itching, acne, rashes, redness, hives, and eczema. Pay close attention to a patient's skin. If there are noticeable problems, be sure to inquire about his present feelings and find out if he is experiencing guilt, anger, or stressed emotions. Let him know that practicing relaxation techniques such as meditation, yoga, or tai chi can help with the situation. Anybody with a skin problem should also be advised to see a dermatologist.

Take care to avoid working body treatments on rashes, broken, or irritated skin. This can be painful for the patient, could spread the problem, or the irritation could be contagious and contact could transfer it to you. Also avoid working treatments on cuts, bruises, sprains, injuries, and new scar tissue. Massaging around a skin problem can be helpful, but only do so if it feels good to the person. If a patient has varicose or spider veins, do not press on the veins, as this can intensify them. Instead, brush or feather your fingers lightly over them.

The skin is also at high risk for cancer. Skin cancer is the fastest developing cancer among citizens in the United States at this time, and yet most cancers are curable if they are caught and treated early on. Skin moles are early clues to cancer, and you should advise any patient with a mole to have it checked regularly by her doctor. Changes in the shape, color, size, or appearance of a mole can be indications of a growing cancer.

There are several precautions that everybody should take to avoid the chances of developing skin cancer, and these include wearing a sunscreen with an SPF (sun protection factor) of at least 15, staying out of direct sunlight between the hours of 10 A.M. and 2 P.M., when the sun is at its strongest power, wearing protective clothing and hats with wide brims when you go outside, and making it a priority to see a dermatologist at the first sign of anything unusual.

The Basics

Massage can be applied with brisk circular strokes as a stimulating therapy or in long, deep strokes as a soothing treatment. The type of tissue manipulation depends on what a patient needs. If a person has to get up and go to work or partake in strenuous exercise, then you don't want to perform a deep and soothing massage. In this case, the treatment needs to be stimulating rather than relaxing. If a patient is uneasy, anxious, stiff, or needs relaxing, then the massage can be calming and soothing.

There are a few contraindications under which massage should not be applied, and it is important that you take extreme care to adhere to these situations. A patient suffering from cancer or tumors needs to consult with a physician before any massage treatment is given. Also, you do not want to massage a person with a fever, an infection, or a viral disease. Any person with blood clots, circulatory problems, or a heart condition should have massage treatment okayed by their doctor as well.

Massage during pregnancy can feel great, but you need to be careful not to press on the abdomen during the first four months, and only massage the area very lightly afterward. Some essential oils may not be suitable for a pregnant woman, and any herbal treatments should be discussed with her physician. If you are administering a massage to a patient with an injury, be sure to support the injury comfortably with a pillow and massage around the injury, not directly on it. The same goes for broken skin, rashes, eczema, inflammation, swellings, burns, and other skin problems.

Many people follow the saying, "No pain, no gain." I am of the school of thought that says, "More pain, insane!" If something hurts, then the body is sending a clear message to stop the treatment. With any type of bodywork you need to end the treatment on an area if the patient complains of pain. Stop the movement and ask the patient to see a physician about the cause of the internal pain.

For a massage treatment, you will need an appropriate environment. Use a room with low light, as harsh lighting can make person feel like he is in a doctor's office. I like a fairly warm room, as well. Muscles contract when they are cold, releasing adrenaline. We want to relax the muscles and ease away tension and adrenaline. You can play soft, relaxing music to provide gentle background sounds, just make sure that it is monotonous, as you not want to find yourself massaging in rhythm to the beat. You want to find your own inner massage rhythm.

For bodywork treatments, a massage table or padded floor is the perfect working surface. A very firm bed can be useful if you do not have a table, but a cushiony bed is too soft for a proper massage treatment. Place a thin pillow under the person's head for comfort, and one under the knees to help alleviate lower back stress. Use plenty of towels and blankets to cover the exposed areas of the body when you are not working on them. You do not want a patient to become chilled.

During treatment, a patient can be nude, or she can choose to keep her undergarments on. It depends on how comfortable the patient is with you and her own nudity. Never insist that a patient get undressed if she expresses a desire to remain partially clothed. And unless you know a patient intimately, leave the room when she undresses and let her undress alone to the level with which she is comfortable. Provide a large bath towel or sheet that the person can use to cover herself. I like to have a smaller set of towels to wrap around the areas of the body that I am not currently working on so they do not get cold. This also helps to make the patient feel safe and secure.

You need to pick a suitable massage time. Do not massage a person after a big meal. The pressure is too difficult on the body, as the system is occupied with digesting food. Be sure that the patient does not drink before or directly after a massage. Alcohol before a massage can induce nausea, and alcohol after a massage can have intense effects on the person, as massage therapy speeds up the body's absorption process.

In your work you need to understand and respect the personal bodily limits of your clients. You want to approach a partner with calm, sensitive hands that are not invading. Try to mold your hands to the shape of the patient's muscles. There is a fine balance to massage; you don't want to press so hard that you hurt a patient, but not so lightly that you tickle the patient, either.

Different people have different levels of tolerance. Some people cannot handle deep tissue massage and need lighter, softer strokes. Always start a massage with light strokes, as it may take some time for a patient's body to soften and open up to the treatment. When the patient relaxes and yields to the massage, you can then move into applying deeper strokes. As you progress with your massage work your hands will become attuned and sensitive to the specific needs of each body.

Always massage deeply toward the heart and lightly away from it to facilitate the flow of toxins to the heart so they can be purified. Slide your hands down the arms, legs, and torso, but be sure to apply the hardest pressure on the upward stroke. For an active massage to stimulate the body before exercise or work, make your strokes brisk and stimulating. Use a stimulating essential oil mixture and techniques such as chopping and kneading. For a soothing massage, use deep slow strokes like heel pressure and a relaxing oil.

When you are performing a treatment, you want to be in continuous contact with a patient's body as much as possible. To lose contact with a patient's skin can be distracting for him. Be sure to place all oils within reach and have bottles that are easy to open and pour with one hand. If you need to use both hands for something, like rubbing them together to spread oil on them, you can gently rest an elbow on the patient's back in order to continue the contact.

If you are giving a shoulder, neck, or arm massage, have the person sit up straight with her back supported and her head held erect. For a full body massage, lay the patient on a flat surface like a blanket-cushioned floor, table, or hard bed. If you plan to do a lot of massage, you may want to invest in a special massage table. They are a little bit costly but are well worth the investment.

No matter where the patient is positioned, you want to ensure that you have enough room to move around him. Make sure that you are sitting or standing in a comfortable position when you deliver the massage; you do not want to get a cramp and need a massage as well! Keep your spine straight and relaxed, and do not strain your body to reach an area. Move or ask the patient to move so you can reach him better.

Be receptive with your patients. Ask for feedback and check your hand pressure levels throughout the massage. Ask your partner to tell you if the strokes are feeling good or if they need to be harder or lighter. Have her point out any areas of tension that need to be massaged. You need to be flexible in your work, adapting the massage techniques to compensate for a patient's injuries or sensitivities.

Often a person may feel overly emotional during or after a massage treatment. This is a normal response. To be accepted and loved is a powerful experience that can provoke deep emotions. As a healer, you need to be there for your patients and let them know that any reaction is okay and will be welcomed.

The Oils

I like to massage with oil, as lubrication allows the hands to glide smoothly over the skin and prevents pulling and friction. Be sure to pour the oil onto your hands, and rub them together; never pour oil directly onto a patient's skin. Use it sparingly; you want just enough to coat your hands and allow them to glide over the skin. The oil can be warmed before a massage, just make sure to test it on yourself first so you don't burn the patient.

A basic massage oil is called a carrier oil or a base. For a base oil, I prefer almond or grapeseed oil, as both are smooth, pure oils that are easily absorbed and do not spoil easily. You can add essential oils to a base oil in order to enhance the therapeutic effects of a massage, but be sure to never use essential oils directly on the skin, as they are too potent and will cause irritation. Add essential oils to the carrier oil only when you are ready to use it, because they greatly decrease the shelf life of the carrier. In 25 ml (5 teaspoons) of base oil, you can add about twelve drops of essential oil. This will be good for about three massages and will last six to eight weeks as long as it is kept in a tightly stoppered bottle in a cool dark area.

In the following section I have included recipes for both stimulating and soothing oils, as well as information on several essential oils that are beneficial for specific ailments. Be sure to discuss with your patients the oils you are using and tell them why you chose those oils. You need to be certain that the patient does not have any allergies to an oil you are using. Let him smell the oil to see if he likes it; you do not want to be massaging with an oil that a patient may dislike, as this will make the massage an unpleasant experience for him. Also, do not use oils that have adverse reactions on you. As you massage, the oil will absorb into your skin and hands, so you must like the smell as well.

Experiment with different essential oils in your work. You can use from one to four essential oils in a mixture with a carrier oil. I recommend that you use one to two oils when you are first starting out, as this gives you a chance to learn how each oil affects the body. It can also be nice to use an essential oil aromatherapy diffuser in the room during a massage treatment. Consult with chapter 7 for more information on the various essential oils. Adding essential oils to a massage is a wonderful way to enhance the healing benefits of the treatment, and I suggest that you try a few of the following oils in your work.

Basil

An antiseptic, basil is a powerful essential oil that alleviates sinus congestion, bronchitis, and indigestion. It is an uplifting scent that can relieve mental fatigue and help clear the mind. Basil oil should be avoided during pregnancy.

Chamomile

Chamomile oil is a sedative that is extremely good for skin. It moistens dry skin tissue and works to soothe inflammation and sunburns. The essential oil aids the body in many ways, halting diarrhea, alleviating muscular aches and menstrual cramps, and soothing ulcers; it even works as an antidepressant.

Eucalyptus

A powerful essential oil, eucalyptus is a natural antiseptic that is effective for bacterial and viral infections. It is a cooling oil that is used to fight colds, flu, congestion, throat problems, bronchitis, herpes simplex, and pimpled skin. Eucalyptus oil is also an anti-inflammatory that helps to alleviate swelling, rheumatism, arthritis, and muscular aches and pains. It further stimulates, cleanses, and strengthens the kidneys.

Lavender

Lavender oil is a beneficial essential oil that is a must in any healer's collection. It is an antiseptic oil that heals burns and scalds, reduces inflammation, nausea, and the pain of headaches, controls diarrhea and vomiting, and it can further help to alleviate muscular pains, aches, rheumatism, cystitis, and cramps. It is also a powerful sedative, with its soothing essence promoting mental relaxation and working to remove stress and tension.

Rose

Rose is an antiseptic and cleansing essential oil with a pleasant scent. It relaxes the body, promotes circulation, strengthens the digestive system, and is very beneficial for the skin as well. I find rose to be an emotionally soothing oil, helping to greatly relieve a patient's depression, stress, or grief.

Rosemary

A powerful stimulant, rosemary oil helps relieve coughs, colds, heartburn, headaches, and stomachaches. It also does a wonderful job cleansing and toning the skin. Rosemary further stimulates and strengthens the memory and works to promote mental clarity. Because it is a highly potent stimulant, rosemary should be avoided during pregnancy.

Sandalwood

A rich-smelling oil, sandalwood is a relaxing oil that is profoundly calming on the body. It has antiseptic and soothing effects that relieve coughs, sore throats, inflammation from asthma, vomiting, heartburn, and nausea. It is also good for skin irritations and itchiness and helps relax patients suffering from anxiety and tension.

A Relaxing Oil

Add the following to 25 ml (5 teaspoons) of a carrier oil: three drops of lavender, three drops of rose, and three drops of sandalwood.

A Stimulating Oil

Add the following to 25 ml (5 teaspoons) of a carrier oil: four drops of rosemary, four drops of eucalyptus, and four drops of basil.

The Strokes

The nine basic massage techniques that we will learn include the large-area stroke called effleurage; specific manipulations of kneading, squeezing, wringing, rubbing, circling, and chopping; the light stroke of feathering; and the limb-balancing technique of stretching. These movements can be either stimulating or relaxing, depending upon the intensity of the pressure you apply. There are other valuable hand techniques in massage therapy, but these nine are the easiest to learn and experiment with when you are first starting out. Used together, they will allow you to administer a very effective massage.

Effleurage

This is the basic massage stroke that begins all massage. It is a gentle sweeping stroke that is used to spread oil over the surface of the body and works to loosen and relax the muscles. Oil your hands and stand before your partner's head, starting the massage in the center of the upper back, fingers pointing downward, and molding the palms and fingers to the shape of the body. Slide your relaxed hands down the back, spreading the oil over the skin and feeling for hard or knotted areas of tension. Cover the whole area of the back using a greater pressure toward the heart and a lighter pressure away from it. Use more oil when you need it. Fan your hands out over the lower back and hips, and then bring them up the sides of the ribs and back to the starting position. Effleurage can be used on the arms and legs as well. Starting at the wrist or ankle, slide your hands firmly up over the limb, and when you reach the joint, separate your hands and slide them gently down the outside of the limb. Always begin a massage with effleurage. It can also be used as a fill-in stroke when moving between the various areas of the body.

Squeezing

This is a technique that involves firmly squeezing the individual muscles. It is usually done after effleurage to further loosen and relax the muscles. Use both hands to firmly, but gently, squeeze an area, always working in an upward motion toward the heart. You want to form a V with your forefingers and thumbs and squeeze the V into the muscles, being careful not to pinch the tissue. Work up the entire length of the muscles of the shoulders, back, chest, legs, and arms. At the elbow and knee joints you want to ease up on the applied pressure. Squeezing is mainly done to prepare the body for deeper strokes.

Kneading

Kneading is a technique that involves squeezing and rolling the muscles, in much the same way that you would knead dough. The hands work alternately, lifting and squeezing the rolls of tissue on the body's fleshier areas like the thighs, abdomen, and buttocks. Using your thumb, press into the muscles and push the tissue gently away from you, and then roll the flesh back to your thumb with your fingers. Repeat the pulling and rolling process with your other hand, creating a rhythmic movement. Kneading is a deep, releasing movement that drives out tension. It is done with firm strokes, but you need to be careful not to knead directly over the bone. Also, watch that you do not dig into the muscles or pinch them. For this technique your hands need to be well oiled, but not too oiled or they will slip off the tissue. You will need to experiment and find the right amount of lubrication. Use your body weight to support your kneading strokes so that you do not stress your hands.

Pulling

This is a nonspecific muscle-releasing technique that is always done at the sides of the body. The stroke pulls against the person's own body weight to relax and ease entire sections of the body. Start with your partner lying on his chest. Lean across his body and place your first hand slightly beneath the far side of his lower hip. Keeping your hand soft and molded to the body shape, pull the tissue up toward you and then let go at the end of the stroke as your hand slides over his lower back. Repeat the pulling motion with the other hand a little higher than where you first started. Continue with the alternating hand motion, working fully up the back to the underarm. After you finish one side, switch your position and pull the other side. You can also perform the technique on the sides of the abdomen and chest when the patient is lying on his back. I like to use pulling as an in-between stroke to progress from one part of the body to another, like moving from the back onto the shoulders and arms.

Wringing

Wringing is a technique that is used after kneading when the muscles are thoroughly loosened and relaxed. It involves a gentle twisting motion of both hands in opposite directions. Wringing is performed in continuous movements and literally works to wring stress and tension from the body. It is a good technique for the back of the calves, the thighs, and the arms. Place both hands, fingers pointing away from you, on the lower calf, and push the muscles away with one hand while drawing the flesh back toward you with the other. Move up the leg, maintaining the stroke with gentle, continuous movements. Be sure to use a lighter pressure when wringing the arms. This technique can also be done on a fleshy back, where there is a good deal of bulk to wring.

Circling

Circling is a round, all-encompassing movement that opens up the body. Use circling to soften the effects of deeper, stronger strokes like kneading, and also to move from one part of the body to another. Place your hands flat against the skin and move them in precise, controlled circles. You can use both hands working in alternate directions, or, to apply deeper pressure on areas like the lower back, you can put one hand on top of the other. Use broad strokes and make big circles over the back or the buttocks, alternating your hands so that the strokes flow in one continuous motion.

Heel Pressure

The use of the heel of the hand permits deeper penetration into tight or knotted areas. Tilt your wrist back so that your fingers are raised, and apply pressure in small circles with the heel of your hand to an area. Be sure to use your body weight to properly administer the movement. On the buttocks and hips, circle your hand firmly over the contact spot and then move over the area with larger circling movements. The technique is good for removing tension in the hips and the buttocks, and can also be applied on the limbs. When working on the limbs, always apply the pressure on the upward stroke as you move your hands toward the center of the body. Work the leg muscles in strips, circling up the length of the leg. On smaller areas of skin, like on the arms, use your thumbs (instead of the heal of your hand) to apply pressure in circles.

Chopping

Also called hacking, chopping is a percussion movement that works to stimulate an area. It increases the circulation to the surrounding section and is an essential part of a stimulating massage. Only chop after you have thoroughly warmed up and worked a targeted area. To perform the stroke, bring the outer edge of your hand down lightly and sharply onto the tissue and then snap it up again. Chop rhythmically over an area, alternating hands and being sure to keep your fingers loose to produce the chopping sound. Chopping works well over the shoulders, back, buttocks, and thighs.

Feathering

Feathering is a soft, light stroke that uses only the fingertips to gently brush the body. It is a delightful stroke that can be performed to connect one section of the body to the next. It also works to bring the patient's attention back to the body on a sensual level. Start at the top of the back, leg, or arm, and stroke the tips of your fingers down the body, alternating hands to produce a continuous rippling feeling. Feathering can be done to finish one section before moving onto the next area, and it is also performed as the final stroke to end the massage.

Stretching

Stretching is a simple technique that works to expand and lengthen the body. It is a beneficial action for the neck and the legs, as it reduces muscular tension around joints. Stretching should always be applied after the muscles have been thoroughly worked. Make sure your movements are smooth and fluid, and be careful that you do not pinch the tissue. Pull with a gentle, consistent force when stretching a patient's limbs; never yank on them! Always release the stretch when you encounter resistance.

To stretch the neck, cup the hands under the base of the skull and pull the head firmly back toward you and then release the movement. For a leg stretch, cradle the heel of the foot in your palm, lifting the leg up slightly. Place your other hand over the top of the foot and slowly pull the leg back toward you. The movement of the leg is meant to come from the hip. When you feel resistance, stop the stretch and lower the leg. You can also stretch out the arm, gently, making the movement come from the shoulder joint. I like to end a massage with stretching, repeating each stretch twice.

You need to warm up your arms and hands before practicing the strokes or performing a massage treatment on a patient. Following are a few stretches that I recommend you repeat several times. Lace your fingers together and outstretch your arms in front of you, and then again directly over your head. You should also do a few arm circles in both directions to loosen up the shoulders. Then work on the hands. Make your hands into fists and squeeze them gently for a moment, then open and extend the fingers as wide as you can. Do this several times to warm and stretch out the fingers. Try a few finger waves. This is where you open your hand fully and then curl each finger into the palm in a smooth wave motion, starting from the little finger and progressing down to the index finger. Perform the wave a few times on each hand.

When your hands and arms are warm and stretched, then you can concentrate on opening your hand chakras. Rub your palms together briskly to open the hand energy centers, and then hold them a few inches apart and visualize energy gathering between them. Focus on feeling your energy coming from the heart center and running down your arms to collect at the palms. Move your hands apart a bit more and feel the energy stretch out like an elastic. Then push them back together and see the energy grow and concentrate between your hands. It is important that you take the time to awaken your energy before a treatment because, as a masseuse, you are not only affecting the physical body of a patient but the auric field as well.

For this reason you also need to be conscious of your own energy vibrations. You do not want to project negativity onto a patient. The more you work with your energy, the more your sensitivity to energy will increase. This knowledge will enhance the bodywork treatments. Consult with chapter 8 for various techniques and exercises to increase your proficiency when working with energy.

Administering a Massage

When you begin to administer a massage you want to be fully prepared. Perform the treatment in an undisturbed place that is warm and comfortable, and ensure that you have warmed oil, tissues to absorb any excess oil, and towels to cover the patient; play some soft, soothing music. Set a time limit on the treatment beforehand so you and the patient know how long it will last. Remove all jewelry and have your partner remove her jewelry, too, so you avoid pulling on it or getting oil on it. Keep your nails short and filed, and always wash your hands before and after any treatment.

Make sure you know what kind of treatment the person needs. Does he have allergies or aversions to a particular essential oil? Does he need a stimulating or soothing massage? Find out where he wants to be rubbed and where he may not want to be touched. Ask if he has any injuries and, if so, tailor your work accordingly. Be sure to ask for feedback so you know how he is feeling during the treatment. The following is an idea of a massage technique that can be used as a guide for you to adapt as you wish.

Center yourself with a few minutes of deep breathing. Warm up your arms and hands and open your hand chakras. Approach your partner with confidence, making your movements fluid and smooth. At the moment of initial contact, place both of your hands, palms down, on the person's back, and just breathe for a moment. Let your energy blend with the patient's own auric field. This allows her to get used to your presence.

We start the treatment on the back and hips, as they are the largest continual surface of the body and allow us to apply many different strokes. Have your partner lie on his stomach with his arms at his sides. Cover the patient's arms and legs with towels when you are working on his back so he does not get cold. Stand above the person and pour a bit of oil into your hand; rub your hands together to coat them with the oil. Position your hands together at top of the back. Point the thumbs down and, using an effleurage stroke, run the hands down the back, separating and fanning them out at the lower back to glide over the hips. Smooth the hands up the sides of body, then around the shoulder blades and back to the original position. Repeat these long, gliding strokes for a few times until the whole back is coated with oil.

Now change position so you are behind the client, at her feet. Begin to use circling movements to press deeper into the tissue, working up the sides of the spine from waist to neck. Then knead up one side of the body, starting at the waist, being careful not to pinch the flesh. Repeat the kneading on the other side.

Starting at the base of the spine, use the pressure of both your thumbs to work the tissue on each side of the backbone in small circles, moving up the back to the neck and over the shoulders. Be sure that you are pressing inward and into the muscles, not into the bones. Finish the back with a few light feathering strokes.

Then circle the hands over to the hips. Make small pressure circles with your thumbs over the hips, beginning from the spine at the waist and circling out over the hip bone. Finish the area by pulling up the sides of the body to the shoulders.

Knead the shoulder area and use the thumbs to apply small circular pressure over the neck. Gently stretch out the neck, and then progress to the arms.

For an arm massage, use a few drops of oil. Grasp the hand of your partner in yours and stroke the outside of the arm, from the wrist up, with your free hand. Repeat the effleurage stroke on the outside of the arm, beginning with the wrist again. Apply a kneading technique to the arm, focusing on manipulating the tissue on the fleshy areas of the upper arm and into the shoulder area. Then use your thumbs to make small circles of pressure up the sides of the arm. Wring the whole arm and stretch it gently. Finish the treatment with a few feathering strokes down the arm. Be sure to repeat the movements on the other arm.

At this point I like to circle my hands down to the hips and focus on the legs. For a leg massage, begin by oiling the leg with long, gliding effleurage strokes. Stroke firmly up the legs and gently on the downward stroke. Do not apply pressure to the backs of the knees. Use the kneading technique on the fleshy area of the upper thighs, then wring out the leg from ankle to hip. Finish the treatment with a few feathering strokes and two gentle leg stretches. Repeat on the other leg.

Add to this basic massage by working on the parts of the patient's body that need more attention. If the patient wishes, she can roll over to receive massage on the front of the body. Press lighter here, especially around the abdomen. Work the front of the arms and legs the same way you worked the backs of them. Remember to tailor your strokes to the patient's needs and sensitivities, and always ask for feedback.

Aftercare

After a massage, permit the patient some time to lie still for a while. You do not want to rush him, as the body needs time to absorb the treatment. Allow him a few moments of privacy to enjoy the pleasurable feelings. I really need this downtime after my own massages and find that my clients do as well.

Offer the person some water to help facilitate the internal cleansing process. Advise him to avoid showering for at least one hour to allow the skin time to fully absorb the essential oils. Ask him to avoid alcohol for a few hours as well, as the absorbency of the body is vastly increased with a massage treatment.

Properly administered massage has the power to make us feel loved just through simple, intimate, and direct human contact. It is a healing therapy that promotes love, and with love we can heal all. There is nothing more satisfying than seeing a person accept love—seeing her body unraveling and opening up to relaxation and healing possibility.

7

Healing with Herbs

The most ancient form of medicine practiced by man, herbal healing is the use of plants to prevent and treat illnesses and diseases. Herbal healing includes medicinal treatments made from plant material, and also the use of the concentrated essential oils of plants—an herbal healing treatment known as aromatherapy.

*U*ntil the twentieth century, herbal medicine was the basis of all medical treatment practiced in this world. Much of our modern day medicine is derived from the herbal remedies of the past. In North America we are now experiencing a resurgence of herbal medicine, a green revolution that is reawakening human consciousness to the incredible powers of natural plants.

From a plant's unique combination of active compounds we can heal injuries, cure disease, alleviate stress and mental anxiety, and promote wellness and personal health. Plants are milder on the body and have less damaging side effects than conventional medicines. Herbs are the pinnacle of the physical treatments, the densest, the most concentrated. They connect us with the earth energy that streams through this planet. Flower, leaf, stem, root, and seed all hold potent medicine inside their tissues, natural energy that is powerful enough to rebalance and recharge our own energy. Herbs have been described as tuning forks—gentle, natural medicines that work to facilitate the body's own innate healing process. Plants tell the soul soothing stories; they give us unconditional gifts of healing greenery and love.

Herbs can be used gently on a daily basis as vitamin and mineral supplements. They provide a natural way to nourish the body, unlike chemically processed vitamins. Stronger doses and more potent plants can be used in specific healing situations. Herbal treatments often require a longer duration of usage, but, as you know, healing cannot be rushed.

Plants are powerful medicine that can be used to heal problems and injuries that you know are not serious, such as small wounds, insect stings and bites, occasional headaches, upset stomach, indigestion, gas, minor diarrhea and constipation, colds, menstrual cramps, occasional insomnia, bruises, minor muscular pains, sprains, and very minor burns.

But herbs cannot replace the use of antibiotics in the case of actual infections, and herbal treatment cannot replace regular physician care. Do not attempt to self-diagnose and medicate a serious problem like fever, flu, persistent constipation or diarrhea, chronic sore throat, internal damage, extreme pain, consistent nausea, or any condition that worsens or persists for more than three days. Never diagnose and medicate children, as ordinary signs of minor illnesses can actually be symptoms of very serious diseases and problems.

For a diagnosed illness, the use of herbs can aid in the treatment of the problem, but any treatment should be discussed with the attending physician first, as some herbal remedies may interfere with prescription drugs. If a woman is pregnant or nursing, then the use of herbs should be discussed with her doctor as well, as some herbs can be harmful to a pregnant or nursing woman. If a person feels worse after taking an herbal treatment, she should stop the treatment and see a physician. She may have developed allergies to the plant.

The Action of Herbs

How do certain herbs work on the body? In this section we will discuss different terminology and how each type of herb affects the physiology of the body.

Adaptogenic: Herbs that assist the adrenal glands and work to increase the body's resistance to stress.

Anthelminitic: Anthelminitic herbs help destroy and expel intestinal worms.

Anti-inflammatory: Herbs that have the property to reduce inflammation of the body's tissues.

Antimicrobial: An herb with antimicrobial qualities aids the body's own natural immunity, strengthening resistance to infective microorganisms. Some antimicrobial herbs are antiseptic and directly fight disease-causing organisms.

Antispasmodic: Herbs that relieve cramping and tension in the muscles.

Carminative: A carminative herb helps the digestive system to function smoothly by reducing inflammation, working to soothe the gut wall, and helping to expel gas from the tract.

Diuretic: Herbs that cleanse the body through increasing the production and elimination of urine.

Emmenagogue: An emmenogogue is an herb that stimulates the menstrual flow and supports the female reproductive system.

Expectorant: Herbs that work to stimulate the removal of mucus from the lungs.

Hepatic: An herb with hepatic properties aids the functioning of the liver, toning and strengthening it.

Laxative: Laxatives promote bowel movements. They work by one of three ways: by increasing the production and excrement of bile, by triggering peristalsis, or by providing bulk for the system.

Nervine: A nervine is an herb that has a direct effect on the nervous system. Nervine stimulants activate and increase nerve activity, while nervine relaxants soothe the system, easing anxiety and tension.

Herbal Treatments

There are many ways to use herbs. You can brew teas from leaves and flowers for common afflictions, make a decoction from tougher plant material like bark and roots, use herbs steeped in alcohol to make a tincture, treat sores and sprains with a wet compress or poultice, or ingest herbs dried in capsule form. In the use of any herbal treatment, avoid mixing herbs, as each herb works best by itself (although you can add mint to flavor a medicine to make it more palatable).

In America, there are laws that prohibit people from growing and distributing herbs for other people. It is okay to grow herbs for your own uses, but you need to buy your herbal supplies from a reputable dealer if you want to use them to treat others. Look for clean, identified plant material that is bright in color and has a strong odor.

In the following section I will discuss various ways to use herbs in treatment, but be sure to refer to the information on the individual plants included at the end of this chapter for appropriate uses of each herb and possible side effects.

Herbal Tea

An herbal tea is made from an herb steeped between five to ten minutes in boiled water. It is also called a *tissane*. A single dose of tea is one teaspoon of dried plant material to one cup of water. If you are using fresh plants, then one tablespoon of fresh equals one teaspoon of dried herb. Since dried herbs are available all year round, most recipes give the amount needed in terms of dried material. You get the best results if you use loose herbs and strain the liquid afterward, rather than using a tea bag or an infuser. Always use pure distilled water instead of tap water, and boil the water in a glass, china, or enamel pot. Add the herb to the hot water, and then keep the container covered as the herb steeps to prevent the volatile oils from evaporating. Never use milk or cream to dilute the tea, as milk weakens the power of the herb; use honey or lemon juice to sweeten and flavor the tea instead. A usual dosage is one cup of fresh tea three times a day before meals, and one more cup at night before bed. Do not wake up to take a dosage in the night, as the best healer is often a good night's sleep.

Decoctions

A decoction is made from tougher plant material like roots and bark that need to be brewed longer than leaves to extract the active constituents. Follow the same proportions of water to plant material as for a tea, but be sure to crush the herb first to release its essence. Add the herb to a pot of cold water and bring the mixture to a slow boil. Reduce the heat and simmer for about fifteen to twenty minutes, stirring occasionally. Remove from the heat and place a lid on the pot to steep the herb for about five minutes. Strain the liquid and then use honey to sweeten, as bark and roots can taste somewhat bitter. The dosage of a decoction is the same for tea: one cup three times a day and another before bed. A decoction will last for about three days in the refrigerator.

Herbal Compresses

A compress is a hot or cold dressing that is applied to the body to soothe aches and pains. For a hot compress, use a clean rag and soak it in hot, freshly brewed tea or decoction; you can also use essential oil from the chosen plant to make a compress—simply add seven drops of the oil to the hot water instead.

Wring the excess water from the dressing and place it on the skin, and then, in order to hold the heat in, cover it with a piece of plastic film and a small towel. Be careful that the compress is not so hot that it burns the skin. When the compress becomes cool, you can replace it with another one. Keep it on for at least two hours. For a cold compress, soak the rag in the hot liquid, but allow it to cool in the refrigerator before applying it to the afflicted area. A cold compress is used for swelling, bruises, headaches, and recent sprains.

Poultices

A poultice is a mash of crushed plant material that is held against the skin by a bandage. The herb is mashed and then mixed with a small amount of boiling water. Apply the hot pulp directly to the skin, and secure it with a cloth or gauze bandage. A poultice is often more effective than a compress for internal use. It, too, is applied to alleviate aches and pains, but it is also used to draw impurities and infection out of the body.

Herbal Tinctures

A tincture is an amount of plant material that has been prepared in a mixture of water and alcohol. Many alcoholic extracts can be potentially toxic, so it is best that a patient consults with his doctor before experimenting with tinctures. Tinctures are purchased as commercially made products from a reputable supplier and will last about two years. A normal dosage is about ten drops of the liquid placed directly under the tongue, or added to a half a cup of warm water and drank.

Capsules and Tablets

Herbal remedies can also be taken in pill form. Natural health-food and vitamin stores have many herbal remedies available. A normal dosage of treatment is one pill twice a day taken with a large glass of water.

The Herbs

There are many more useful herbs than the ones I have presented here, but it is important that you learn some of the most common and most versatile ones first. The twelve herbs included are easy to find and use and are effective for a wide variety of complaints. As your herbal knowledge base grows you can branch out and experiment with using other herbs.

Aloe Vera *(Aloe vera)*

A succulent perennial, aloe vera is a desert plant that has narrow, prickly edged, fleshy leaves. The leaves hold a clear gel that is applied as a valuable first-aid treatment for skin injuries. The leaves also emit a sour juice called bitter aloe, which has an intense laxative property and should not be taken internally. Aloe vera is easy to grow and requires very little water.

How it works: Fresh aloe juice is an excellent emollient, or skin-softening substance. It contains allantoin, a material that activates the immune system and facilitates quick healing of the skin. It provides instant relief from scalds, sunburns, small wounds, bites, and other minor skin irritations. Aloe also works to prevent the wound from becoming infected, as the gel dries and forms a protective antibacterial barrier.

How to use it: Pick an aloe leaf, split it open, and gently rub the clear liquid directly onto the skin. It will dry quickly, creating a natural bandage. Apply as needed.

Side effects: Aloe vera has no side effects when applied topically. In rare instances, individuals have skin allergies to the plant. Aloe juice should not be ingested, as it could be potentially toxic.

Asian Ginseng *(Panax ginseng)*

Sometimes called Korean ginseng, Asian ginseng is used by the practitioners of traditional Asian medicine. An adaptogen, ginseng helps the body react to stress and boosts the immune system.

How it works: Ginseng has warming properties that work to activate the systems of the body. Compounds called ginsenosides stimulate the adrenal glands, helping the body respond to stressful situations. They help the body maintain balance and also support the functioning of the immune system.

How to use it: Dried ginseng root is powered and taken in capsule form. The liquid extract is also available.

Side effects: Ginseng has been known to overstimulate the body, increasing blood pressure and causing heart palpitations, diarrhea, insomnia, and agitation. People with high blood pressure and diabetes should have ginseng use okayed by their doctor, as should pregnant or lactating women. Ginseng should not be taken for more than two months at a time unless under the advice of a medical specialist.

Basil *(Ocimum basilicum)*

A popular culinary herb, basil is a bushy-branched annual that has a square stem opposite shiny, green-toothed leaves. Small white or purplish flowers grow in whorls of six at the ends of its branches. Basil is an herb that is easy to grow and dry. It is used for many purposes, including as a carminative and an emmenagogue. Fresh basil poultices are also applied on insect bites and stings.

How it works: An infusion of basil leaves works as a carminitive, relieving gas, cramping, and digestion pains. Extracts of the leaves have been found to possess soothing properties that inhibit the poison from insect stings and bites. It can also bring on menstruation and stop cramping.

How to use it: Tea made of basil leaves is drank to treat minor nausea, gas pains, diarrhea, colds, and to induce menstruation to end cramping. Eating the fresh leaves is known to lower the risk of cancer. A poultice of mashed basil leaves draws the poison out of an insect sting or bite and helps stop irritation and itchiness.

Side effects: Basil has virtually no side effects, although a few individuals may develop skin allergies from the leaves.

Burdock *(Arctium lappa)*

A biennial plant, burdock has large waxy leaves that are roughly heart shaped. It bears clusters of purple tubular flowers and small hooked burs. Burdock root and leaves holds powerful medicine that is used to treat a variety of conditions including skin irritations, liver and kidney problems, and ailments that affect the female reproductive system.

How it works: Burdock contains polyacetylenes, substances that work as antibacterial cleansers. A poultice of mashed leaves applied to the body acts as an external antiseptic, healing minor wounds and skin irritations such as eczema, cysts, pimples, and acne. Burdock root also works as a hepatic. It strengthens the liver, binding toxins in the gut and flushing them out of the body. It can be used to treat liver disease. This marvelous plant also has the power to heal the kidneys and stop urinary problems, stabilize blood sugar levels, help ease the outbreaks of herpes, soothe the stomach, and cure chronic digestive problems. Burdock root is a valuable medicine to women, as this powerful emmenagogue heals internal feminine problems; it eliminates the overgrowth of yeast, dissolves ovarian cysts, and strengthens the womb. Burdock is also an anticancer and antitumor medicine.

How to use it: Dried burdock root and leaves can be taken in capsule or tincture form. The plant material can also be made into a tea. Burdock is a plant that works slowly, and it must be used over a few months to see results.

Side effects: Burdock should not be taken by pregnant women, as it is known to be a uterine stimulant.

Clove *(Syzygium aromaticum)*

The clove tree is a broad evergreen that bears little flowers that are picked and dried to produce the aromatic cloves used in many culinary dishes. Cloves are a preservative and have antimicrobial powers.

How it works: Eugenol, a powerful substance found in cloves, acts as an antibiotic that kills disease organisms. It is best extracted through tea made from the cloves.

How it is used: The tea is taken to kill intestinal bacteria and to destroy the germs that cause traveler's diarrhea. A drop of clove oil can be applied directly on a toothache to numb the pain; one clove can be placed on the tooth and bit down on for relief. A poultice can be used on the skin to heal cuts and bites.

Side effects: The oil of cloves can cause irritation in some people. It should never be ingested.

Dandelion *(Taraxacum officinale)*

A perennial herb that is considered a pesky weed, a dandelion actually holds strong power within its cells and is a valuable healing plant. It is useful as an antimicrobial, a diuretic, an emmenagogue, and a hepatic.

How it works: Dandelion's dark hairless greens are edible and are extremely rich in potassium, vitamin A, and vitamin C. They have been proven to have an antibacterial effect against bad bacteria, including the germs that cause staph infection, pneumonia, tuberculous, and diphtheria. Dandelion leaves also heal the kidneys and urinary system by removing blockages and promoting urination. The root of the plant works as a liver strengthener. It helps to flush toxins out of the body and, thus, is known as a valuable herb to use to prevent cancer and tumors. Dandelion root is also a stabilizer of blood sugar levels and aids in controlling diabetes. Often called the woman's healer, dandelion root heals ailments of the uterus, ovaries, and breasts. It eases menstrual cramps, internal inflammation, PMS symptoms, yeast infections, and helps fight breast cancer.

How to use it: The leaves can be eaten in salad or made into tea that is taken for chest pain, healing of the urinary system and kidneys, to enhance circulation, and to stimulate the appetite. A tincture or dried capsules of dandelion root can be ingested to prevent and heal cancer, stabilize blood sugar levels, strengthen the liver, heal women's complaints, and help to cure digestive problems. Dandelion can be combined with burdock for tough inner problems.

Side effects: Be careful that you are not using dandelions gathered from lawns that have been treated with pesticides. Some people may have allergic reactions to dandelion.

Echinacea *(Echinacea angustifolia)*

Also called coneflower, echinacea is a hairy perennial shrub that grows about two feet tall with narrow oblong leaves. The plant bears single stalked flower heads, with purple or white flowers that have orange-brown centers. The root, stem, and leaves are used to increase the strength of the immune system, making echinacea an effective antimicrobial against bacterial and viral infections.

How it works: Echinacea stimulates and boosts the immune system, as it increases the production of leukocytes, the white blood cells that work to protect against attacking viruses and bacteria. It restores normal body functioning and is taken to treat infections like colds, the flu, sore throats, coughs, and recurring yeast infections.

How to use it: You can buy capsules in health-food stores or take the dosage in tincture form. A normal dosage of echinacea in tincture form is up to thirty drops of extract in warm water taken three times a day. Echinacea should be used for no more than two weeks continuously.

Side effects: Echinacea should not be taken by those people who are allergic to members of the sunflower family, such as ragweed and daisies. Generally, side effects associated with the use of echinacea are rare.

Garlic *(Allium Sativum)*

A perennial plant that grows up to two feet long with flat pointed leaves and an edible bulb composed of small cloves, garlic is a powerful healing herb. In cooking, it can be used in all savory dishes, hot or cold. It is a potent antibiotic that can be eaten to cure colds, sore throats, coughs, infections, intestinal disorders; to lower cholesterol levels; and to boost the immune system.

How it works: Containing vitamins A, B_1 (thiamin), B_2 (riboflavin), and C, plus a natural germ-killing chemical, garlic prevents heart attacks and strokes, as it raises the level of good cholesterol in the blood and decreases the level of bad cholesterol. It works to lower blood pressure, thins the blood, and reduces blood clots. Garlic also contains a natural antibiotic called allicin, which prevents and fights infections. It is used in respiratory infections. Furthermore, the plant has been found to reduce the risk of contracting stomach and colon cancers.

How to use it: To benefit from garlic's healing properties, you can either eat it in food, or pieces of it can be swallowed raw like pills. There are also garlic supplements available in pharmacies and health food stores.

Side effects: Garlic has been known to cause heartburn, flatulence, and halitosis. Because it naturally thins the blood and reduces clotting, it should not be taken with anticoagulant drugs, medication that is taken to thin the blood.

German Chamomile *(Anthemis nobilis)*

German chamomile is a perennial herb that grows up to twelve-inches long, with fine feathery green leaves and small daisylike flowers that have yellow centers with white petals. The flowers emit a sweet odor similar to the smell of apples, and are used to treat both internal and external conditions.

How it works: Taken as a tea, the flowers are a relaxing nervine that possess mild sedative properties. They have a relaxing action on the nervous system, working to decrease anxiety and promote sleep. They also work to ease the digestive system and reduce internal inflammation. Chamomile has a beneficial effect on the skin as well, as it opens the pores and soothes irritation.

How to use it: Chamomile tea is taken for indigestion, upset stomach, menstrual cramps, and to reduce pain and swelling. It can also be ingested just for relaxation or to cure insomnia. The cooled tea is often used as a rinse for the body to soften and soothe the skin.

Side effects: If you are allergic to ragweed, daisies, or chrysanthemums, you should not ingest chamomile, as it can sometimes cause rare but serious allergic reactions. A large amount of chamomile, anything over three cups, should not be taken at one time, as it has been known to cause vomiting. The plant also causes skin allergies in some individuals.

Horehound *(Marrubium vulgare)*

A member of the mint family, horehound is a perennial with a square woolly stem that grows up to three feet tall. It has an expectorant action and is useful for relieving coughs.

How it works: The leaves of horehound contain marrubin, a substance that irritates the lining of the throat and causes the removal of mucus from the body.

How to use it: A horehound infusion of fresh or dried leaves can be sweetened with honey to taste and imbibed every six hours. Or, you can eat the fresh leaves chopped in a bowl with a teaspoon or two of honey.

Side effects: There are very few cases of horehound causing adverse side effects. Some people may have allergies to the plant, and others may dislike its bittersweet taste.

Peppermint *(Mentha piperita)*

A perennial herb growing three feet tall, peppermint has toothed oval leaves on a square stalk of purple-pink colored flowers. A time-honored healing remedy, peppermint aids in digestion, eliminating gas, diarrhea, and other digestion problems. It also has antimicrobial properties.

How it works: Peppermint oil contains menthol, a powerful aromatic chemical that does several things: it helps to soothe stomach complaints by stimulating the gallbladder and encouraging bile secretion, supports the muscles of the stomach and intestines, and it also reduces internal inflammation. It eliminates intestinal gas and relives indigestion. Menthol also has strong antimicrobial properties that work to kill organisms that cause digestive problems. It further is used to clear congestion in the head and upper respiratory passages.

How to use it: A tea of fresh peppermint leaves has many therapeutic effects. It can be imbibed as an after-dinner digestive aid to relieve gas and to stop mild stomach problems. It stops diarrhea, colic, colds, fevers, and kills internal worms. Peppermint can also be added to flavor other teas and decoctions.

Side effects: Pure peppermint oil contains the potent chemical menthol and should never be taken internally. Even the menthol component of peppermint tea can be too strong for infants and very young children and can cause a choking sensation.

St. Johns Wort *(Hypericum perforatum)*

A perennial herb, St. Johns wort has yellow five-petaled flowers and opposite paired leaves. The leaves release a potent red oil when crushed. Used as a natural antidepressant, St. Johns wort also has antimicrobial properties and is currently being tested as a medicine to fight the virus that causes AIDS.

How it works: The plant contains chemicals that improve the mood and raise the spirits by increasing the action and amount of transmitters in the brain. It further possesses antiviral, antibacterial, and anti-inflammatory properties.

How to use it: Dried St. Johns wort leaves are taken in capsule form as a natural antidepressant. The extract is also available in tincture form and is applied externally to relieve muscle tension and facilitate the healing of wounds.

Side effects: Side effects include a sensitivity to sunlight, dryness of the mouth, and occasional instances of nausea. St. Johns wort may interact with prescription medicines and birth control pills, so it is important that usage be discussed with a doctor before taking the herb.

Aromatherapy

Aromatherapy is defined as the use of essential oils for therapeutic treatment. Sometimes called the soul of the plant, essential oils are the odoriferous active constituents found in the branches, leaves, flowers, and roots of plants. These concentrated medicinal constituents are extracted and then used in minute quantities in various healing and preventative therapies. Aromatherapy is a generally safe healing therapy because it does not have the negative side effects associated with conventional treatments and antibiotics. It is a very effective therapy because the small molecular size of the oil particles are able to easily penetrate bodily tissues. Essential oils are used in aromatherapy treatments such as bathing, inhalation, or massage, but they should never be taken internally, as they are too concentrated and could cause damage to the body.

Aromatherapy is helpful for immune deficiencies, as certain essences can be used to stimulate the immune system and energize the body into healing action. The minute plant essences can enter skin and penetrate the bloodstream directly, promoting health. They can help the body build immunity, fight infections through their antibacterial and antiviral properties, heal skin disorders, alleviate clogged sinuses and chest congestion, and work to detoxify the digestive system. Aromatherapy is a beneficial treatment to clear up colds, the flu, headaches, and muscular aches and pains.

Aromatherapy can also be applied to produce changes in the neurochemistry of the brain, transforming and stabilizing emotions. As the aromatic molecules are inhaled, they create signals that travel to the limbic system in the brain, the mechanism that regulates heart rate, breathing, hormone balance, blood pressure, and memory. The signals can subtly alter perceptions, memories, and emotions, stimulating or sedating brain waves depending upon the type of essential oil used.

Specific scents like rosemary and sage boost beta brain waves and work to stimulate the body's systems, while other aromas like chamomile and rose increase alpha waves and promote relaxation. Aromatherapy can be used to treat anxiety, depression, insomnia, grief, mental imbalances, and stress. In fact, it is a particularly good treatment for relieving stress—a valuable therapy for the healer, as many illnesses caused and/or triggered by stress.

Basic Information

Aromatherapy is fast becoming a popular healing treatment, and there are a great deal of aromatherapy products available on the market today. But the key to an effective healing product is to choose one made with natural essential oils. Many products being sold are actually made with synthetic fragrances rather than the raw constituents, and for your healing treatments you want the real thing. To prevent purchasing manmade oils, look for a company that specializes in aromatherapy oils and labels its products as essential oils rather than perfume essences. Avoid buying your products at the cosmetic counter or in bath shops where product fragrance is often more important than natural ingredients. A good way to tell if you have a natural product is by looking at the price. The price of essential oils varies from oil to oil, so if you find they are all the same price, it is a sign that the products contain perfume essences instead of essential oils.

You also need to be sure that the oils you are buying have been stored in dark bottles out of the sun. Sunlight depletes and weakens the active constituents of the oil. Because many pounds of plant material is needed to produce only the smallest amount of essential oil, natural oils can be very expensive, and you will want to take good care of your supply. Keep your products in a dark, cool spot like the refrigerator or a cupboard. Kept this way, an essential oil will last for at least a year. If an oil appears cloudy, then it is past its prime and needs to be thrown away. And be sure to get an accurate dropper cap so you can control the amount of oil you are using in your treatments. Because the oils are made from such concentrated chemical constituents, small amounts of the essence will go a long way.

With any aromatherapy treatment, you want to start with a small dosage and watch for allergic reactions. For a first experience with an oil, try a skin test using two drops of the oil mixed in a tablespoon of a carrier oil, like olive or almond oil. Rub a bit of the mixture on the inner arm and wait twelve hours for a possible allergic response such as redness or itching. When using any oils, always be sure to protect the eyes, as the essences can be very irritating. Never ingest essential oils, as they are too potent for the body.

Most essential oils actually need to be diluted in a carrier oil before they are applied on the skin. When an essential oil can be used full strength, it is referred to as using the oil "neat." Any oils that can be used neat are specifically identified. Never apply an oil that needs to be diluted full strength on the skin, as it can cause severe reactions. It is best not to use essential oils on a woman who is pregnant, as some oils could perhaps trigger a miscarriage or provoke an allergic reaction.

Be sure to let a patient smell the oils you want to use in order to check for compatibility. People are instinctively drawn to the healing scents they need, as the fragrances we like are connected to the body pheromones we excrete at different times in our lives. Patients always know what is best for their bodies. Also, if a patient does not like a particular scent, this is when you can find out, instead of when it is diffused through the room or slathered over part of his body.

Aromatherapy Treatments

Inhalation

The distribution of essential oil particles in the air is an effective treatment for respiratory problems or to charge the environment with mood enhancers or calmers. Oils can be misted in a room through a spray bottle or vaporized through a room with an electronic diffuser. Put a drop of oil on your pillow to help with insomnia. When studying, add a drop to a page of your book to help reduce mental fatigue.

Skin Application

A very effective way of using essential oils is through skin application. Skin is extremely absorbent, and the oil quickly affects underlying muscles and nerves. But you should never apply any essential oil directly to the skin, as it is too powerful. It must first be diluted in a carrier oil or water. Oils can be applied in a hot or cold compress to relieve sprains, muscular pains, injuries, cramps, and skin problems. See the preceding herbal treatment section for information on using oils in compresses. They can also be applied in massage. Refer to chapter 6 for information on using essential oils in massage treatments. Apply a few drops of diluted peppermint or rosemary oil to the temples to aid with headaches. In a bath, essential oils can be added for relaxing or stimulating the body, depending on what is needed. Use five to ten drops of oil for a full bath.

Steam Inhalation

Steam inhalation is used to treat respiratory problems such as colds, congestion, and sinus ailments. It can also be used to relieve headaches. To use essential oil as an inhalant, add five to ten drops of oil to a bowl containing three cups of hot water. Drape a towel over your head and slowly and deeply inhale the steam for about ten minutes. Repeat the treatment no more than three times a day. Asthmatics should not engage in steam inhalation.

The Oils

Although there are many useful essential oils, I have only included eight here. These eight oils are common beneficial oils that can be used to treat a great variety of conditions. Start with them, and as your knowledge grows you can add more oils to your medicine bag. Keep notes of your experimentation with each oil.

Chamomile *(Anthemis noblis)*

Chamomile is a very useful oil with vast therapeutic properties. It is a calming, soothing oil with mild sedative properties that is excellent for the skin. Rub a few drops into the stomach and solar plexus to calm an upset stomach, physical stress, menstrual cramps, indigestion, vomiting, and diarrhea. The oil can also be applied to the temples and forehead to ease the effects of a migraine, hysteria, and nervousness. Chamomile oil is good for all forms of skin care, including eczema, herpes, broken capillaries, spider veins, and minor irritations. Chamomile blends well with the scents of lavender and rose. If you are allergic to ragweed or other members of the sunflower family, do not use chamomile oil.

Eucalyptus *(Eucalyptus globulus)*

Eucalyptus oil is a powerful therapeutic oil that has antiseptic germ-killing properties. It has a positive effect on the immune system and is used for colds, the flu, coughs, asthma, and internal bacterial infections. You can place three to five drops of eucalyptus oil in the bath, or add the drops to boiling water and breathe as an inhalant infusion. For colds, inhale the steam two to three minutes, five times a day. When mixed in a carrier oil, it can also be applied as a topical rub on the chest and neck to fight internal infections. Because of its anti-inflammatory action, it further works to reduce arthritic pain when applied topically. Eucalyptus is also effective against herpes; apply a few drops of the oil several times a day directly on the lesions. Never take the oil internally, as it is highly poisonous. Eucalyptus blends well with the scents of lavender and tea tree.

Lavender *(Lavandula officinalis)*

The heady scent of lavender is a favorite among most people, and, indeed, lavender oil is the most versatile oil, as it is beneficial for a vast amount of common problems. It possesses a high ester content and sedative properties. It lowers high blood pressure, relieves muscular aches and painful cramps, and helps digestive upsets. It is the best oil to use for skin problems like acne, burns, boils, dermatitis, high blood pressure, mild rashes, and it contains antivenomous properties to help heal insects bites and stings. To deliver skin treatment, lavender oil is very effective when added to a patient's bath water. It also has a mind-balancing action, and inhaling it can calm fits of hysteria, nervousness, anxiety, anger, and depression. For stress or shock, put ten drops of lavender in the bath water. It is a soothing scent, and misting the oil on your bed sheets ensures a calm gentle sleep. Lavender is not to be taken internally, as the oil may be poisonous. Lavender blends well with the scents of chamomile and rosemary.

Peppermint *(Mentha piperita)*

The zesty smell of peppermint is a favorite and has many healing properties. Add a low concentration of essential oil to the carrier, as it can be irritating for the skin. Rub the mixture on the abdomen and solar plexus for colon problems, irritable bowel syndrome, indigestion, and vomiting. Peppermint oil is a stimulant, so be sure to use it during the day, as it can keep you up at bedtime. It stimulates the adrenal cortex and boosts the mental process; spritz some on a handkerchief and inhale it if you need a mental energizer for an exam or in a meeting. It also fights migraine, colds, and coughing. Peppermint harmonizes well with the scents of lavender or rosemary.

Rose *(Rosa species)*

Rose oil is a tranquilizing essence that is used primarily for skin care. It can be added to bath water and massage oil to aid circulation and help heal veins and stretch marks. It also cleanses toxins from the blood and relaxes the body. Massage it into the stomach to purify the uterus and treat female problems. Inhaled or rubbed on the temples and forehead, rose oil works to lift depression, sadness, and grief. Rose blends fine with most essences, but it harmonizes especially well with chamomile and sandalwood oils.

Rosemary *(Rosmarinus officinalis)*

A pungent spicy herb, rosemary is an intense stimulant. When inhaled, it increases energy response in the brain, boosting the memory and promoting clarity of thought. Use rosemary oil in the bath to flush out the system and eliminate toxins in the skin. It speeds up the metabolism of the outer skin cells and, thus, regenerates the skin. It also raises low blood pressure, alleviates fatigue, and helps ease the pain of rheumatism and arthritis. Use rosemary in steam inhalation for colds, flu, bronchitis, and catarrh. Rosemary oil rubbed on the hair acts as a tonic, stimulating hair growth and eliminating dandruff. The scent blends well with peppermint and lavender. Because it is such a stimulant, rosemary should be avoided during pregnancy, and care should be taken to avoid putting the oil directly on the skin without diluting it in a carrier oil first.

Sandalwood *(Santalum album)*

The heavy sweet smell of sandalwood is a relaxing sedative that soothes respiratory problems like chest colds, coughs, bronchitis, and catarrh. Hailed as an aphrodisiac, sandalwood is also used in massage oil to cure impotence and frigidity. Sandalwood blends well with rose and works exceptionally well by itself.

Tea Tree *(Melaleuca alternifolia)*

One of the most powerful antibiotic essential oils, tea tree is a valuable oil. Its healing properties include antifungal, antibacterial, and antiviral effects. When inhaled or applied on the body, it stimulates the immune system and can be used to fight infections. It can be applied neat as a topical antiseptic to treat acne, athlete's foot, warts, rashes, herpes, insect bites and stings, and minor wounds. Tea tree oil blends well with lavender.

8

Healing with Energy

A profound healing treatment that has evolved from the ancient practice of laying on of hands, energy therapy works to remove blockages and deficiencies in the body's energy field, creating health through restoring proper energy alignment and flow.

*E*nergy therapy is a powerful healing system that encompasses many aspects. This chapter aims to build upon your growing knowledge base of energy, beginning with a discussion on understanding and perceiving personal and universal energy, and ending with an introduction to aura therapy treatment. The three subsequent chapters cover specific chakra healing treatments, and working with the vibrations of colors and crystals in order to align and balance the personal energy field.

We know that the body is an instrument composed of far more than flesh and bones. It also has an amazing electronic component. The body functions as an extensive communication system that hinges upon the individual cell's ability to send electronic messages to each other. Receptors in the synaptic gaps receive these electrochemical impulses that the brain then translates as thoughts. External electromagnetic frequencies from sources like radiation, electronic equipment, or even another person's own electronic vibrations can affect the body's electronic functioning.

But the body does not just communicate in electronic impulses, it is literally composed of moving, living bioenergy. Even the smallest atoms of the body break down into energy and space. The flow of electrons in the nervous system of the body creates an electronic and magnetic field, known as an *electromagnetic field*. Every molecule in our universe is actually a piece of a giant moving electromagnetic field, called the *universal energy field*.

The energy field that emanates in layers from a living body is part of the universal energy field and is called the *human energy field*. Generated by the body, the human energy field interacts with the other environmental fields. The part of the human field that we can learn to see is called the *auric field*, or the *aura*. The aura is accompanied by twelve major energy pathways, called *meridians*, that run down the body from head to toe.

Down the center of the body runs the center meridian, and it is supplemented with a linear arrangement of seven major energy concentrations called *chakras*. At the top of the head lies the crown chakra; at the center of brow is the third eye chakra; at the hollow of the throat situates the throat chakra; directly between the breasts is the heart chakra; just above the navel is the solar plexus chakra; below the navel lies the sacral chakra; and at the very bottom of the spine, in the perineum, we find the root chakra. There are also minor chakras located in the palm of the hands and the souls of the feet. The chakras are openings to the auric field that allow energy to travel in and out of the field. (See chapter 9 for detailed information about the chakras.)

The auric field completely infuses and encompasses the body, acting like a psychic shield. It appears in various layers of thickness, states of motion, and color intensities that can be read to reveal the physical and emotional health of the organism. A skilled reader can study the aura and diagnose disease and sickness in a person, both of the body and of the mind. Your personal aura is an extension of you; it contains your feelings, thoughts, memories, personality traits, even traces of your past experiences. We carry everything around in our energy. Our intimate connections to others even remain in our energy, which is a reason why we experience so much pain, grief, and anger when we break

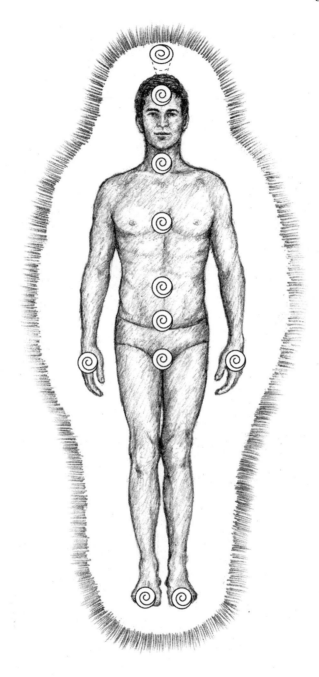

The Aura and Chakras

up with a partner. The aura has been called a *soul record,* as it contains the total experiences of the soul. It becomes stronger as spiritual ability and personal power increases.

Through various electronic techniques such as Kirlian photography and aura imaging, the colors of the aura can be electronically viewed and photographed. The photographs reveal some very interesting phenomenon. If you cut the tip off a plant leaf and then photograph the leaf, the image will show energy surrounding the leaf. But it will also show energy outlining the missing section, completing the original shape of the leaf. The leaf possesses an energy vibrational field that remains even when it is physically severed. The aura is seen to be a blueprint of the physical body, and the field is still left in the space once occupied by the leaf tip. I believe that this residual energy helps to produce the phantom limb effect felt by individuals who have lost an appendage.

In moments of extreme emotion, intense movement, or profound concentration, we can generate large amounts of personal energy vibrations. Under these types of extreme conditions, electronic photography has shown that with the increased vibrations the aura expands outward and its colors intensify. We see physical examples of these increased energy vibrations in the case studies of individuals who have produced superhuman strength necessary to lift cars of their trapped loved ones and perform miraculous feats of strength in times of danger. In Kirlian photography, energy vibrations and colors appear to intensify in the hands of healers when they are performing healing work.

The aura is constantly in connection with external electromagnetic fields every second of every day. It is what is called an *open system,* where energy naturally flows in and out of the field and the body. Some vibrations that the aura interacts with are natural energy that emits from other living things, like the energy from plants, humans, pets, and the environment, while other vibrations are unnatural, like the fields from electronic equipment such as television, radios, computers, hydro towers, microwaves, fluorescent lights, and cell phones. When such vibrations are detected by our nervous system, they are interpreted as either positive or negative and dealt with accordingly.

With a healthy aura, external energy vibrations flow through it and do not get assimilated into the field. But when we are stressed, sick, or simply not spending the time to regularly cleanse the aura, energy tends to get stuck in the field and accumulate there, in much the same way that an air filter becomes clogged with physical debris. Since thoughts are simply energy, a person's own negative mental biases and self-created judgments can clutter up the field as well. Excess energy creates blockages and deficiencies in the body's energy flow and must be dealt with, as it can eventually affect the functioning of the physical tissues of the body.

The physical body exists in a direct relationship with the aura; what happens to one level happens to all levels. The health of the life field has an immediate connection to the health of the nervous system and the glandular system. If the flow of energy becomes obstructed, the blocks can crystallize in the tissues of the body, resulting in inferior cellular functioning, degeneration, illness, and even disease. Specific organs of the body can be adversely effected, and problems in communication, emotional comprehension, and mental processing are also a result of a poorly functioning energy field.

The energy field contains important clues to subtle happenings of the mental and physical self. It has been said that when you come down with a cold you have been carrying it around in your aura for at least a week, and, indeed, Kirlian photography has shown that plants have displayed energy problems in their auric fields long before they have manifested as physical signs of the disease.

Fortunately, a skilled energy healer can detect and correct blockages, agitation, and deficiency in a person's energy field before these conditions can manifest as serious problems. What an energy healer does is identify problems in the energy flow, and then she works to neutralize them. In energy work, the healer becomes a conduit for the universal energy force, channeling healing, and cleansing spiritual energy from the universe into her body and out through her hands so that it enters into the patient's aura.

Through basic hand work we manipulate the aura, focusing on smoothing out excess accumulations of energy and filling in areas of deficiency and physical illness with positive healing vibrations; and we can also pull clumps of energy out of the field in places where there is a congestion of unwanted energy, like at the site of an infection or tumor. In this way a patient's energy field is aligned and balanced. In energy therapy we work to restore a smooth flow to the body's entire energy system and reestablish the clear rhythmic energies needed for health.

A scientific explanation for the effectiveness of energy healing lies in the study of ions. Positive ions are formed when an atom loses an electron. High concentrations of positive ions are associated with crowded, stressful places and environments where people are experiencing extreme emotions. In situations where people are exposed to high levels of positive ions, they have been shown to exhibit signs of frustration, irritability, confusion, and lethargy. They also manifest symptoms of nausea and headaches. Winds from the desert (for example, the Santa Ana wind) carry positive ions that make people feel agitated and irritable.

On the other hand, high levels of negative ions are found in natural peaceful spots, such as by trees, waterfalls, mountains, and rivers. Negative ions are associated with peacefulness, tranquillity, and positive feelings. They are needed to maintain the strength of the immune system and, thus, work to protect the body from illness and disease. They make us feel good. When we are angry or stressed we create positive ions and a lower count of negative ions in our energy fields and in our surrounding environment. In energy therapy the healer moves his hands over places of illness or injury, picking up positive ions and transmitting a flow of electrons to the field in order to create a higher level of negative ions. In this way balance and healing takes place in the field. Negative ionic therapy is also used in the treatment of burn victims.

Touch is an instinctual reaction of healing. When we are injured we are naturally led to touch the sore spot, and we all know that a kiss can make it better. Research into energy therapy has shown that touch effectively reduces pain, alleviates anxiety, and calms the autonomic nervous system. It produces a relaxation response: the breathing slows, blood pressure lessens, muscles relax, brain waves slip into the alpha state, and metabolism idles down. It also increases the level of hemoglobin in the red blood cells, bringing more oxygen for the body to use. It further boosts the immune system by restricting the cells that suppress helper T cells. T cells aid the body in fighting disease, and the more of them we have, the stronger the immune system will be.

The healing of the aura will facilitate healing of the body's tissues. Energy therapy can be applied to ease symptoms of PMS, speed healing of wounds, lessen nausea and vomiting, combat fatigue, stress, and headaches, heal colds, the flu, and provide pain relief. Virtually any ailment can be treated with aura therapy, including heart disease, skin diseases, stroke, internal inflammation, infections, eyesight and hearing problems, mental and emotional difficulties, neuromuscular problems, skeletal ailments, digestive upsets, circulatory problems, and respiratory conditions.

And even when energy treatment cannot completely heal a problem, it can still be applied to eliminate pain and provide physical comfort. Energy therapy can be used in conjunction with other treatments, as the effectiveness of all therapies is greatly increased when healing energy is channeled and directed toward the process. It has been compared to giving a person's weak car battery a boost. It is truly an excellent form of healing and is often used in Lamaze classes. An ancient form of energy healing used in the East is known as *Reiki*, and today in the West nurses in many hospitals are learning about the healing power of personal energy and are using it to heal their patients in a form of energy therapy commonly known as *therapeutic touch.*

With energy healing there is a strong energy link that forms between the patient and the healer. The healer channels energy to the patient, and she is benefited in the process because the healing energies pass through her body before they are given to the patient. The patient can be benefited by the healing energies as well, but we must remember that it is the patient who ultimately decides how to use the energy. If a patient is open to change, then an energy healing can facilitate an extreme transformation. It allows a person access to her own truth; it connects her soul with the spiritual energy of the universe and brings this connection to a level of conscious perception where it can be applied in daily life. It enables the client to understand personal cycles and patterns. She is able to let go of old pain and give up unneeded biases and limitations. It brings about the ability to see one's true life path and make honest choices. Experiences are then seen as lessons, and personal responsibility can be seized.

This is why, as energy healers, we can help disperse unwanted energy from a patient, but we alone cannot remove it completely. Problems, pain, depression, and frustration are created by the patient and ultimately must be removed by the patient. We can heal a blockage or an energy deficiency, but if the patient does not modify the initiating mental or behavioral patterns, the condition will start again. Problems are really gifts in disguise, chances for a person to learn new, more positive ways of living. It is in moments of discomfort that we are lead to discover new choices about the way we wish to exist. Energy healing brings problems, tension, and blockages from the body to the conscious mind for examination. A healer does not offer a quick fix, but allows an individual a valuable opportunity for learning about himself and his needs.

When we work with energy we are using intuitive knowledge. Energy manipulation puts us in touch with ourselves. It trains the senses to be aware, to tune into the smallest flicker of feeling, the slightest change in form. We learn to listen, to feel, to perceive the messages of the body. Expect to experience changes in your life as you develop your skills as an energy worker. You are forming a connection to pure energy, to spirit, and as you do so, your connections on other levels will increase, too. You may become more emotional, intellectual, or tactile. As your awareness of energy grows, you will become more perceptive, able to pick up on subtle clues about people and to know things that are seemingly unexplainable.

Some people have concerns when experimenting with personal energy. It is important that you understand that there is nothing to fear. Personal energy is a natural force that belongs to you, and you can call it up and let it go at your own discretion. If you have ever taken martial arts, then you will recognize personal energy as the Chi of the body.

Viewing Energy

Energy is real and concrete. It is hard to see, but through practice you can learn to physically view the universal energy field, as well as specific energy fields around living bodies, with the naked eye. The following exercises are various techniques to begin to help you perceive energy fields. It is important that you work through them in the order that they are presented, as each one builds upon the knowledge and skills you have learned from the previous one.

The universal energy layer is most visible against the backdrop of blue sky on a clear, sunny day. If you look hard enough, you will see little squiggles of white energy that seem to flit in and out of existence and leave a slight trail behind. The entire universal energy field vibrates in rhythm, and you can notice a pattern change in different weather conditions. On cloudy days there will be less energy balls, and they will move slower, whereas on bright sunny days the energy balls are larger, brighter, and move at a faster rate.

With practice it is also possible to see the aura around living bodies. Children are naturally able to see auras, and we can notice this in their drawings. Their artwork frequently portrays colors surrounding a person's head and body, and they often draw sad or sick people as black. The following are some exercises that I have found to be useful in learning to see auras.

It is easiest to start with the aura of a tree. A tree is such an enormous organism that it produces a large, quite visible, and very strong aura. In fact, the heat energy generated by a tree makes the air under it an entire degree warmer than the surrounding environmental air. The best time to view a tree's aura is at dawn or twilight. Choose a fairly large tree that stands alone and position yourself about twenty feet away. Look at the ends of the branches of the tree. You are looking for a filmy, greenish-gray outline that surrounds the tree. The energy field will extend about six inches out from the tree form and will move as the tree moves. It may be hard to see at first, and sometimes it helps to squint your eyes a little bit. Have patience, and if you can't see it around one tree, try viewing another.

Here is an easy exercise for seeing your own aura. Put your hands together and press your index fingertips to each other. Then separate the tips a little bit and look between them. You are looking for wispy strands of energy that vibrates between them. You may need to take your eyes in and out of focus a few times to see it.

The following exercise for seeing auras can also be useful. Stand a partner up against a dark background and try to view the energy field around her. Look for color or energy movement emitting from her body. Dim lighting can often be helpful in this process. Sometimes it is easier to see an aura against naked skin. Again, have patience. You may not see colors, but gray mist, like the tree. Do not worry if you cannot see the colors of the aura. With time and practice you may see them, or you will learn to clairvoyantly perceive them.

As a psychic, I perceive the colors of the aura rather than visually see them. I visually see a person's aura as a clear field that surrounds him and penetrates into a deeper field of the environment's universal energy, but the fields I see are not normally in color. As a person moves, he sends waves of his energy outward to interact with other energy waves. The field gets its actual colors in my mind, clairvoyantly, where I perceive them according to the intensity of the energy flow.

I must say, though, that the energy fields of certain significant individuals always flash in color for me, and all babies glow, as their energy is so pure and new to this world. Dangerous people and situations are always surrounded in dark reddish-black color pulses as well.

But mostly, I see a clear shimmery bubble around living things. So when are you looking for the aura, do not be discouraged if you cannot see colors. Instead of looking for a colored energy line that emits around someone, watch what the person does with her energy. People send off waves of energy as they respond to stimuli, such as when they move around in their environment and interact with each other. The best way to see energy movements is to observe people in the stresses of their everyday lives. When people are stressed, their energy level speeds and increases. It expands outward, and it is much easier to see. Watch the people waiting on a crowded street for the bus, a couple having a disagreement, a man frustrated with the job he is doing. As tensions rise, the energy vibrations increase and become agitated.

Try viewing the aura of different people. More spiritually advanced people will radiate a stronger aura than others. An interesting exercise is to have a person stand up against a wall and intensely concentrate on different emotions, like love, anger, fear, or hate. See if you can tell a difference in the energy color or its expanse around the body as he focuses his feelings. The higher the level of spiritual advancement a person has, the farther the aura extends, also. Ancient writings tell of the Buddha Gautama, whose aura could be seen for six miles. You can try all these exercises facing a mirror to experiment with viewing your own aura.

The fundamental colors of the aura remain constant, while others fluctuate with our emotions, health, and mental state. Serious problems can be indicated by splotchy, muddy, or missing colors from the aura. We see energy colors through the filters of our own energy's colors, and so color perception is very subjective. I have included a common guideline of meanings. In general, aura colors should be clear, strong, and vibrant. Weak, faded colors of low intensity indicate a need for aura energy healing. Dirty colors tainted with black indicate illness, and breaks or patchy areas without color show energy blocks in the body.

Red is the color of life energy, passion, sex, and healthiness. It indicates a high energy level and a zest for life. Fighters of freedom have a lot of red in their auras. Red that is blackened can indicate anger and stress held in the body, or intense self-worship to a fault.

Orange is the color of clear emotional flow throughout the body. A warm orange shows a person in touch with her emotions. It indicates an individual who is cheerful, positive, and life-affirming. A dirty orange indicates emotional blockages in the system. It can also depict a person who is extremely selfish and needs to work on sharing.

Yellow is the color of the intellect and the flow of thoughts through the body. A bright, shiny yellow indicates mental stableness, joy, and enthusiasm for life. A sickly yellow is an indication of disease, and denotes mental illness if around the head.

Green is the hue of good health, healing, and the ability to manifest creations. The color should be a bright clean green. A person with a lot of green in his aura is going through some intense evolutionary changes in his life. A black-green color indicates sickness, deceit, or greed.

Blue shows a clear-headed person who has good communication skills. It identifies an emotionally collected individual who has a reflective personality. A faded blue indicates emotional sadness, and a murky blue can indicate deep emotional imbalance and depression.

Purple is a powerful color that indicates spiritual wisdom, psychic development, and wholeness of the soul. It stimulates awareness, depicting a mystical person who has a strong spiritual ability.

Black, or an absence of color, is an indication of disease, injury, or blockage in the tissues that it surrounds.

Feeling the Aura

It is also possible to feel the aura, and, again, it is easiest to begin with a plant. Be aware that different flora give off different vibrations. Pass the palm of your hand over a growing plant. Can you feel its hum, like a tingling in your fingers? The life force of the plant is considered to be a sort of consciousness, a spark of divine energy. You can also feel the electrical energy of crystals. Hold them in your hand to feel each crystal tingle or vibrate in your palm. As with plants, each crystal will give off its own personal energy vibration.

To experiment with perceiving the aura on a larger scale, try walking in and out of the area under a big tree, and see if you can feel the difference in the air. Your skin may feel tingly, or the hairs on your body may rise. The air may feel charged or warmer. After this exercise, try walking in and out of a grove to see if you can sense the combined magical energy of trees. Spend some time sitting under a tree to merge your energy with its energy and become one.

The following exercise for feeling the human aura can be a very powerful experience. Close your eyes and run your open palm along a person's head, about two inches away. Concentrate, and you can feel the force of energy that she emits. It will feel warmer than the surrounding air. Push ever so lightly on it, and it will resist slightly, much like a weak version of the force that repels two same-poled magnets when you try to place them together. You can feel this energy all over the human body, through clothes, leather, even a cast on a broken appendage.

With a partner, try the exercise we did previously, only this time feel your partner's energy as he thinks intense thoughts of anger, sadness, love, or joy. See if his energy feels differently during various emotional states. You can also have him think intensely about different areas of the body, and, as you will see, when you feel the area that he is focusing on, the energy there will grow and intensify. Your personal energy is an extension of you, and it flows where your attention goes.

A healer feels a client's field this way, looking for weakness or breaks in the aura that they can channel energy to in order to heal and repair the problem. You can also feel your own energy all over your body. Try it, and you will see that it feels different than other people's. Each of us is a unique being, and our personal energy flows show this.

Using the Hand Chakras

In energy work, personal power can be collected in the hand chakras and used to promote healing. Energy enters the crown chakra, travels through the brow and throat chakras down to the heart, and then comes out of the heart chakra and is directed down the arms and into the hand chakras. You can control this flow of energy, directing it to either blast it out the hands, or you can close the flow of energy down and just hold it contained within the hand chakras. You can also take outside energy into the hand chakras and send it up the arms into the body's own energy system. Through practice, you will become efficient at running energy. You will be able to focus on transmitting energy even in a chaotic situation.

As an energy healer, you are channeling energy, not generating it, so you need to open a channel for universal energy to pass through you and into the patient. This is done through visualization and breathing. It is important that you visualize opening the energy center on the top of the head, the crown chakra, and accepting flow through the body. We cannot generate energy from our own fields to heal another, as this would deplete our energy and weaken the field, and eventually harm the body. We must open the crown to accept a direct energy stream from the universe. I visualize it as a beam of light that penetrates through me.

To begin, rub your hands briskly together for a few moments to stimulate the hand chakras, and then hold your palms facing each other about an inch apart. Visualize energy entering your crown chakra, traveling through the body and running down your arms into your hands. Use the inward breath to pull energy through your crown chakra into the body, and the outward breath to push the energy into your hands. Concentrate, and you will feel the energy grow between your palms. Your hands will begin to get warm and will perhaps feel tingly. The space between them will fill with your energy, and you will need to move your hands farther apart to contain the energy.

The energy between your hands is flexible and can be molded. Move your hands to shape the energy into a ball, or spread them wide apart, stretching the energy thin like an elastic, and then feel it contract as you push it back together. Try throwing the energy ball at a candle, an incense smoke stream, or the surface of water. You will cause movement, more than just the natural disturbance produced by your arm moving through the air. Your energy is real, tactile, and concrete. It is hard to see, but we can easily see the results of its manifestation, the same way we see the results of the wind, but not the invisible element itself. You can enlarge the energy ball; feel more energy flow down your arms and add to the energy sphere until it is the size of a huge ball.

Here is an exercise to try with a partner. Have your partner gather her energy in her hands, and place your hand in and out of her energy ball. Can you feel a difference, a tingle, a warmth, a subtle resistance? Now have your partner place her hand in and out of your energy. Can you feel when she enters your field?

You can also send energy blasting out of your hands. Extend your arms out into the room and project a blast of energy out of your hands. This will clear any energy blockages you may have in the upper body. You can then close your palms to stop the flow of energy out of your hands. Open them slightly again, and focus on collecting your energy in your hands without sending the stream out. After you experiment a while with your hand chakras, you will find that you will not need to close your hands to collect and hold the energy without sending it—it will simply happen with your will.

Most energy healers feel the right hand is used to project energy and the left hand is for receiving energy. I am stronger at projecting energy with my right, but I can use either hand to project or receive. Through experimentation you will discover that either hand can be used to project or receive energy, although you may be more efficient at a specific technique with a definite hand.

Try house cleaning with energy. Project your energy out of your palms to blast away negative energy in your home. See your energy as a colored stream that pushes other energy away. Direct this other energy outside through a door or an open window. This type of energy cleansing should be done about once a week to facilitate smooth energy flow around your home. It can also be done in the office or in hotel rooms to cleanse the area of negative energy.

When you are done playing with your energy, you can push an energy ball that you have created into the solar plexus chakra, and your body will absorb it back into its system. You will need to close your chakras as well. To close the hand chakras, simply close your hands or shake them a few times, while envisioning them closing. Visualize the crown chakra closing like a big eye that shuts. The crown chakra never really closes, as we are constantly running energy for survival, but visualization helps close it down to a manageable level for normal functioning. It is important that you use visualization to close any chakra that you open, as the body cannot run full energy streams all of the time. The chakras are delicate centers that can burn out when there is too much energy running through them that is not being directed at a purpose. Possessing the knowledge and skills to work with personal power demands that the practitioner take responsibility for that power and follow proper procedures.

Energy Healing Techniques

There are several techniques that are necessary in energy work, and they include shielding, palm induction, aura smoothing, massaging the field, pulling energy, and adding energy. Each technique will be thoroughly discussed in the following pages.

When you practice these techniques it is important that you open your senses and allow yourself to feel the connections to the power. Energy therapy is a healing meditation, so you need to be slow and precise in all your movements. Before you begin, stretch your neck and arms from side to side to open up energy centers, and visualize your crown chakra opening and drawing universal energy into your body. When performing the techniques, keep the fingers of the hands held close together, as scattered fingers mean scattered energy.

Remember that energy flows where attention goes, so the location you direct your mental and physical focus is where the energy will collect. Maintain your full concentration on the person you are treating, and be sure to set personal concerns aside while you are administering a treatment. Visualization is very important in energy healing, as the mind needs to tune into the energy of universe and the energy of the person that you are healing. They deserve your full focus, as improperly working with energy can cause a person to manifest problems. Practice the visualization exercises described in chapter 3, "Healing and the Mind," to refresh your mental visualization powers and to improve your concentration and focus.

Shielding

As an energy healer, it is important that you protect yourself and make a conscious effort to avoid taking in other people's energy problems. I know healers

and counselors who constantly (and often unknowingly) absorb their patients'
pain and negative energy in dangerous attempts to heal their patients, but this
only creates disease and anguish in their own bodies. People who practice
without safeguards for themselves are dishonoring their own spiritual energy,
and, subsequently, they become affected with cancers, tumors, and diseases
that destroy the immune system and attack the organs. Their bodies are trying
to process energy that is simply not their own, and they do not possess the
internal tools to deal with such foreign vibrations.

A healer is an emphatic guide, not a dumping ground for another person's
negative energy. To protect yourself against taking in unwanted energy, be sure
to shield yourself when working with energy. Shielding is a process of directing
energy to the outermost layers of the aura in order to enhance the protective
energies around the body. Use visualization to guide universal energy into the
shield. Stand up and imagine an outer ray of white spiritual light entering the
body from above you. Breathe in the white universal light through your crown
chakra and your mouth on the inhale, and breathe it out into the aura on the
exhale. See your aura grow and strengthen, and feel it expand around you, creating a protective shield. This shield will insulate you and deflect any negative
energy. A shield should be created before you begin a healing treatment, and it
also can be used as a protection device in any situation where you feel threatened.

It is common for new energy healers to experience minor illnesses like a cold
or nausea at first, as their energy field detoxifies and learns to expel external
energy. If this happens to you, focus on strengthening your own system
through visualization and physical hand work. Reread the mental exercises in
chapter 3, and use the healer's meditation to reconnect to your inner healer.

If you find yourself becoming emotionally overwhelmed while performing a
treatment, stop the treatment and take time to recenter your personal energy.
Strengthen your shield and ground out any excess energy using the following
waterfall technique. Emerging the arms in cold running water is another useful
technique to prevent energy from being drawn up the arms and into your field.

If you cannot seem to concentrate during a treatment and feel dissociated
from the experience, or if you feel overloaded and hypersensitive, then you

need to end the treatment and focus on taking care of yourself. An enormous part of healing is knowing your own limits and being able to judge when it is time to heal and give energy and when it is time to withdraw and conserve energy.

Directly after administering a treatment, I suggest that you wash your hands, as this works to physically and psychologically break the flow of energy from the healer to the patient. I also perform a visualization to clear my energy field. I visualize that I am standing under a ray of white light that cascades over my body, like a waterfall. As the purifying light passes over me, it washes away negativity, energy blockages, and foreign vibrations from my aura. The white light cleanses my field and grounds any excess energy to the earth. I focus on being open to letting go of that which I do not need. I also suggest that you drink water to hydrate your system, and make it a habit to always eat after working with energy, as you need to replenish your personal energy level (foods containing proteins or carbohydrates are good choices).

Palm Induction

An assessment of the patient's energy field is performed with a technique called palm induction. Palm induction, or scanning as it is also known, is a nontouch hand movement where you slowly sweep the palms in a flowing motion over the patient's aura, feeling for sensation. Scanning is not a medical diagnosis, but it is a way of simply looking for changes or differences in the energy field.

Scanning can be done over clothes or against bare skin. I always scan the body from head to feet; I like to do it with my hands positioned side by side. You can close your eyes if that helps you to focus on the client's field. Take your time and slowly progress over the body. Do not scan too close to the body, as the immediate body heat can interfere with the energy-sensing (you want to be about three inches from the skin).

Generally, you should feel resistance, a slight pressure that will be warm and will also flow smoothly. The energy field should be symmetrical and feel the same on both sides. A huge pressure or extreme heat in one spot indicates a blockage and a buildup of energy. This can happen in the case of a physical inflammation. An energy congestion can also feel like a bulge in the field. Imbalances in the field will feel agitated or quivery beneath the palm. An area of coldness or lack of feeling indicates a deficiency in the energy field where energy is leaking from the field. A void center or a place of no sensation can be caused by a wound or an infection.

In treatment we strive to balance a problem and use an alternate method of treatment, so in the case of coldness we put heat into the field, and vice versa; with a deficiency we add energy into the aura; with a blockage we remove the excess energy; and in the case of agitation we work to smooth out the field.

Smoothing

Smoothing is an aura-sweeping hand motion that is used to smooth out any agitation and bulges in the aura. It clears the energy and gets it moving and flowing correctly, facilitating a healing response. It can be applied as a pain management technique and is very useful for calming babies.

To perform a smoothing, gently sweep the palm of your hands over the field, about three to four inches away. I like to sweep from head to toe, following the natural path universal energy travels through the system. Use your hands to smooth the energy down the body. Be sure to always use long sweeping motions and take the flow right down to the feet to connect the energy to the earth and facilitate grounding. As you sweep, make sure the energy does not gather somewhere else, like the neck or shoulders. Use palm induction to check for areas that may need more work.

Massage

Massage is the technique of stimulating the energy field in order to activate it and facilitate healing. Open your palm chakras and concentrate on creating energy in your hands. Hold your open palms an inch from the head and move your fingers in small circles over the head, using your hand energy to gently massage the aura and knead out the energy. This healing touch technique can be used all over the body and especially in areas that need physical healing. Try it on your own face and head, and you will see how much more alive you feel after performing this exercise. I use massaging to activate the field before I perform specific techniques of adding or removing energy.

Pulling Energy

Pulling energy is a technique used to remove excess and unwanted energy from areas of the field. Use this motion over an area where there is an energy blockage or when there is physical pain or an injury. It works really well over a scratchy throat to prevent it from becoming a full-blown sore throat. It is also effective at stopping a head cold when administered over the throat and nose. In the case of pain, as we break up congestion we remove pain from the body. After I pull unwanted energy, I always add healing energy back to the aura and perform a smoothing to facilitate even flow.

To perform the technique, use your thumb and fingers in a pinching motion and pull the energy out of the area. So you do not fill the room with unwanted energy, either hold it in your hand and charge it with white light to purify it before letting it go, or you can flick it into a bowl of water. It will cling to the water, and after the treatment you can wash the water down the drain to dispose of it.

When you are pulling energy you need to focused on removing and disposing the energy. Do not absorb it into your field. Be very aware of your own energy and emotional levels. If you feel that you are taking in energy, stop the treatment and shake both hands vigorously, or you can emerge your arms in cold running water. Spend the time necessary to strengthen your aura and ground out any excess energy before continuing the treatment.

Projecting Energy

When we project energy we specifically transfer healing energy directly to a patient's aura. This technique is performed over an area that has physically damaged tissue, or an area that has an energy deficiency. It can be used on any part of the body that has any sort of problem, including the head, eyes, ears, face, throat, neck, back, chest, arms, torso, legs, ankles, and feet. It also works to eliminate pain and tension.

Open the crown chakra and visualize energy coming from above, entering the body and traveling out through the arms and hands. Hold the hands over the area to be worked on, gently touching the skin ever so slightly. If an area cannot be touched, then hold the hands directly over it, as close to the skin as possible. Direct universal energy to balance the energy field and fill it with healing energy. You can imagine it as a beam of golden light that brings health and pain relief into your partner. Envision this energy fixing the problem; see it repairing tissue, destroying bad cells with love and healing vibrations, or reknitting a broken bone together.

The energy flow will rise and ebb during the treatment, and you will feel the sensation change in your hands. The flow increases gradually, building up until there occurs a point when you intuitively know the treatment is working. After a while the flow will start to taper off and there will cease to be sensations. At this point, I like to stop the treatment and scan the field to check for balance. If there are still problems, then I repeat the treatment.

Practice these energy techniques on your husband, your dog, even your houseplants. Every living thing benefits from energy therapy, but it works best on babies because their development is rapidly occurring and their minds are very open, on animals because they, too, are open and do not have biases and mental limitations, and on accident victims because the injury has not had time to attach at cellular and mental levels.

Over time your mind will become very efficient at holding concentration and focus, and your body will the build muscle tone needed to be able to easily run and manipulate energy. Energy healing is a natural skill that our ancestors practiced readily, and it does not take long for a person to reclaim this important knowledge.

An Energy Treatment

The following is an example of a healing treatment performed on a patient to speed the recovery of a broken arm. The case study is divided into steps so you can understand the various levels through which the treatment progresses and see how the techniques are applied.

We begin the treatment by holding an in-depth consultation with the client. I advise you to be careful about who you treat, as healer and client become connected during the energy treatment. Energy therapy is a dual process that changes both the healer and the healed. If a client looks and feels offensive to you, then you need to consider your own system first. There is nothing wrong with telling a person that it is not the right time for you to administer a healing. If a client is hesitant, he must be made to feel comfortable with you and the treatment before you begin.

What is the client looking for in a treatment? As a healer, what do you think the client needs? You and the client should decide on a course of action. Briefly discuss with the client the steps of the procedure, including deep breathing, aura awareness, guided meditation, and aura contact and manipulation. Advise the client that the energy will continue to flow for up to forty-eight hours following the treatment, and she should expect to notice physical and emotional changes in that time.

Be sure to set a time limit at the beginning; it should be flexible so if you need more time, you can use it, but you and the patient should have a general idea of how long the treatment will be. A deep state of relaxation and the infusion of energy into the system can drastically alter a client's perception. For acute problems, a treatment lasting no longer than thirty minutes is appropriate. I'm more inclined to treat a person who is new to energy treatment for ten minutes several times a day instead of administering one long treatment. The body can only take so much intense energy concentration, and we do not want to overload the centers.

The room should be warm and comfortable. Have the patient recline on her back, unless, of course, the injury or ailment is located on the back of the body. Place a pillow under the head and knees for comfort. Have the patient lie with her head to the north, as this aligns the spinal cord with the magnetic energy of the earth. Keep her legs uncrossed and remove tight belts, glasses, and jewelry to help the energy flow freely. As with all my energy work, I like to have a patient remove her socks and shoes to ensure consistent energy flow through the body and a good grounding connection.

While the patient relaxes into the position, take a moment to ready yourself. Close your eyes, focus on the flow of your breath, and begin to breathe deeply, opening the crown chakra and drawing the light and vitality of the universe into your mind and body. Center your mind on the healing work to be done, and ask your inner healer to provide guidance. This is the time for you to completely release your own personal issues so you can open your spirit to the healing energy of the universe. As I have said before, if you find you cannot let go of personal concerns, then you should concentrate on healing yourself first. Full focus is needed with all healing therapies, but it is especially essential with energy work, as energy vibrations are so sensitive and can be manipulated with even the slightest thought.

In the italicized passages, I have included suggested comments to say to the client to guide them through the treatment. Be sure to say them slowly and calmly. Do not rush the patient; by paying close attention to the energy and breathing patterns of the patient, you will perceive when she is naturally ready to progress to the next step. Let the patient set the pace, and remember the power of silence.

> *Relax. Focus only on your breathing. Breathe in through your nose, inhaling deeply into every cell, taking in clean fresh air. And then exhale out of your mouth. Push the carbon dioxide out of your lungs, clearing the passageways, opening up the energy centers of your body. And inhale again, taking in pure healing air. Exhale. Keep breathing and filling yourself with air. The air makes you feel healthy and strong, and these feelings flood through your body.*

Now have the patient visualize her energy, seeing her aura surround her as a safe, healing field of light.

See a white bubble of light around yourself. The energy bubble is your own healing energy that radiates out from your body. It is a blanket of energy that protects you and surrounds you with love. In your bubble you are safe and warm and loved. Can you see the energy? Can you feel it? What does it look like? What does it feel like?

Continue to reassure your partner that she is surrounded by her own healing energy and that it is a positive force, especially if she was initially apprehensive about the energy work.

Use your hands and senses to begin to scan the energy field for blockages, heat, coldness, energy deficiencies, or agitation. Take a mental note of all you uncover. I like to tell clients exactly what I am doing, as it helps them to feel comfortable with the treatment.

I am scanning your energy field to look for any imbalances or blockages. Just relax and continue to breathe deeply. Good.

After I have made my assessment, I always ask the clients to use their mind to scan their body. The clients know their bodies best of all, and know on a cellular level why the disease is taking place. Our job is really to show them what they already know. Through visualization, they may discover unconscious energy patterns and blockages, images of forgotten childhood trauma, or fragments of past lives, where damage to a previous body is affecting them in their present lives. Having the client look within also allows me, as a healer, to judge my own findings against those of the clients.

Now we are going to use some basic visualization. Use your mind to go within your body, to go deep down into the cells. Each tiny molecule of blood and bone and tissue is a living entity that sustains you. What do you see inside your body? Describe to me what you see. Do you see a problem, a blockage, a tightness, a color? How does your body feel? Is there a pain, tingle, heat, or cold? Are there organs or areas that feel tight or are not functioning smoothly?

Allow the patient enough time to see her body and formulate responses to the questions. It may be hard for some to vocalize their visions. Energy colors can be very useful to a patient, especially to one who is new to energy work. Often a patient will perceive something but will have no idea how to describe it, and colors can work wonderfully. If a patient picks up something, take the time to explore it with her. Encourage your partner to talk about and share with you whatever she desires.

Do you see any images or symbols? What is your body telling you?

As the healer, you may receive some visual images, and you can gently bring them up to your client. If they make sense, use them, but if not, simply let them float away. If you think they are crucial to the patient's health, you can file them in the mind to use in an aftercare discussion.

It is also important that you not judge or try to explain what the patient is seeing. This is a time for gathering information, not interpreting it. It is useful to write any images and phrases down for the client so she can consider them later. If the client experiences an emotional response during mental scanning, speak gently and support her through it. Encourage her to focus on her breathing, and let her know she is loved.

If you need to move the treatment along, it can be useful to ask the client to notice any positive body feelings. Often we lose track of the positive because we are too focused on the negative.

Are you aware of any smooth-flowing places of energy? Where does it feel good inside your body? What can we do to make the rest of the body feel good?

At this point I start the physical work of the aural treatment, beginning with smoothing to get the client relaxed and used to aura manipulation. I perform an energy massage to stimulate and open the field to prepare it for receiving the healing treatment. I then concentrate on balancing and aligning the energy, pulling out any excess energy, and filling any deficiencies. I rest my hands very lightly over any areas that need to be filled so I am just slightly touching the skin. For about five minutes I send healing energy into each area, visualizing the energy filling and healing the tissues of the body.

I find the use of affirmations to be very powerful tools in an energy healing treatment. A patient's transformation begins with the actual healing, but it must follow with changed behaviors in order to maintain the wellness. Affirmations can help implement these positive behaviors. While I work on the energy field, I may have my partner repeat an appropriate affirmation.

There will come a time when it is appropriate to end the session. You will naturally know when you have depleted your energy and when the patient has received all the energy he can infuse into his system. When you end the treatment, finish with a smoothing to balance out the field, and then perform a scan. The aura should feel balanced and should be clear flowing, any pain that the patient was experiencing should be reduced, breathing patterns should be calm and relaxed, and the skin should look better—it should be glowing with vitality.

> *Slowly return your attention to the present and this room. When you feel ready, open your eyes.*

It may take several sessions for the healing to occur. Problems take a long time to develop, and they may need a long time to work themselves out. Do not try to solve everything in one session. You need to be aware that some people may not be healed, as it is not possible to heal someone who does not truly want to be healed.

Aftercare

Do not rush a patient to get up. He has just been through an emotionally intensive journey and needs time to relax and adjust. Advise him to drink lots of water to flush toxins out of his system. Discuss with him any images that may have surfaced during the treatment. Explore them, and see if they make sense and can help aid with the healing energies. Also, discuss other possible treatments that you want him to consider, such as diet and nutrition, vitamins, herbal treatment, professional help, or meditation in order for him to change the behaviors that created the problem. Take the time to encourage the client to repeat his affirmations at home, as this will activate the seeds of change that were planted in the healing.

And remember aftercare for yourself as well. Ground out any excess energy from your shield and close your crown chakra. Spend time replenishing your energy. Eat some carbs, take a bath or a nap, have a cup of herbal tea. Remember, you need love and healing vibrations as well. Take a few moments to perform an analysis of the treatment in your healer's journal.

Energy therapy is really an art form, the physical weaving of vibration and pulse into structure. It unleashes the energies of health at a deep cellular level, facilitating balance. It is a therapy that is a strong preventative measure, and it is one of the best ways to keep the body healthy. A clear-flowing and balanced field promotes wellness and, in times of need, healing.

Practice the techniques as much as you can. It takes dedicated study to learn the intricacies of energy healing. In time, your hands will become sensitive, and strong healing connections will form between you and your partner. As they do, strong connections will be created in you. You will be opened to the true essence of your soul, and through this you will experience profound healing transformations of the self.

9

Working with the Chakras

The chakras are openings in the auric field, and through them we give and receive all forms of energy. In energy healing they can be used to tell the health of the body and to treat many problems and diseases.

The chakras are small, four-inch wide circular shaped energy concentrations that pulse and spin within the body's energy field. The word chakra actually comes from the Sanskrit language and means "wheel." The chakras are openings in the auric field that can receive and give all forms of universal energy. They are like little vortexes that are composed of layers of light energy and vibrate in the frequencies of the corresponding colors of the spectrum. The chakras have been described as flowers with petals that open and close at the front of the body, and stems that remain constantly open at the back of the body. The chakras are polar, with the flowers emitting positive vibrations and the stems giving off negative electrical pulses. Most of the body's energy and its colors are created by spinning layers of the chakras.

There are seven major chakra points in the auric field, and many minor ones. The major centers are located in an anatomical line that runs down the middle of the body, beginning at the top of the head and ending at the perineum, the sensitive area between the anus and the genitals. At the top of the head we have the crown chakra. Energy is naturally drawn from the universe like a laser beam into the auric field through the crown chakra, and flows down through the body into the third eye chakra, located in the center of the forehead. It further pushes downward to the center at the hollow of the throat, the throat chakra. Here the energy is drawn further down into the heart chakra in the center of the chest, and can continue down to the solar plexus chakra, located between the navel and the sternum, or it can be pushed through the arms and out the minor chakras of the hands. From the solar plexus chakra, energy travels down into the sacral chakra, found just below the belly button, and then continues onto the root chakra at the base of the spine. Here it grounds out to the earth and also travels down the legs to ground out through the minor chakras of the feet.

Energy can also be pushed upward through the body and exited through the crown, or it can enter from the environment through any of the chakras and can be pushed out of them, especially at the heart center and the palm chakras. Each chakra naturally is either a receptive center that normally receives energy, or a projective center that gives out energy, but each chakra can, and indeed must, take and give energy as needed in order to maintain a healthy system. A damaged or blocked chakra cuts the field and body off from receiving the full amount of the vital energy it needs, and also stops the release of excess energy out of the system. This can eventually create illness and disease. A chakra that is excessively open stops the release of excess energy out of the system, and it also takes in too much energy and projects it into the aura. A person with an excessively open chakra is exposing themselves to overburdening the system with energy, pain, and emotional vibrations that are not their own, and this opens the system to physically manifesting illness and dis-ease.

The energy of the crown chakra vibrates at the highest frequency, as it receives the pure spiritual light of the universe. As the energy travels through the field and body, it slows down, causing each chakra to vibrate at a slower frequency than the one above it. Thus, we find that the crown, third eye, and throat chakras are associated with the higher vibrations of spirit, psychic intuition, intelligence, and communication, while the three lower chakras, the solar plexus, the sacral, and the root, deal with the slower, more denser aspects of life, like the gut instinct, the emotions, and the physical body. The heart is the central chakra, sitting balanced between the heaviness of the root and the lightness of the crown. The two groups of chakras are often referred to as the higher and lower chakras, but this simply pertains to their placement. One is not less spiritual than other; all are equally important.

Each of the seven chakras influence different biological functions and are associated with specific organs of the body. They are also connected to the glandular system, as each chakra influences specific endocrine glands. The endocrine glands are the important tissues that secrete the body's control hormones in order to regulate physical and emotional processes in the body. They affect moods, personality, health, development, and growth. If one chakra is out of balance, the whole health of the energy system and the body is adversely affected.

The root causes of a lot of energy problems can be found in the chakras, and they can be read like meters to tell the health of the body. The chakras naturally open and close to accommodate the flow of life, but an injury, traumatic event, or an emotional imbalance can cause some or all of the chakras to open far too often and far too quickly. This can damage the sensitive receptors and create an overstimulated center that constantly needs energy. Physically, an overstimulated center creates a drain on the body's energy and can manifest problems of the emotions, the mind, and the body.

A projective chakra that is excessively open runs too much energy out of the body. It is literally blasting out energy, and if a chakra like this is not shut down and resized, it can blast until it finally burns itself out. A blasting chakra can be very damaging to the body, as it interferes with proper grounding, leaving a person feeling flighty and unsettled, and it also constantly engages the body's energy to project outward, depleting the personal energy level and giving the auric field no chance to take in energy for replenishment. This leaves the body very susceptible to disease, as it simply cannot spiritually give all the time. Like the ocean wave, there must be an ebb and flow to personal power.

I'm sure you have met people who have excessively open and blasting chakras. They throw off waves of energy that you can actually see and feel when they enter a room, are very animated and scattered, have ten projects on the go and not one completed, can't remember where they parked their car, and constantly give off vibrations in the form of chitchat, advice, or physical help. On the surface they may seem exciting and free-spirited, but it is these people who manifest serious problems like chronic fatigue syndrome, and are often afflicted with debilitating strokes. They are ungrounded and unstilled, and are simply giving too much of themselves away.

An extremely open receptive chakra is one that is taking in far too much external energy. This leaves the system open to manifesting illness, stress, diseases, and mental and emotional difficulties, depending on the specific chakra. Many therapists, nurses, counselors, and caregivers have receptive chakras that are far too open, and as a result, they take in too much pain and emotional baggage that is not their own. It is one thing to be empathetic, but it is quite another to embody the pain of others. The aura and body cannot process high levels of external energy that is not our own, and these people often manifest cancers and tumors from the foreign energy that is constantly entering their bodies.

The chakras can become clogged with excess energy and cease to function at full efficiency, in the same way that an air filter becomes hindered with particles of dust and debris. Low physical activity, poor diet, a repetitive lifestyle, a stagnant spiritual attitude, lack of challenges, a negative self-image, a pessimistic environment, and physical and mental abuse are all factors that can lead to chakra clogging and blockage. Blockages and energy fluctuations in chakra movement will deeply affect a person's energy level and well-being, and can cause disease and illness.

A chakra that is cold and barely moving is the sign of an energy center that is shut down. Several closed chakras is an indication of a person who is emotionally withdrawn and recoils from connections with others and the spiritual energy of the universe in general. Both projective and receptive chakras can close and isolate a person from receiving or giving spiritual energy. People with closed chakras are usually suffering from long-term pain and emotions and have locked these feelings deep inside of themselves. Spiritual isolation, as with physical isolation, leaves the body very susceptible to illness and disease.

Closing off a chakra, or several chakras, is a natural defense mechanism that the body and mind engages in to protect the self from receiving negative vibrations in times of dangerous or stressful situations, but if there is no positive situations to facilitate the reopening of the chakras, they can become sealed and will not promote the reciprocal give and take of a normal energy flow. Closed chakras are the most difficult to heal. An individual with a closed chakra will often defend her closed chakra vehemently, as it is a defense mechanism that she sees as necessary to her survival. Change is very hard for all people, but opening to new situations and possibilities is the hardest for those people who want to hold on to the pain and energy from the past. Again, we may feel an overwhelming need to help the person, but the work of transformation has to be done by her.

I often see sealed chakras in suicidal, pain-ridden individuals and abused children. Children with this problem are withdrawn and essentially guard their energy flow in normal interactive situations, but if pushed, some of them will act out violently, both in their physical actions and in their energy flow. Before they lunge, their actions are proceeded by a burst of energy shooting out of their chakras like a flare of the sun. They blast extremely intense energy streams out of their projective chakras before they recoil and shut the centers down again. This is so severely damaging to the auric body, as it burns out the sensitive centers, wrecks havoc on the normal grounding process, and stresses the auric field immeasurably. It also shows the kind of inner pain and turmoil these children are suffering. When we are really angry we exude that same rush, but it is not damaging in healthy chakras that are naturally open. I'm sure you have felt this rush flowing in yourself as you react in moments of anger.

Part of the job of an energy healer involves learning to diagnose the condition of the chakras and then working to strengthen the centers to enhance physical health. Through meditation and practical manipulation, the chakras can be cleared, opened, and resized to facilitate healing. We will first learn how to detect and physically manipulate the centers, and then in later chapters we will learn how to use crystals and colors to heal and enhance the power of the chakras.

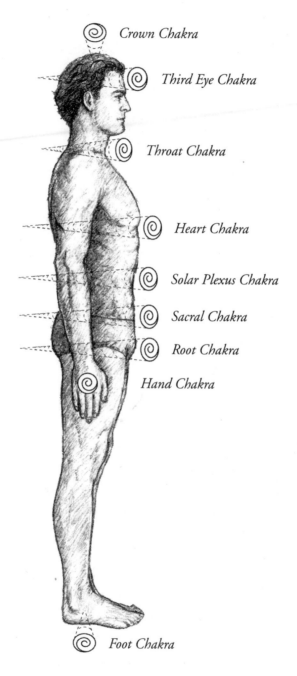

Crown Chakra

Third Eye Chakra

Throat Chakra

Heart Chakra

Solar Plexus Chakra

Sacral Chakra

Root Chakra

Hand Chakra

Foot Chakra

The Chakras

The Chakras

In this section we will discuss each of the chakras individually, and include details on specific problems. It is important to realize that the following descriptions are simply my own understandings and interpretations of the energy centers based on my research and experiences. Energy work is defined by the individual experience, so as you create connections to the chakras, you will formulate your own ideas and understandings.

The Root Chakra

The first chakra is known as the base or root chakra. It is located in the perineum, at the very bottom of the spine. Although in diagrams the root chakra is often shown as facing forward, the open flower of the chakra is really an anchor point with the earth, as it projects downward between the legs and grounds energy out of the field and into the earth. Physically, it is connected to the blood, the pelvis, the legs, feet, and spine, and can be used to treat problems associated with these tissues, including high or low blood pressure, strokes, poor circulation, lower body ailments, and paralysis. The root chakra is considered to be the seat of power in the body's energy system, called the *psychic heat* or the *fire of life,* as this projective energy center is associated with our basic primal life energy and is the force behind our survival instincts.

Connected to the adrenal glands, the root chakra helps direct the hormones in the fight-or-flight response, producing the energy that enables people to perform superhuman feats in times of stress, or allowing them to flee from danger. As humans we naturally feed on adrenaline rushes, going to scary movies, taking roller coaster rides, and visiting haunted houses. Root chakra adrenaline rushes keep the energy system alive and moving, acting as a natural mechanism to clear clogged pathways and prevent life from becoming dull. In spiritual terms, the upward rush of energy is called a Kundalini rush, and can also be performed during yoga to fuel the chakras with spiritual energy.

The root chakra is concerned with our very first relationships. If the connections we shared with our parents were strong, then we will possess well-developed first chakras, as we were supported and provided with the firm foundations we need to tackle the challenges of life. If a person did not have strong connections to his parents, then he has to do some healing of the root chakra. The root chakra also creates the primal intensity behind the human sexual drive. Primary sexual energy is not really about the erotic connections formed between individuals, which is the function of the second chakra, but it is about sexual lust, the drive to orgasm, the need for personal satisfaction.

The color of the root chakra is a healthy red—powerful and alive. Red is the color of the warrior, the part of ourselves that has the ability to take care of the self and our loved ones, to manifest what we need, and to provide security, protection, and material requirements. Stones of the root include the red ruby, bloodstone, and smoky quartz.

The root chakra should be envisioned as a bright red-colored disk about four-inches wide that swirls just above the genitalia. People with a clear-flowing root chakra are well grounded and have a strong respect and appreciation for their bodies; they also possess an understanding of their needs and responsibilities in life. Connection to the root chakra gives us our fundamental requirements: security, firm foundations for our goals and dreams, preservation and protection instincts, acceptance of the self, the ability to manifest what we need, sexual pleasure, and the essential link to primordial earth energy. The root chakra is connected to the crown center, and with any problem in the root chakra you should also check the condition of the crown chakra.

Excessive Energy in the Root: An individual with an excessively large and open root chakra is experiencing extreme survival issues in her life. This projective chakra opens naturally to protect the self from danger, and should shut itself down when the danger has passed, but if it remains open and blasting, the chakra will not be able to receive energy, and it will not be able to properly ground the entire auric system, either. A blasting root sends constant streams of energy upward to protect the body instead of grounding universal and excess personal energy downward.

A blasting root chakra can cause an individual to manifest physical obsessive behavior, such as being overly concerned with cleanliness, orderliness, attention getting, material accumulation, sexual gratification, perceived problems and faults, and a lack of acceptance of body size and its limitations. Obsessive behavior is an overcompensating mechanism that occurs because the individual feels an intense need for security, as he is ungrounded and not connected to the essential energy of the earth. The earth is our Mother, and without connection to the material plane, we experience a void in our lives, and we feel like we never can get enough love, security, attention, and so on. And, indeed, we are not getting enough nourishment on a physical energy basis, as we are separated from the earth. With a closed root chakra our needs as humans cannot be met.

It is very stressful and debilitating to have a root chakra blasting protective energy continuously, and if a person experiences this, it is an important clue to the tension and negative vibrations he is receiving consistently on an energy level. It demands a close look at his environment, and the need to make the necessary changes to create an atmosphere that is more secure and relaxed. A healing can reshape and subdue the blasting root center, but it is essential that the potentially dangerous and stress-producing elements are removed from the person's lifestyle, or the chakra will begin to blast again.

Deficient Energy in the Root: A person who possesses a small or closed root chakra is shutting out her life's energy and her essence of purpose. This is an escape tactic that can happen consciously or unconsciously to prevent mistakes or errors, but constant attempts to deny one's purpose is spiritually limiting and causes imbalances. We often unconsciously close down the root when we are feeling out of control and afraid that we are giving too much of ourselves away. It happens in an attempt to regain control in our lives. But cutting off the grounding portal does not provide us with control; rather, it increases problems, as it prevents grounding of the stressed emotions and thoughts. It manifests as pain, denial, uncertainty of purpose, difficulty in stable relationships, and powerlessness.

A deficient root chakra does not empower the other chakras. It provides no survival energy to the system and creates a situation in which the person cannot deal appropriately with dangerous situations or even provide the self with essential needs. A person with this problem cannot manifest abundance in his life, achieve goals and aspirations, experience fulfilling sexual orgasms, or even begin to have a clue about what they want out of life, or what they can do in life. Again, they are cut off from the essential earth energy and, thus, are lacking common sense, practicability, confidence, the ability to make direct choices and follow through with them, and acceptance of the self and its potential. A healing can connect a person's energy system to the essential earth energy and provide a firm foundation to create primary needs.

The Foot Chakras

The root chakra is connected to the foot chakras, the energy wheels that exist in the center of the arch of each foot. The foot chakras ground the body to the earth. Grounding is a powerful way to replenish and stabilize the body's energy. We ground through food, meditation, massage, or sex, but most of all we ground through linking the body to the earth. We can do this by lying directly on the ground, or it can be done through the root and foot chakras. They can facilitate the downward path of energy to allow for the grounding of negative emotions and stress into the earth for cleansing of the self, or they can pull earth energy upward to charge the body with power. The foot chakras are smaller than the other chakras, and can open and close much more frequently. Healthy foot chakras support an individual's energy base and create a grounded, stable person.

The Sacral Chakra

The second chakra is a receptive center known as the sacral, or the reproductive chakra. It is located in the lower abdomen, from the top of the pelvic bone to the belly button. It is associated with the reproductive organs, the spleen, bladder, kidneys, intestines, and the skin, and problems with these organs can be treated from the sacral chakra. A healthy reproductive chakra should be a warm orange-colored center that spins below the navel. The second chakra drives the reproductive system and fertility on all levels. It also governs the emotions and the intimacy between people in both sexual and nonsexual connections. The sacral is the center of profound transformation on the emotional level. This is where we truly feel things—deep down in the pit of the gut. Great healing transpires at the second chakra—healings of the soul. Stones of the sacral include the warm energies of the carnelian, amber, and citrine.

When the sacral chakra is spinning well, an individual will possess a healthy awareness of emotional commitment and her own sexuality. Those individuals in touch with the second chakra's energy maintain a strong sense of community and are not afraid of being open and vulnerable with others when forming intimate connections. They like to socialize and have close-knit friendships. The sacral is the place of emotional sexuality, especially for women, as right inside the center lies the womb, uterus, fallopian tubes, and ovaries. A woman with a healthy sacral chakra is able to create strong sexual connections without sacrificing her own independent identity to the relationship.

The sacral is the womb center, the sacred fire from which creativity and artistic energies spring forth. From this originative place babies grow, anchored to the body of the mother, and fed from the mother's own energies. A healthy sacral creates healthy babies with secure emotional connections and flexible temperaments. On a symbolic level, the sacral is the seat of the inner child, where love, humor, creative impulses, trust, innocence, and imagination run freely. Artists, musicians, dancers, sculptors, writers—the creators of our world—often have strong sacrals. Those in touch with their child energies have healthy chakras, also. Their systems are infused with natural healing vibrations and nurturing energy, and they are able to easily flow with the changes and movement of life. Individuals who experienced childhood trauma often need work on this chakra.

The sacral is also connected to the digestion system and the small and large intestines. This is the place of moving and clearing of energy. The small intestine's role is to decide which nutrients to take out and use and which ones to pass on as waste. At the sacral, this physical cleansing operation is applied to the emotional layer of our lives; here we sort through and process emotions, feelings, impressions, experiences, sensations, perceptions, and biases. We keep what is necessary and pass it up to the gut intelligence of the solar plexus chakra for mental consideration. The large intestine's job is to let go of the physical waste from the small intestine, to pass out the unnecessary. On the emotional level, the sacral facilitates the downward elimination of inessential things: worn-out relationships, old emotions, pains of the past, ineffective emotional biases, and misconceived notions. It passes this unwanted energy down to the root for disposal and grounding. Work on the sacral is appropriate to help cleanse energies that are no longer necessary from the system.

When we encounter uncertainty and emotional stagnation in life, we experience constipation, physical blockages in the pathway of the body's elimination system. On the other hand, when the exchange of emotions happens too quickly, and we feel frazzled and out of control, then we experience diarrhea, an overloading and overprocessing of the system. The physical symptoms of diarrhea and constipation are important clues to the emotional health of the sacral, and work on this center can help alleviate these chronic digestion problems. The sacral is linked to the throat chakra, and problems in the sacral may also manifest in the throat, and vise versa, so it is essential that you check the health of the throat as well.

Excessive Energy in the Sacral: This receptive chakra is an extremely sensitive center that has the ability to be empathic and sympathize with another person's feelings and emotions. It opens naturally during lovemaking and in moments of deep emotional bonding with another, but it can very easily open far too wide and take in an excess of foreign energy. Constant exposure to the stress and pain of the world is damaging, as it overloads a person's emotional system and interferes with her own feelings. It also prevents proper elimination and grounding of excess energy.

Particularly, I find exposed reproductive chakras on nurses, massage therapists, counselors, psychologists, relief workers, and other people who help those in need. Many of these people have problems with processing anger, sadness, depression, guilt, confusion, and emotional connections. They simply do not know how they feel, as they are distanced from their own emotions and are overburdened with other people's feelings. They are emotionally out of control and experience intense explosive feelings. They also tend to hold on to hurtful emotions and painful experiences from their past, compounding the problem.

Emotional overloading can also manifest in physical problems, such as diarrhea, fatigue, immune system deficiency, prostate and testicle problems, ovarian cancer, and other reproductive complications. I see many people with exposed chakras who have excess weight that accumulates in the abdomen area; this is because, in an effort to protect itself, the body will physically pad itself in attempt to stop the intake of all this external energy.

For those who have difficulties processing emotions and maintaining positive connections, second chakra work is essential. People with excessively open reproductive chakras often have problems with relationships and personal boundaries. They can possess a martyr mentality and frequently attract abusers in their lives. Often they are unknowingly manipulative and self-serving, manifesting traits of excessive dependency on others and overindulgence of food, sex, and material goods. Besides a resizing of this chakra, a healing must also include ways for a patient to set up personal defense systems and avoid taking in an excess of emotional energy.

Deficient Energy in the Sacral: A closed reproductive chakra indicates a person who is disconnected from his emotions. Often, these people are withdrawn and can be rather cold and emotionally distant. Strong connections to others are important for healthy, loving relationships, and humans need the emotional response in order to be spiritually whole. I often see career-driven women with a closed reproductive chakra, especially if they have not had children and instead channeled their creative energy into building a career. A lot of men also have closed second chakras, as society often forces men to be emotionally distant. Physically, a closed sacral can manifest as constipation, digestive upsets, emotional guilt and resentment, and problems with sexual performance and reproduction including frigidity, impotence, and sterility. It also cuts a person off from his natural childlike energies and dulls creativity and enthusiasm for life.

A closed chakra needs to be opened immediately in order to create emotional balance in one's life, facilitate creative expression, and to open the self to healing experiences. It can be helpful for a patient with a newly opened chakra to associate with emotional people in order to connect with their empathic energy. Bodywork treatments like massage can also release emotions, and it can be beneficial to explore these types of therapy. Please be aware that a healing of the second chakra can cause profound emotional release in a patient, and this will require your sensitivity.

The Solar Plexus Chakra

The third chakra is the chakra of the solar plexus, and it is located under the rib cage right between the navel and the sternum. It is a projective energy center that is concerned with the intellect and the direct effect of thoughts on the body's physical systems. This chakra is often called the *abdominal brain,* as it is directly connected to the lower part of the brain, the medulla. On the left side of the body, it is further associated with the organs of the stomach, spleen, and the endocrine gland of the pancreas, while on the right side lies the liver and gallbladder, and to the back are the kidneys. The color of the solar plexus is the bright hue of yellow, and its stones are the citrine, amber, and tiger's eye.

A healthy solar plexus chakra enables a person to have a powerful mind/body connection. It allows for effective interpretation of the second chakra's emotional signals, and also grants protective energies to the body through the power of knowledge and awareness. Rationalizing, thinking, perceiving, and making logical and rational judgments are the processes of the solar plexus. It is further responsible for the innate intuition that comes straight from the gut; the indescribable ability that lets you intuitively know when something has happened to your child or that a stranger is dangerous. With normal functioning, the energy of the solar plexus is alert and actively in contact with the intellectual layer of the self. It is associated with the stomach, where the breakdown of tangible things into understandable, useable parts occurs. This applies to the physical digestion of food, but on a mental level it also applies to ideas, messages from the body, emotions, perceptions, insights, thoughts, and impressions.

The solar plexus distributes and processes lower chakra energies. That fluttery feeling that occurs in the stomach when you are nervous or are in a potentially dangerous situation is, in part, the efforts of the solar plexus chakra trying to protect the self by spreading out energy. Centering is a technique used in martial arts that involves pulling the energy of the body into the solar plexus chakra to steady and prepare the self for physical work. In martial arts it is believed that the solar plexus is the seat of personal power, the inner sun, and the center of the Chi.

Work on the solar plexus is appropriate when one needs centering in his life. A resizing of the chakra helps an individual find self-fulfillment and mental or emotional balance. At the solar plexus we breathe deeply, expanding the diaphragm and filling the body with the life force of air. Here we also fill the body with power. A healthy solar plexus is expressive and energetic, stimulating the system with protective and motivating energy. It is the place of inner strength for the self and must be strong to promote a healthy body. With any problem in the solar plexus, it is important that you check the health of the third eye chakra as well, as the two are linked together and problems in one will affect the other.

Excessive Energy in the Solar Plexus: A third chakra that is excessively open picks up far too many vibrations and overloads the mind with stimulus. It causes an individual to become overly intellectual, to the point where she overanalyzes situations and becomes very judgmental, critical, and demanding. Perfectionists often have excessively active solar plexus chakras. An extremely exposed solar plexus also leaves a person open to be consumed with other people's thoughts, and this can cause mental confusion, preventing clear thinking and rational decision-making.

I also find that people who are suffering with paranoia and severe anxiety possess extremely active solar plexus chakras. They perceive dangers lurking everywhere. The center is taking in too much energy that the body cannot ground out as the chakra is blasting energy in an attempt to protect the self. It is very disruptive and unsettling to be carrying around extreme fear and mental anxiety and have a chakra that is constantly flooding the system with protective energy. It never allows the self to relax and stresses the body immeasurably. When we overprocess energy in the solar plexus, we become physically afflicted with ulcers of the stomach and headaches of the mind.

Resizing the chakra or even closing it temporarily can alleviate many of these kinds of problems. People with a solar plexus chakra problem should also work on the third eye chakra, for it is connected to the solar plexus. A healed solar plexus chakra will bring positive feelings about the self, mental centering, and an overall sense of safety.

Deficient Energy in the Solar Plexus: When the solar plexus chakra is closed and experiencing a deficiency in energy, it indicates that the person is in denial of her mental defense systems. The solar plexus chakra is the protective center that gives us our gut warnings and, if closed, it prevents a person from perceiving warning signals about potentially harmful situations. This is obviously very dangerous. A closed chakra also prohibits mental understanding and a rational look at the truth of a situation. A person with this problem is insecure and lacks confidence, and is often depressed and confused mentally. Sometimes she can be overly competitive and self-centered, as she is distanced from perceiving the loving energy of the second chakra.

Drug addicts often have closed solar plexus chakras; they cannot center themselves and are constantly denying themselves a logical look at their lifestyles and the damage their patterns are causing themselves and their loved ones. I also see closed solar plexus chakras in women who have been with abusive partners. They did not pick up on the warning signs of a harmful relationship, as they were distanced from their essential survival awareness skills. Healing this chakra can begin to facilitate centering of energy, awareness, and truthful cognition about a situation; it also brings the ability to clearly recognize a potentially harmful path and make smart, direct choices.

The Heart Chakra

The energy of the fourth chakra is driven by the positive, receptive power of the heart. It is the special place where our personal energy holds a true connection to the goodness of life. The heart chakra allows us to feel love and forgiveness, compassion and peace. The heart center sits balanced in the human energy field, being the central chakra of the body's energy system, uniting the first three higher chakras with the lower three. Through its spinning motion, it generates the healing color of pure emerald green. Stones of the heart include the emerald, jade, and rose quartz. This chakra rules the heart and the circulation of blood, of course, but is also associated with the lungs, thymus, and immune system.

The heart is the center of the soul, the focal point of the energy system. It acts as a collective energy core that maintains the body's energy balance by facilitating communication between the physical nature of the first three lower chakras and the spiritual nature of the three higher chakras. Energy flows downward from the heart, deep into the instinctual and emotional layers of the stomach, and out the physical root of the body into the earth; it also cycles from the heart upward to the crown chakra, passing through the communication center of the throat chakra and the psychic center at the brow. The heart adds loving vibrations to the physical chakras and grounds the intense spiritual energy of the higher centers. Energy is also pushed out from the heart down into the arms, and travels out through the hand chakras so that we may use our hands to direct personal power.

A healthy heart chakra brings tenderness, love, and laughter to the self. It allows us to forgive ourselves, to heal the ugly scars of the past, and to release unnecessary energy. Through the powerful energy of the heart we learn to be flexible, to love the self unconditionally. Only when we hold healthy, loving connections with ourselves can we create powerful bonds with others. The heart allows us to accept the truth in our relationships, both with ourselves and other people. At this center the physical desires of the root and the emotional attachments of the sacral are transformed into the pure sacred love of the heart.

We experience the goodness of life and are filled with humanitarian energies, peace, and love.

As the central functioning chakra, the health of the heart is essential to the whole energy system. A big part of energy healing involves work on the heart center. A healthy heart chakra creates balance between the body and the spirit, whereas an unhealthy heart chakra creates a harmful mind/body split. Often a heart chakra healing will facilitate the healing of the entire energy system. Treatment of the heart chakra is necessary for the healing of immune system disorders like HIV and AIDS, lupus, arthritis, chronic fatigue syndrome, cancer, lung problems, circulation conditions, emphysema, pneumonia, and physical heart problems. It is also effective for healing people with emotional problems and for those who lack self-esteem and self-love.

Excessive Energy in the Heart: A heart chakra that is extremely enlarged is a center that is feeding on too much external energy and not enough internal love energy. As a society in general, we all need to learn to love ourselves, to give ourselves unconditional acceptance for who we are and the trials we have been through. But an individual with an enlarged heart chakra cannot fully love himself, as he is seeking attention and energy from outward sources. This receptive chakra is constantly needing energy and will take it from whatever sources it can get it from, healthy or unhealthy. This is why so many women stay with men whom they know are not good for them.

The heart chakra is the balance center between the spiritual and the physical aspects of a person, and when its attention is constantly directed at seeking more and more external energy, the lack of self-fulfillment creates a spirit/body split. A person with this problem will try to be selfless and completely giving in order to receive the energies of attention, love, and approval in an attempt to fulfill her intense need for love. And we all know that, of course, one cannot be giving and altruistic all of the time. We live on a physical level where food, sex, money, the body, emotions, withdrawal, self-preservation, and even selfishness are a necessary part of a balanced life. It is extremely exhausting and endlessly frustrating to be pulled in these two directions, striving to live in a physical world and yet trying constantly to live up to the expectations of the spirit in order to receive love.

And because the system is not being fueled by self-generated love energy, but by external energy, the current does not cycle naturally through the system but creates an enormous blockage in the chakra. The energy builds up in an attempt to feed the vacuum caused by the person's extreme need. This is physically damaging to the system and the body, as we cannot take in an overabundance of external energy. We simply do not have the innate tools to deal with things we have not created, and it manifests as disease and illness.

As humans, we all have emotional requirements, but people who possess an excessively open heart chakra have extreme needs. Often passive on the surface, they exhibit needy, critical, and melodramatic behavior and attempt to control others through guilt and a martyr attitude; for example, "I give you everything, so why do you treat me this way?" or, "I sacrifice so much for you and get nothing in return."

Personal energy must be focused on loving the self first before a person can support a healthy emotional commitment with another. A healing can soothe the heart chakra and unite a spirit/body division, as resizing the chakra draws its energy inward into the self, providing the much-needed self-love and support. I know that healing my own heart chakra brought an enormous change and balance to my life, as it taught me to love myself before seeking love from others. It allowed me to see that I was a good person who didn't need to be fed by external approval. It is important that the healing is accompanied with positive affirmations that build self-esteem and promote self-love.

Deficient Energy in the Heart: A heart chakra that is small or closed is a sign of a person whose soul is cut off from love, laughter, joy, and trust. We see this reflected in our language from the phrase, "He's got a small heart." There is no enchantment in a person's life when the heart is closed. We naturally close off the heart at times, such as when we are hurt by a loved one. "I'll never love again," we say, building walls and locking our personal bonds of attachment deep inside the soul. But most walls are temporary, for if they were not, we would die. The souls of very few people can survive a hermetic lifestyle, because life is essentially about connections. We connect to the self and the strength of personal power, to each other and the bond of love, to the universe and the spiritual energy of life, and we cannot deny these essential connections.

People who shut off their heart energy in a defense attempt to deny connections live without love in their lives. They suffer from fear and anger, and eventually manifest cancers and immune deficiencies. They do not live a happy life and tend to die early, alone. A closed heart means a deadened spirit, a lack of energy and possibility.

It is so important to heal the heart chakra, for it is the central chakra of the body, and when it is weak, the entire system is imbalanced. A healing opens the heart to touching, communicating, and loving. When we discuss crystal healing, we will talk about rose quartz as the best healing stone for a heart chakra. It works wonders at healing, allowing one to see tenderness and love in the self and all places. Love can truly heal all, make everything well and whole. This is really the essence of spirit, this love, this tenderness for all things.

The Hand Chakras

The heart chakra is connected to the hand chakras, the energy focal points that exist in the center of the palms. They are slightly smaller than the other chakras, and mainly behave as channels that conduct energy. Usually the dominant hand acts as a sending or directing chakra, and the submissive hand a receiving chakra; although, through concentration, either chakra can send or receive energy. Like the foot chakras, they open and close much more frequently than the body's other focal points. Used by masseuses and energy healers, the hand chakras allow energy to be directed out from the heart and the rest of the body. Healthy hand chakras facilitate balanced give and take relationships, and also manifest a positive energy flow through the entire bodily system.

The Throat Chakra

Known as the throat chakra, the fifth energy center of the body sits above the hollow at the base of the neck. Connected to the throat, eyes, neck, muscles, thyroid, and nerves, this projective chakra rules communication and the ability to manifest creatively. It is seen as a bright sapphire-blue disk. A person who has attuned to the power of the throat chakra can create positive lines of communication and can clearly articulate her thoughts. Spiritual leaders, speakers, and motivators usually possess strong throat chakras. This communication center is where we express ourselves to the world. In a healthy throat chakra we truly experience the moment and understand our needs and responsibilities as creatures of this earth. The primary stone of the throat chakra is beautiful blue energy of the turquoise.

You can treat the throat chakra to balance the metabolism of the body and for all throat problems, including soreness, tonsillitis, larynx problems, communication blockages, anger and rage, guilt from harmful words, stage fright, expressiveness, singing concerns, and vocal power control issues. It can also be used to treat problems of the eyes, ears, muscles, nerves, and conditions like anxiety, nervousness, and creative blockages. With any throat chakra problem you need to check the health of the sacral as well.

Excessive Energy in the Throat: A throat chakra that is too big and blasting provokes a person to talk far too much. We all know someone who cannot listen because he is talking too much, and often in his ramblings he does not speak the truth; he will make excuses, lie, cover up, and blame. There is a disturbing victim mentality present here; a person with an out-of-control throat chakra cannot speak the truth, as he does not accept responsibility for the self and the reality of his situation.

A person with an aggressive throat chakra is loud and complaining, just like a stubborn two year old, and she will defend her victimization with a very strong and enthusiastic communication ability. This only compounds her problems, as it works to attract unstable, often abusive individuals whom she will let victimize her, manifesting even more negative energy situations.

Complaining and blaming only throws barriers and blockages up in the face of a problem; these tactics do not allow a person to work through the problem to find its hidden gift.

Sadly, I see many people in this world with fifth chakra problems. A throat chakra healing makes a person take responsibility for himself; it allows him to begin to speak the truth. He moves away from excuses in himself, and finds that he cannot handle evasion and pretense in others as well. When one starts to perceive and live out situations as they truly exist, the truth will open doors to change and new opportunities. Expect that a throat chakra healing will transform a patient and shake up his world, and also expect that this may be very frightening to some. And believe me, a person with excessive throat chakra energy will certainly let you know about the transformation occurring in his life. Be aware that it may take several healings to resize the chakra and get the energy flowing in a normal measure.

Deficient Energy in the Throat: The fifth chakra can just as often be closed, and this indicates an individual who is withdrawn and rarely expresses her personal energy. We see a victim mentality here, too, only this type of person is a quiet victim who suffers inside with great resentment because she cannot voice her needs. She experiences helplessness, confusion, unhealthy dependency, extreme shyness, emotional depression, and difficulties with changes. By holding throat chakra energy within, the blockage can create many physical problems, such as chronic throat ailments, neck problems, headaches, earaches, and stuttering.

A healing of a closed throat chakra is just as transforming as a healing of an exposed throat chakra. It allows a person to become expressive and communicative in his wants, and it brings to a person the ability to assert and create his own journey. The patient will be opened to change, as he discovers new interests, switches jobs, leaves a partner whom he is not compatible with, and is finally ready to seize new opportunities. This is a healthy, honest way to deal with the world, but it presents changes that are often hard, especially at first. For some people it may take years for them to find their true voice. Often opening up a throat chakra will trigger a rebound action that will cause the chakra to open up far too much. So with any healing of this nature, you will need to check the chakra in a week or two and resize it again if necessary.

The Third Eye Chakra

The sixth chakra is the receptive energy center that aligns with the third eye. It is located in the center of the forehead between the eyebrows and the hairline, and its color is the brilliant violet of clairvoyants and mediums. This chakra is associated with the bottom of the brain, the eyes, the ears, the nose, the face, the nervous system, and the pituitary gland, which is a remnant of a third eye that never developed over the process of evolution. The third eye chakra is an extremely conscious psychic center that rules higher level intuition and conveys the ability to perceive energy vibrations on a psychic level. Mystics have always talked of the third eye as the passageway to psychic knowledge. A healthy brow chakra allows an individual the ability to see on other levels, giving her a comprehensive vision of the world and her part in it. The primary stone of the third eye is the amethyst, with its strong psychic and healing vibrations.

Through the brow chakra we are able to transcend the body and see the truth on other realms: past, present, and future. It provides us with layers of learning. A healthy sixth chakra allows a person to see the root cause of a situation and make an objective, unemotional judgment. It brings truth, inner knowledge, and wisdom. We need to have healthy third eye chakras to make positive decisions, to see behind excuses, distractions, and pain in order to find the true causes of a situation. This chakra is also the center that interprets spiritual guidance from the universe and from within our own inner recesses. With its health we have no need for an accumulation of material things, as we have wealth of truth and fulfillment in our lives.

Treat the third eye chakra for sinus problems, cold and flu, eye problems, ear infections, nose problems, headaches, stress reduction, insomnia, and clouded thinking. It can also be worked on to promote clarity, the ability to see what is needed, and to enhance clairvoyance and psychic skills. With any problems in the third eye chakra, you need to check the health of the solar plexus as well, because the two chakras are linked.

Excessive Energy in the Third Eye: When a third eye chakra is extremely open, it has the tendency to take in far too much psychic information and fill the mind and body with harmful clutter. The ascertaining systems of the self simply cannot process all that foreign energy, and they will overload and cause a person to start feeling like nothing makes sense. The open chakra creates an inclination to be overly logical, too rational, too idealistic, and exceedingly analytical—to the point where the thinking process begins to interfere with normal functioning. A person may even start to become obsessive, manipulative, and egomaniacal in an attempt to regain some mental control in his life. If left unchecked, excess energy overloading can eventually cause hallucinations, nightmares, insomnia, headaches, migraines, confusion, anxiety, extreme paranoia, and fear.

I have seen psychotics and frightened clairvoyants with excessively open third eye chakras, and it is not a pretty sight. As a psychic, my third eye center is naturally very open, but when I am stressed it opens enormously and causes me to pick up on all kinds of unimportant vibrations. I often have to physically downsize my third eye, which feels a little like I am slipping a helmet over my head. It cuts me off from all but the most intense psychic vibrations, but it is a necessary action in some chaotic situations.

It is very important to get this chakra under control. It can wreck havoc on a person's life, especially if that person has latent or untrained psychic abilities. Excessive energy in the psychic portal can be very disturbing and can drive some to the brink of suicide. If the third eye chakra is out of whack, then the whole energy system needs cleansing and healing, as the chakra will have been infusing the system with all kinds of extraneous energy. Be sure to especially look at the health of the solar plexus chakra, for as the linked partner of the third eye center, it will need specific healing as well.

Deficient Energy in the Third Eye: A deficiency of the third eye chakra is a very dangerous thing, as it cuts a person off from receiving energy on a psychic level. Without being able to access her psychic intuition, an individual cannot fully process information, analyze a situation, or make objective judgments. A blockage in this center prevents clear perception of the subtle behavioral patterns of people, and it prohibits an awareness about the real truth of a situation. It leaves a person open to make potentially dangerous choices. With a closed chakra, we do not trust ourselves and doubt our intuitive skills and abilities. A closed chakra further cuts a person off from her spiritual path and personal destiny. A blockage can manifest in mental problems like distress, confusion, bewilderment, headaches, fear, and phobias.

A healing of this chakra opens a person to his psychic energy, allowing him to see the truth in situations and receive spiritual guidance and insight. He begins to live his spiritual path. We all need to experience the truth of our personal journeys; honest spiritual experiences are the essence of the soul. It also reconnects a person to his innate psychic ability. We all have psychic skills, its whether we develop them or not that determines the extent of our powers. Even those people who do not believe in psychic powers use them unknowingly to make judgment calls about situations in their lives, and we must have healthy third eye chakras in order to ensure our survival in this world.

The Crown Chakra

The seventh chakra is known as the crown chakra and is located on the very top of the head. The mystics called this last center the "thousand petaled lotus," as it is the expressive chakra that receives the pure spiritual energy of the universe. It is connected to all the other chakras, and must be healthy in order to facilitate a strong energy flow through the body. The crown chakra is linked to the higher levels of the brain, the scalp, and the pineal gland. It is associated with the color white, as white is light that is made up of all other colors. In the spectrum it is also charged by the color violet, but I like to use a general purple for the third eye chakra and white for the crown. Stones of the crown include the brilliant whiteness of the diamond and the clear quartz.

A person who possesses a healthy crown chakra has an understanding of his self and his place within the universe. The center rules enlightenment of the self and contains the accumulation of the individual's spiritual destiny here on earth. Most healers have a healthy crown chakra, as they are able to be a channel for immense spiritual power without losing themselves in the energy flow. It takes a lot of personal effort and understanding of the self to manifest a strong seventh chakra. A crown chakra that spins clearly brings divine inspiration and knowledge to the self and facilitates an awareness of one's true spiritual path.

Work on the crown is appropriate for the treatment of headaches, seizures, shock, studying and retention of knowledge, memory problems, depression, anxiety, and other mental conditions, balancing the creative and logical sides of the brain, and to stimulate the endorphins for pain relief. The crown chakra is also the center to work on in order to tap into higher consciousness and receive insights from spirit.

Excessive Energy in the Crown: When a person's seventh chakra is excessively open, it is an indication that he needs more spiritual energy in his life. The chakra is trying to take in more celestial energy in an attempt to compensate for a mundane, unspiritual life. This creates an overflow of energy that is coming from an outside source instead of a self-fulfilling flow, and can lead to migraine headaches, confusion, frustration, depression, and even anger and manipulative behavior. The body cannot ground the excess energy fast enough. A healing can subdue the excessive needs of this chakra, but a person with this problem needs to look at ways to increase the enchantment in his life.

We all require magical, mystical, enlightened lives for the spirit to be at peace, but we need to find this spiritual fulfillment from within. We do this by seeing the magical in the everyday, finding the beauty in the laughter of children, experiencing the wisdom of the universe, having gratitude for the good things in life, taking the time to get out into nature to see the wonders of our planet, enjoying the spontaneity of life, sharing the love bond with others. By simply appreciating the little gifts of everyday living, we increase the enchantment of our lives and heal the crown chakra.

Deficient Energy in the Crown: A closure of the crown chakra is a dangerous thing, as it is an attempt to deny the spiritual energy of the self and the universe. This really creates a life without magic and enchantment, and it leads to severe depression, hopelessness, frustration, chronic pain, and cancers. I have seen severely closed crown chakras in several people who have attempted suicide. When you deny your spiritual path, there is no pride in the self. Every day is a chore, as there is no purpose or meaning to your existence.

A closed crown center shuts down the entire energy system, and it is so important to get a closed chakra under control before it can do permanent damage to the mental and emotional levels of the self. Opening it up allows a person to perceive experiences in a positive light and to begin to honor the beauty and spiritual purpose of the self. People with this problem also need to see the magical in the everyday, to spiritually connect to the beauty and enchantment of life.

Chakra Healing Techniques

Healthy chakras are expressive and aware of each other. They are connected together and work in harmony to prompt the entire energy system to function at peak efficiency. The vibrations of each chakra will flow with the energies of the next, transmitting energy up and down the system to promote balance.

Each of the spinning energy vortexes is composed in layers, so when we treat problems in the chakras we solve them in layers as well. The more you work on the chakras, the deeper through the various energy levels you will go, and the more you will discover; and, thus, the more you can change. A deeper-seated healing will require several sessions.

Be aware that often after a treatment we will see a reversal of chakra problems. If a chakra is too open, a healing can cause it close right down, or when it is opened in a healing it can open far too wide. You need to keep an eye on the chakra and have the patient periodically check them, too. It is her chakra, so she has the best chance of knowing what is going on with it.

During a treatment we can work on all the chakras or on one individually, according to our assessment of a client's need. With a problem in any chakra, you may also need to work on the chakra that is connected to the first, as an imbalance in one can affect the other, however subtly. The primary chakra pairs consist of the root and the crown, the sacral and the throat, and the solar plexus and the third eye, with the heart acting as the focal point in the system. There are different pairings of the chakras used in other healing treatments, but these are the pairings I use, as I find they are very effective. So when we treat a chakra we want to consider the health of its complementary chakra as well, because we may need to treat it to reestablish a balance in the flow.

In any healing you should also focus on treating the heart chakra, as it is the central equilibrium point of the energy system, and strengthening it will facilitate healing of the entire system.

Palm Induction

We read the chakra centers through the technique of palm induction, where we manually sense each chakra to assess for differences in feeling or sensation. To begin, practice the technique on yourself. Lie on your back and run your open palm slowly over your body, directly down a center line from the crown to pelvis. Focus on sensing each chakra, and feel for the concentrations of energy under your palm. The chakras may tingle or possess variations in temperature. They should be warm and moving, but should not feel too hot or too cold, or move at too frantic or too slow of a pace.

An active chakra will be hot from usage, like the throat chakra of a speaker, but in normal resting condition chakras should be warm and not possess an extreme temperature. An extreme hot temperature chakra indicates an energy center that is overused and excessively open. An excessive chakra can also feel very wide—wider than the normal four inches of a healthy chakra.

A cold temperature chakra or an energy center you cannot detect indicates a deficiency of energy in the chakra. It is closed and is spinning very slowly.

Balanced chakras all spin in the same direction. An imbalanced chakra will gather all energy to it and feel agitated. It will be moving frantically.

During your physical assessment, use your inner intuitive vision to see the color that the chakras are predominantly displaying. Is the chakra color clear, cloudy, or pale? Listen to your inner wisdom to find out what each chakra is saying to you.

Clearing a Chakra

A chakra that has an excess accumulation of energy and feels agitated under the hand needs to be smoothed. When smoothing, apply the same technique that we used to even out general imbalances in the energy field. Use your palms in gently flowing motions to smooth out the energy from the center. I like to smooth the chakra with one hand smoothing up and the other smoothing down, and smooth the center out to the sides with one hand smoothing to the right and the other smoothing to the left.

Opening a Chakra

When we resize a chakra we use our hands to physically manipulate the center. To open a closed chakra, have the client lie down and use your hands to pull the energy center apart. Make small spreading motions across the body, directly on the chakra center, with your palms and fingers. Literally drag the energy center open while using visualization to see the chakra expand. You do not have to drag the energy far; dragging it to the next chakra is fine. Just be sure that you drag the energy in all directions; begin by using one hand above the center to draw the energy upward to the crown, and simultaneously use the other hand to draw the energy toward the root; then move your hands to the two sides of the chakra in order to draw the energy out from the sides. Have the client focus on mentally expanding the chakra and projecting energy out through it while you physically open it. You should also visualize the chakra opening and see energy shooting out of it. I like to work the chakra in layers, so I begin to open it from all sides about five inches from the body, and repeat the spreading technique at three inches, one inch, and then directly touching the skin. You can even put your hands into the chakra and swirl the energy around in a clockwise motion to facilitate movement of the chakra. When you open a chakra, make sure it does not become excessively open. Be sure to use palm induction to check it and resize it smaller if necessary.

Reducing a Chakra

To reduce the size of a chakra, it is again best to work on the patient when she is lying down. Stand beside the patient and hold your hands apart over the chakra, palms down. Cup the chakra between your hands so that you have made a frame with your fingers and thumbs around the energy center. Slowly bring the hands together, narrowing the circle between them, like a camera lens closing. Envision the chakra becoming smaller, and have the client visualize it closing as well. When your fingers and thumbs on each hand touch each other at about a three-inch diameter, have the client exhale forcefully to seal the chakra at this size while you physically tighten your hands together to lock the chakra in place. Again, since the chakras are composed in layers, you can work on them in layers at five inches, three inches, one inch, and directly against the body.

Connecting the Chakras

The chakras need to share energy links with each other in order to maintain a healthy system. To connect the chakras together, have the patient lie down in a comfortable position with his shoes and socks off and his legs uncrossed. Open your chakras and channel energy in your hands. Starting at the crown chakra, hold your palms on the lowest layer of the chakra directly against the body, and send energy through it. Have the client visualize a ball of golden light entering his crown chakra. Slowly move your hands down through the chakras, drawing the light through each of them. The client should visualize the light connecting each chakra in the system. As you reach each new chakra, place your hands directly on the center and have the client inhale the energy from your hands, pulling it deep into the chakra. Placing your hand on the chakra helps the person process the energy. On his exhale, have the client focus on pushing the energy out the soles of his feet. If you or the client feel any resistance from any chakra, pause and explore it. What messages is the body giving you?

This technique stimulates and activates each chakra, and establishes a free flow of energy through the system that connects the chakras to each other. The client can perform this exercise by himself at home to connect and clear the energy of the chakras.

You can also place each hand on one chakra to connect two of them together. Project energy through each hand into the two centers, and have the client inhale deeply, pulling the energy into the body; feel it flowing between the two centers. This technique is useful to strengthen the link between the complementary pairs of chakras, working to clear and balance the energy flows.

Pulling Energy

When there is unwanted energy in a chakra, or you are treating a chakra for a specific problem, use the technique of pulling energy to remove the unwanted vibrations from the center. Pulling removes toxic energies and helps to move them out of the energy system. Move the palm counterclockwise to pull off energy; you can circle the palm inside the chakra and scoop up excess energy into your hand and dispose of it, either by pulling it off and holding it in the hand to mentally charge it with white light to purify it before letting go of it, or by flicking it into a bowl of water that you can rinse down the drain later. After removing energy, I like to add positive healing vibrations back to the system to facilitate healing.

Adding Energy

You can focus healing energy into a chakra to help aid patient with a specific ailment. Open your personal chakras and channel universal energy through your system and out of your hands. Place your hands directly on the chakra and focus on sending healing energy into the area. Have the patient inhale deeply to receive the energy and visualize the energy penetrating deep into the system, healing the problem. Be sure to close down the chakras after you are done working with them.

Self-Chakra Activation

You can perform this standing meditation to activate and center your own chakras before healing work. It can also be wise to teach it to a patient who has a lot of chakra problems. Self-balancing can be done every day, just be sure to stress the importance of closing down the chakras after the balancing. The procedure of opening or awakening the chakras is a spiritual process that encompasses concentration and visualization.

We begin with the root chakra. Stand and firmly plant your feet about shoulder width apart on the ground. Concentrate on envisioning the pure red energy of the root chakra. It swirls clockwise in a disk about four inches wide inside your pelvis at the base of your spine. Place one hand on your tail bone and the other on the front of your lower pelvis, and feel the energy swirl between your hands. Focus on making the energy grow and cycle in a smooth motion. As it grows, you will need to move your hands slightly away from your body to create space for the concentrating energy. You can use your hands to shape the disk, creating a well-defined border. You can even put your fingers into the energy, then move it to facilitate the swirling of the chakra.

When you have awakened the root chakra, envision some of its energy running down your legs and pooling in the foot chakras. As long as you live, your chakras generate an endless supply of energy, so you never have to worry about depleting that energy. Each foot chakras should be a smaller disk that grounds you to the earth. Feel the energy move through your feet and enter into the earth, traveling down into its core. If you are having trouble connecting your foot chakras to your root chakra, again use your hands to facilitate the flow of energy down your legs. Grounding your foot chakras to the earth heals energy blockages that are commonly found in the lower body and begins to allow personal energy to travel in its natural flowing state.

When you have awakened your root chakra and the connecting foot chakras, you can then progress to the reproductive chakra. Envision the chakra as a four-inch disk swirling in a warm orange color. The second chakra should be in a straight line above the root chakra, and the same size and shape.

After you open up the sacral, progress to the solar plexus chakra. Envision the energy running through it as a yellow disk that swirls above the belly button. When the solar plexus is open, you can concentrate on centering yourself. Stand firmly with your feet planted about shoulder width apart. Visualize all your energy focusing on your solar plexus chakra. You can aid the visualization process through the act of stretching out your arms and clenching your hands into fists. Inhale deeply, and at the same time, pull your elbows directly back to your waist. Visualize your energy centralizing at the solar plexus with the movement of your arms. Breathe out as you feel your energy center concentrate. Repeat this technique a few times to completely center your energy.

Then continue to advance through the awakening and opening of the rest of the chakras in the same manner. The heart spins with healing green energy directly in the center of the chest, and after opening it, concentrate on feeling some of its energy run down your arms and collect at the hand chakras. Rubbing your palms briskly together for a moment is an easy way to open up the hand chakras. You should envision the energy focusing in each palm, and then blasting out your hands in a steady stream. Feed the projective stream from the energy of your heart chakra. This will clear any energy blockages you may have in the upper body. You can then close your palms to stop the flow of energy out of your hands.

Continue to open up the rest of the chakras using the same technique we used for the first chakra. The throat chakra is a beautiful blue center that turns in the hollow of the throat, while the brow chakra is a spiritual vibrant purple color that sits in the center of the forehead, and the crown chakra spins on the top of your head in a pure white color.

When all your chakras are open, you can concentrate on drawing earth power up through the foot chakras and into your body. You may feel a burst of power as it blasts through your body and out of the crown. Envision the energy running through your body and then recirculating from the crown chakra back down to the root chakra like a fountain. You are being charged and energized with earth power.

You can also breathe in universal energy through the crown chakra, then use your breath to draw the energy through each chakra of the body, and breathe it out through the root chakra with your exhale.

This exercise manifests balance within the body and ensures that the body's energy system is functioning normally. It smoothly links the chakras to each other and stabilizes the energy flow.

After you are finished experimenting with the chakras, you must close them. To leave the chakras constantly open can burn out the sensitive energy centers and create illness and disease within the body. You can imagine the chakras closing in order, from the crown chakra down to the root chakra, like great eyes that shut fully and completely. Most of the energy will drain out of them, and they will slow down their rate of spinning. They will never completely shut and stop, but for our purposes we visualize them shutting to remove the added energy that we have generated. Eating is also an excellent way to ensure that the chakras are fully closed. I cannot stress enough the importance of closing down the chakras.

Adding Chakra Work to an Energy Treatment

To incorporate chakra work into a basic energy treatment, follow the guidelines for an energy treatment. Perform an initial assessment and decide on a course of treatment. Discuss the procedure with your clients.

Have the client lie down and relax with her shoes and socks removed. Prepare yourself to heal, and guide the client though a relaxation exercise and an aura-envisioning meditation. Perform a general palm assessment of the energy field, and then assess the individual chakras, using palm induction to scan the centers for blockages, agitation, or extremities in temperature. Have the client perform a mental assessment of her body, and, together, explore any findings.

Begin the actual aural treatment with a general smoothing of the field, and work on any general imbalances of the field. Then tailor your work to the needs of the individual centers. Affirmations and visualizations may be used here by the patient to enhance the healing work. With any work on the chakras, I like to work on the heart to promote general healing as well.

After treatment of the centers, perform the golden light exercise to connect the chakras together. Perform a general smoothing of the entire auric field. Complete the treatment with a final assessment of the chakras, and note any physical changes in the centers of the body. Gently bring the patient's focus back to the room.

Discuss aftercare procedures with the client, and go over your findings and administered treatment. Be sure to ground out any excess energy and close down your chakras after you are done working with them. Eat some food to further ground out any energy and replenish your own levels.

It takes time to learn the subtleties of energy awareness. Every person's needs and reactions differ, and your treatments must be tailored to the specific vibrations of the individual. You will never know it all; your energy study will continue throughout your whole life. Experimentation will propel you to formulate your own conclusions about the flow and patterns of energy. Through time and practice you will learn the intimate needs and drives of each chakra center, and how best to heal imbalances. In the two subsequent chapters we will add the energies of crystals and color to enhance the chakra and aural treatments.

10

Crystal Healing

An ancient practice, crystal healing involves the application of the energy vibrations generated by crystals and stones to heal imbalances and blockages in the body's energy flow, aiming to restore proper balance and smooth functioning to the entire energy system.

The dynamic art of crystal healing is quickly growing in popularity, as our collective human consciousness is becoming increasingly aware of the transformative powers of crystals. Crystals and gemstones naturally generate immense energy that can be harnessed for both physical and psychological healing treatments, making crystal application a valuable therapy to the alternative healer. Their vibrations can align the energy field, transmit and amplify personal healing energy, and raise the spiritual vibrations of an environment. Crystal healing is an integral part of a comprehensive healing program.

Crystal healing is my favorite type of healing therapy. It is a powerful practice that draws strongly upon the intuition. A crystal healer must be focused, bold, and confident, firmly connected to herself and her own energy patterns. It is extremely important that a healer has experience with centering and balancing her own energy flow before applying the potent currents of crystals to her work, as the stones directly act to focus and amplify all forms of energy. Administered properly, a crystal healing can create extreme changes in the body's energy field, promoting health and maintained wellness.

Growing deep within the darkness of the earth, crystals form in spiral patterns, wondrous illustrative representations of the universal symbol of healing and transformation. Each stone is uniquely individual in its makeup, composed of different amounts of chemicals that are held in fixed internal structures. Under extreme heat and pressure of the dull earth, crystals melt and compress into form. They are the creation of beauty out of basic materials, testifying to the amazing power of growth and change.

But beyond being beautiful, crystals also emit a unique constant piezoelectric charge, which makes them ideal for use in electronic equipment. Able to focus, emit, and amplify natural energy, they are used in watches, lasers, computers, radio technology, radar, and television. Their energy vibrations can also be harnessed and used for healing the energy field of the body. And when used properly, they have the power to increase the spiritual energy of the aura.

In our work we want to use naturally shaped crystals, as raw, unrefined stones are the most powerful for healing. A crystal grows from its base out to its termination, or point. The base is receptive with a negative charge, while the termination is projective and has a positive charge. Under an electron microscope electrons can be seen moving out of the termination, and because a crystal is sensitive to squeezing and pressure, the termination is seen to give off more energy when the stone is squeezed. Because they project electrons, the application of the vibrations from crystals increase the body's negative ion count and work to promote expansive healing. Crystals are truly pure manifestations of energy in physical, tangible form, and they are a valuable, living tool.

We know that the body is much more than just mass; it is also dynamic energy. In the chapter on energy we discussed how energy concentrations can become crystallized in the body, creating damaging blockages, and we studied the techniques of energy therapy to break up and dissolve these blockages. Crystal healing can also break up blockages and promote a smooth energy flow throughout the body. The light energy from the stones penetrates into the aura, soothing physical problems and healing the emotional root sources of physical illness. They strengthen the systems of the body and wash away pain and fear on both emotional and physical levels.

I often find that crystal therapy is more effective than energy work alone, as the stones can heal a deeper-seated blockage. There are literally trillions on trillions of tiny quartz crystals contained in the body; we find silica chemical crystals in the brain, the nervous system, and in the plasma of blood. The body is really a giant crystal; its systems are maintained by molecules of silica. The application of external crystals can greatly affect the functioning of the body's internal crystals. The energy of the stones can strengthen the mind and enable us to better perceive and process information; they bring balance to the energy field by infusing spiritual energy into the body's own electromagnetic field, they amplify energy and increase emotional levels, and they have the magical power to delve into the deepest parts of the soul.

Crystals are used to enhance and focus power through the properties of absorption and emission of light. Certain types of stones, like onyx, obsidian, and other dark stones, are natural receivers of energy and can be used to absorb pain and other unwanted energy, while other types of stones, like amethyst and amber, project energy and can be directed to speed up the healing of cuts, burns, bruises, breaks, and ruptured tissue. Natural clear quartz crystals can be empowered to project or receive energy, depending on how they are shaped. A receiving crystal with a large flat face or wide base is normally used to absorb energy, while a projecting crystal with a sharp point gives out energy.

Crystals can also change negative unbalanced vibrations into positive unwavering vibrations. They further absorb energy, soaking up negative energy and promoting harmony. Crystals can be used to absorb pain and blockages in the system, to speed the healing of injuries, to reduce and soothe emotional problems like stress, anxiety, depression, anger, guilt, and also to strengthen the immune system. Under a crystal treatment, a patient noticeably relaxes, softens, and shifts her perception. Use crystal therapy to supplement an energy healing, and you will see the dramatic power of crystals to heal.

Crystals and Gemstones

There are many more healing crystals and gemstones than I have included here, but this is a good start. The list includes some of the most common and useful clear quartz crystals and gemstones. As you become more familiar with crystal healing, you can expand your knowledge base with other stones.

Clear Quartz Crystals

Clear quartz is an all-purpose healing stone. It channels the vibrations of pure light, containing the full range of energy, as white light holds all colors of the spectrum. It is considered to be a neutral energy stone, as it can be empowered to both absorb or project universal light energy. It further can amplify and intensify any vibrations given to it. Clear quartz crystals come in several distinct shapes that are used for different healing applications, and we will look at these specific crystals.

Activator Crystals

An activator is a type of projective crystal that is used to send direct energy to activate and enhance the body's energy field and the energy of other stones. Normally, an activator is a long, straight, clear quartz crystal that comes to a strong six-sided termination. It possesses an internal structure that brings energy inward through the base and channels it outward through the point. An activator also amplifies energy, and the longer and clearer the quartz crystal is, the greater its powers of transmission and amplification. Activators are usually held in the hand and used to project energy over a specific area or into another crystal. For your healing set you want to look for a large activator crystal that has a strong pulse and clear internal structures with little or no fissures and markings. It should come to a good termination.

Receiver Crystals

A receiver is a clear quartz crystal that is used to absorb unwanted or excess energy. Some receivers have a large flat face that slopes at approximately a forty-five degree angle to absorb energy, while others are often round-shaped quartz crystals that absorb energy through a large base. A receiver is used to pull unwanted energy out of an area, like in a blocked chakra or over an injury to speed healing and rejuvenation. After you use a receiver you will need to use a projector to put positive energy back into the field. Look for a receiver that feels good when you hold it in your hand. It should pulse with absorption properties and signal to you that its job is to absorb and hold energy.

Scanner Crystals

A scanner is a clear quartz that is used to pick up on energy patterns. It can come in any shape; you need to choose a scanner that feels right to you. Some healers do not work with scanners, preferring to use palm induction alone. I like to use a combination of both. Be patient—it may take a while to obtain an accurate scanner. It took me about three years to find mine. The process of scanning with a crystal is explained later on in the chapter.

Transmitter Crystals

A transmitter is a thin clear crystal that can be placed on the body to direct energy; it can also surround a focal crystal in order to activate and enhance its energy. Sometimes I will use large size transmitters placed by themselves to correct the energy flow in an area that has a blockage or a deficiency. A double-terminated crystal projects energy out through both ends and can be used to draw energy between two chakra centers.

I face the termination of a transmitter in the direction I want energy to flow. Pointing a termination away from an area helps remove energy for cleansing and eliminating tension, pain, and blockages. Pointing a termination toward a region provides extra energy for healing, growth, and regeneration of tissues.

Transmitters are often placed surrounding a focal crystal. The terminations can be aligned to point toward the stone in order to intensify the energy of the focal stone in one area, or they can point out from the stone to spread its energy out through the whole system. In your collection, look for two larger transmitters and five or six thin, little transmitters. A double-terminated transmitter is a rare find and can be a very useful tool.

Colored Quartz Crystals and Gemstones

Agate

The agate is a member of the quartz family that is found in many beautiful colors and patterns. It is a subtle but powerful stone that works to strengthen the aura and align the chakra centers, promoting grounding and balance. Place an agate on each chakra point to create a strong energy connection between the centers. In this way it empowers the body's entire energy field and strengthens the immune system. I have also used the vibrations of the agate to heal impurities of the stomach and digestive system.

Agate has the magical ability to heal psychologically through the release of anger and the transformation of negative emotions into positive action. It is wise to meditate with it for issues of anger, animosity, and jealousy.

Amber

Amber is the gold-colored solidified sap from cone-bearing trees. Connected to the earth and the plants, amber is a material that promotes grounding and stability. This magical substance produces a negative electrical charge when rubbed and, thus, is a powerful purifier of the mind, body, and soul. Wear its beads in a necklace to receive protection from disease, fever, and plague; put it on the heart chakra to change the energy of sadness and depression into joy; and place it directly on an afflicted area to cast out pain, viruses, bad bacteria, and inflammation of the tissues.

Amethyst

A dramatic purple quartz, amethyst is a powerful crystal of healing, as its color places it in the highest of spiritual planes. It is a stone of transformation; its vibrations transmit energy and can convert negative energies to positive ones. Give it to people who need its transformative power, and it will grant the wearer inner peace. Worn continually, it protects against poisoning and sterility. Rub it on the body to cleanse blockages from the aura. I have used it to cure headaches by placing it on the forehead and temples. Placed on the heart chakra, it also protects the respiratory system and cures lung problems. Sleep with it under your pillow to overcome insomnia and prevent nightmares.

The amethyst is a powerful stone of psychic ability, connecting a person to his intuition. When placed on the third eye chakra, it promotes the ability to visualize, purifies and clarifies thoughts, alleviates mental anxieties and stresses, promotes cerebral stability on a cellular level, and acts as a potent psychic stimulant. Its energies facilitate enlightenment on both internal and external planes, channeling understanding from deep within the self to the conscious mind and bringing wisdom from the universe to the self.

Bloodstone

Also known as heliotrope, bloodstone is a dark green-colored quartz spotted with red jasper flecks that look like little bits of blood. Traditionally, bloodstone was worn by soldiers in battle to transmit courage and power and give protection from death. Carry bloodstone with you when you are facing difficult situations to give you strength in times of chaos and conflict.

Bloodstone is a cleansing stone: it removes blockages and stimulates energy flow, creating smooth energy transmissions throughout the entire field. Place bloodstone on the root chakra to spread its purifying energies through the aura. The stone can also be used to cleanse the internal organs of the stomach, liver, kidneys, and spleen. Place it directly on the organ to eliminate pain, irritation, and toxins. As its name suggests, bloodstone further purifies and strengthens the blood, lowering blood pressure, healing blood disorders, and stopping hemorrhaging. Soldiers used to bind pieces of bloodstone on their wounds to keep the flow of blood cycling smoothly through the body. For blood purification, place it on the root chakra.

Blue Tourmaline

Blue tourmaline is a stone that is composed of long parallel striations that run from the tip to the base, making the stone a powerful channel for positive electrical energy. Blue tourmaline is a gentle healing stone that can be used to soothe inflamed irritated tissue, as it sends cool harmonizing vibrations into the energy field and the tissues of the body. It can be applied to seal holes in the auric field.

I like to use blue tourmaline on the third eye chakra for calming and relaxing the mind. Here it promotes mental balance and infuses the body with healing energies. It can also be used on the throat for problems involving communication. The blue stone works to soothe the hurt from angry words and transforms negative self-talk into positive vibrations. It also brings the ability to create and manifest goals within the framework of a person's inner truth.

Carnelian

The carnelian is a fiery red to orange agate that can be applied to the muscles to soothe pain, stress, and remove tension. Apply the carnelian to the sacral chakra in order to add energy to the body, increase circulation, and rev up sluggish digestion. Here it also has the power to cure infertility and impotency. The stone can be used for thyroid balancing and adrenal gland stimulation. When placed on the throat chakra and the solar plexus chakra it can help rectify an eating disorder.

Citrine

A member of the quartz family, citrine is a gold-colored crystal that helps an individual get in touch with its personal power. It is a stone of manifestation, providing confidence and security in earthly matters, such as business, the acquisition of material things, and overcoming physical addictions. When placed on the third chakra, the solar plexus, citrine strengthens the center and spreads warmth through the body, increasing the amount of light in the aura. It can be used here to clear unbalanced breathing patterns, unblock the navel area, correct poor digestion and constipation problems, and strengthen the kidneys to alleviate bladder infections.

Obsidian

Formed from lava that cooled very quickly, obsidian is a black, glassy, smooth stone. It is a potent grounding rock. Placed at the root chakra, obsidian works to connect the body to earth energy. It is useful for gathering strength, willpower, stamina, and information about the body. For those people who are experiencing intense emotions that keep them agitated and in an unhealthy emotional space, obsidian can help establish a connection to the body and give protection from emotional draining. It is also a powerful cleanser of the body, strengthening the liver, eliminating toxins, diarrhea, and bad breath. It cleanses the intestinal tract and soothes the stomach. Hold a large piece on the irritated area to experience obsidian's transformative power.

Onyx

The onyx has the remarkable ability to absorb energy and emit very little back out. Use it to absorb negative energy; hold it in your hand and send it all your negative thoughts, worries, and fears. It is useful to carry when dealing with negative people, as it will absorb their negative energy and prevent it from being assimilated into your energy field. Put a big piece of it on your desk to absorb negative energy and criticism in the workplace. Place onyx directly on the skin to draw poison, sickness, diseases, and inflammation out of the tissues. Hold it under running water to cleanse the negative energy from the stone, or bury it in the earth.

Rose Quartz

The pink lady is the stone of self-love, the healer of faults, the eraser of guilt. It is a gentle cleanser of the emotions. Place it on the heart and feel the love of the Mother, pure and true; place it on the brow and hear its wisdom. In the arms of the pink goddess, we are soothed and nurtured, never to be scolded, never to be punished. It teaches us to love ourselves, even when we do not like ourselves. It promotes inner peace through forgiveness and compassion, erasing childhood trauma and releasing suppressed feelings. I have an extra piece of rose quartz that I often give to clients to hold, which helps them process their emotions during a treatment.

In our busy world, we often neglect the true core of love—self-love. This is the place from which we must start all our journeys. Communicate with rose quartz to understand self-forgiveness and letting go. Draw on its power to build self-love and inner respect. Place it under your pillow for dreams that soothe the soul with love. It is the primary stone for the heart chakra, and is a must in every healing I perform. We all have issues with self-love and self-image.

On a physical level, rose quartz is a mild cardiac stimulator. It gently increases circulation and strengthens the heart and lungs. It also heals the skin. Rose quartz works extremely well with amethyst, as the two stones facilitate a balance of emotional and mental energies. Rose quartz goes cloudy when it needs to be cleansed, and I have heard of pieces shattering when they have absorbed emotional energies past their limits. To avoid ruining a good stone, be sure to cleanse it often.

Tiger's Eye

A member of the quartz family, the tiger's eye is a magical stone, as it blends rich brown earth energy with the golden light of the sun. Because of its two colors, the vibrations it transmits are naturally intense. The dark energy is grounding, connected to the earth and physical form. The yellow highlights that run through the stone link it to the golden light of spirit that enters through the crown.

Used to balance the root and crown chakra, tiger's eye facilitates the movement of energy through the body from head to toe. You can place a piece on each chakra to connect the flow of energy from crown to root. I often do this if I am seeing a client for the first time, especially if he has not done previous work with his chakras.

Specifically on the root center, tiger's eye transmits grounding energy, and on the navel it motivates and changes thoughts into physical manifestations. Those of us who cannot get it together, feel spacey, or lack solid foundations for our goals and plans can benefit from the firm footing and deep focus of tiger's eye energy.

Turquoise

A beautiful blue in color, turquoise is a healing stone that offers the user positivity and clarity of thought. It has the ability to break down limiting barriers and boundaries. It holds a strong connection to the spirit and helps us feel sensitivity and empathy for ourselves and others. Its blue vibrations connect him to the throat chakra and the powers of communication. Wear a necklace of turquoise to increase your ability to communicate clearly and successfully, as through its creative vibrations it allows a person to speak his own truth. When used for physical healing, place turquoise on the throat chakra to help soothe and clear an irritated or clogged respiratory system. Turquoise is said to turn pale when the health and safety of the wearer is threatened.

Working with Crystals

The energy of the crystals will influence both the patient and the healer. In working with them you must realize that it is the personal experience with them that determines the nature of the relationship. Crystals are profound instruments of life, love, beauty, growth, and healing. They have a spirit, a consciousness of natural earth energy that resides within, and it is through this inner wisdom that they can lead us to connect with our own inner enlightenment. They enable us to link with our higher selves, to discover the true answers to our problems, to unlock the doors to our healing consciousness. Use them in your healer's meditations to increase the connection to your inner healing wisdom.

It is important to understand that we do not own crystals. They exist as their own individual entities. Healer and stone must form a partnership, working together to achieve purpose. Please respect your crystals and always address them with love and honor. Take the time to learn the intimate functions and limits of each one. This will ensure that you are bonding with them to increase positive energy.

Nothing you can do with them is wrong as long as you do it with love and respect. The crystals will be your guides. They teach us to how to use our own power. I can give you a map of where to place them, but they alone will give you the journey. They will show you what to do, lead you into enlightenment. Your own personal crystals are sacred tools of your healing practice. It is wise to not let others randomly touch and play with these crystals, as they are charged with your own healing energy. Keep them in a special spot, in little boxes and bags or displayed in a place of honor.

I advise you to work your own experiments with crystals. I have discovered that quartz crystals placed with pots of seeds caused the plants to sprout and grow faster than those without crystals. Even plants fed with crystal-charged water grew bigger and faster than those without charged water. Scientific experiments have shown that a crystal placed in water charges the water with the same vibration as the crystal.

In my practice I have found that crystals are unmistakably effective in healing many ailments. As there are many possible patterns of placement, you will need to experiment with different stones to find out which crystals work well together. Documentation can help you to see the patterns that are effective. Keep written results of your experimentation and healing attempts using crystals, and over time you will build solid data detailing the remarkable powers of crystals to transform and heal.

As with all therapies, the best way to learn crystal healing is to apply the stones to yourself in your own healing practice. Select a few key ones and attune to them. They do not have to be the biggest or prettiest, as all a healing stone needs is to feel good when held in the hand. Indeed, it is often the chipped or broken crystals that are the most potent for healing, as these are the emphatic stones that understand our own chips and scars.

When picking your crystals, spend time holding them in your hand, feeling for their individual pulses and listening to their inner messages. Each stone will have a specific purpose, and you can find out what that purpose is by engaging the crystal in voice dialogue. What does it say? Is it a healer of the heart, a soother of the stomach, a mediator of the mind? Sleep with your crystals, bathe with them, dance together, use them for meditation, allow them to play with your inner child and reveal their wisdom. Try to perceive the very essence of each crystal, and carefully note all you discover.

Crystals have the amazing property to be able to hold steady vibrations. Through visualization, you can attune a crystal to work in a specific energy pattern, but only if the energy pattern is aligned with the crystal's natural frequency.

You need to be careful to respect the properties of each crystal. If you use a crystal to absorb energy, then do not use it to give out energy. Each crystal has a specific purpose, and if you attune its energy to work in a certain way, then forcing it to work against its formulated energy patterns can have unwanted effects. If a crystal is used to always absorb negativity, and you suddenly try to use it to give out energy, it will only give out any energy that it has retained.

This does not mean that the crystal is a negative entity; rather, it simply has a specific type of work that it has been empowered to perform, and it functions best within that framework. Crystals simply process energy; just like water and earth they do not perceive energy as negative or positive, they simply receive it as energy. It is human beings who place the consciousness classification on it. Crystals absorb energy, condense it, amplify it, or project it, but they do not label it.

After your crystals have been used for a healing, you need to be sure to cleanse them thoroughly, as they will require release of any vibrations they are holding. If they collect too much energy they can fracture. Once, after a heated argument with a partner, I noticed that a favorite quartz crystal of mine had cracked and broken in two. It had absorbed the negativity in the room until it simply could not take any more.

You should purify your crystals through both visualization and an actual cleansing method. Submerge them in salt water, or hold them under a stream of running water. You can rinse them off in the sink, pointing the termination down to cleanse energy down the drain. Or you can bury them in the earth overnight, as the magnetic energy field of the earth purifies crystals very effectively. When you cleanse them, imagine a vacuum sucking away negative energy. Infusing crystals in a burning smudge of dried sage or sweet grass can also be an effective way to clear energy. Sometimes after a very intense healing, I will give the crystal permanently back to the earth to be cleansed and renewed in the Mother's love.

Crystals also need to be charged in the natural rays of light. They like both sunlight and moonlight. Sunlight is a natural energizer. You can charge them in sunlight during the day to infuse them with the healing energies of the sun, or in moonlight overnight to instill them with the magical energies of the moon.

Crystal Healing Techniques

Projective and Receptive Hand

As with any type of energy work, the right hand is considered to be the projective hand and the left the receiving hand. So when you want to give energy from a crystal to a patient, use your right hand, and when you want to pull energy from the body, hold it in your left hand. A patient would also hold a crystal in his left hand to receive healing vibrations from it.

Aligning an Activator

I always like to align the energy of my activators before I use them. To do so, I hold the crystal in my right hand and touch the termination to my left palm, and then pull the stone back a few inches. I project energy from the crystal into my palm by squeezing it gently and visualizing the stream starting at the base and projecting out the termination. I slowly rotate the crystal slightly clockwise until I feel the energy stream align in my palm. It almost feels like the energy shifts or tightens against my palm. I learned this technique as a child, and I have found that my activators are always more responsive and effective when I take the time to align their energy streams.

Empowering a Crystal

Empowering is a technique that activates a crystal's energy to work with the healer's intention. Empowering is also known as programming, but we as natural healers know that crystals are individual entities that possess a consciousness that cannot be programmed. Instead, we use the technique of empowerment to gently enhance a crystal's vibrations with our own healing intentions. Through visualization and breath work we give our healing intention to the stone, and the crystal's natural power amplifies the vibrations of our intention.

To begin the technique, you need to focus your mind on your intent. Create a clear picture of what the crystal is to do in your mind. For example, if you are using the crystal to help heal a broken arm, then, in your mind, hold the image of the crystal's energy knitting the bone together. Focus the intent in your mind when you inhale, and then breathe it out onto the crystal with the exhale, while gently squeezing the stone to activate its energy. I like to repeat this process several times until I feel the crystal is empowered. An empowered crystal warms, tingles, and pulses more intently in the hand. It is charged and ready to get to work.

Scanning

Another technique that you will need to use is scanning. This is where we use a crystal to read the health of the aura. The cues from palm induction apply here. As you pass the scanner slowly over a patient's body, the crystal may tingle or heat up when it senses a blockage or an agitated spot of energy. It may go cold or pulse when it senses an energy deficiency. As you move the crystal down the body, it may want to stop at certain chakras. Sometimes it may stop between two chakra points, and this means, obviously, that you will want to work on both. When you are experimenting with scanners, use palm induction to double-check your findings. This will help you to determine if the crystal is really an accurate scanner for you. If you do not have a scanner or do not feel comfortable with scanning, use palm induction to scan the energy field during a treatment.

Activating the Energy Field

An activator crystal can be used to activate the energy field in order to stimulate it and open it up to receiving healing energies. Begin by slowly projecting a healing beam from the termination of the crystal into the aura around the perimeter of the body. Work in a clockwise direction, beginning at the feet and moving up to the head, and then back down to feet again. The energy from the activator strengthens and stimulates the electromagnetic field. It is beneficial to do this at the beginning and ending of a crystal treatment to strengthen the field.

Using a Focal Crystal

You can also use the crystals to direct intense energy into areas that need specific healing. By placing the correct healing stone directly onto the skin, you can infuse the body with energy it needs to correct the problem. Amber is excellent for projecting healing vibrations, as is blue tourmaline. I like to dip my crystal in a little bit of oil or water to facilitate smooth movements, and then rub it on the tissue in small clockwise circles while visualizing healing energy from the stone infusing the field and body.

You can also place an appropriate stone that correlates to the patient's need directly on the area and surround it with little transmitters pointing toward it to enhance the energy of the stone. Use your hands to project healing energy over the focal stone and through it, into the auric field. The stone will enhance the energy from your hands. You can also use an activator crystal to send a beam of energy into the focal crystal to enhance its energies.

Projecting Healing Energy

Another important technique is projecting healing energy to an area on the body that has an energy deficiency, or around an area like the head (to treat a headache), a cut, or another ailment. Healing energy can be projected directly onto the body, or it can be directed onto a focal crystal to enhance the stone's energy.

For a general energy-deficient area you can use a large, clear quartz activator crystal. I also find that an amethyst works well as an overall energy-projecting crystal. To project healing energy outward with an activator, hold the crystal in your hands and visualize universal energy streaming out through its point into the tissues of the body. Squeeze the energy beam out from the crystal with the energy transmission beginning inside at the base and emitting straight out through the point. See it penetrating into the auric field, traveling deep into the body. The current soothes, heals, and fixes the problem. Be sure to use a visualization that applies to the patient's specific need.

The activator can also be used in the same fashion to project healing energy through a focal stone in order to amplify the specific healing energy of the stone. I like to touch the termination to the focal crystal in order to align the two different energies. I then pull it back and begin to project energy through it.

Removing Energy

For an area that needs energy pulled out of it, like a blocked chakra or an injury, you could use an energy absorber stone like onyx, or you could use a receiving clear quartz crystal to pull energy out of the area.

To absorb energy, wet the surface of the stone in water to ensure a smooth motion, and then rub the face of it over the area in a counterclockwise direction. I visualize the crystal pulling black poison from the body's energy field. To remove negative energy vibrations held by the patient, have her visualize the exhale of her breath pushing the energy out of the body and into the crystal. To treat the accumulation of stress, blockages, pain, or tension in an area, have the patient focus on pushing the energy out of the body and into the stone through breathing and visualization. In this way, the debilitating energy from diseases and problems like inflammation, cancer, and viruses are removed from the body's energy field and, subsequently, from its tissues.

It is important that you visualize the stone removing and holding this negative energy. You do not want this energy floating freely around or entering into your field. You will need to practice keeping your focus during this technique in order to keep the crystal containing the energy.

In a long healing session, I use several crystals to remove negative energy, as they tend to fill up and cannot seem to absorb any more past a certain point. As you experiment and work with crystals, you will be able to tell when a crystal has reached its limit; they feel heavy and full and vibrate at a much slower level than a fresh crystal.

After drawing out negative energy, I like to replace the absorbing crystal with a projecting one to put positive energy back into the aura and the tissues of the body. After the treatment, be sure that you cleanse the absorbing crystal or stone thoroughly.

The Healer's Boundary Stone

As an energy healer, you can be vulnerable, and a boundary stone is your personal protection device. A boundary stone sits in the room near you and the patient and works to absorb excess energies, protecting you from absorbing this energy yourself. It can be a large piece of an absorbing stone, such as onyx, or a quartz crystal that you have empowered to absorb. Use your boundary stone as an energy shield to absorb the client's pain during an emotional release. If the person is giving off too much energy, you can give him an absorbing crystal to hold on to. It is a wise idea to use a boundary stone, especially for new energy healers. Remember to cleanse it regularly.

Basic Crystal Healing Patterns

There are some standard patterns that can be used on the body as treatments for specific ailments. They are intended as a guide for you to begin your knowledge. Crystal healing is an intuitive therapy, and natural healing patterns will evolve as you work with the stones.

For an injury like a fractured bone, sprain, cut, bruise, or burn, you want to place one quartz activator above the injury and one below, with the two terminations pointing toward each other. The energy they direct will be used to fuse and heal the tissues. You could place a healing focal crystal over the injured area as well, as long as it does not hurt the patient. Amber or blue tourmaline would be a good choice.

For general body problems, you can use a triangular position. With an upper body problem you want to place a crystal on each of the shoulders with the terminations pointing toward the neck, and one stone at the navel with the termination pointing up. In the case of lower body ailments, place a crystal on each upper thigh, with the terminations pointing up, and one on the navel with the termination pointing down. This position directs energy to the torso area for healing.

For an arm problem, place a quartz on the shoulder with the termination pointing down the arm, and then position another in the center of the palm, pointing up.

For heart disease, lung disease, or breast cancer, you would want to place three quartz crystals in a triangular position with one on each breast, pointing into the heart chakra, and one on the throat, pointing down. We are aiming to break up the blockage and get the energy moving through the body system and out of the heart.

To heal a leg injury or problem, place one quartz on the hip pointing down, and one on the ball of foot with the termination pointing up.

For a healing of the mind, I place a crystal on the third eye with the termination facing up to the crown to open up the mind. This technique is effective for mental work, as not only is the mind receiving energy naturally through the crown, but the crystal channels an energy stream up from the body and pushes it into the mind. Here we connect to higher consciousness, and it allows us to move emotions up through the body to process them logically.

When you point the termination down into the body, then we turn the attention inward, into feelings and a deeper subconscious. We push the energy down through the body, and it links the mind to the physical layer. This position is appropriate for physical healing of the body.

For specific problems, the colors of the stones is also important. Inflamed, irritated internal and external tissues need soothing, cooling, blue-colored stones like turquoise, blue agate, or blue tourmaline to counteract the angry redness of swelling and inflammation.

An area that is cold and numb or pale with poor circulation needs the warmth of red stones like rose quartz or carnelian. Have the patient breathe the color vibrations of the stone into the area and visualize the vibrations healing the tissues.

Green is used to project growth energy, so use a green stone like green agate or bloodstone for regrowth of bones and rejuvenation of tissues.

Black stones absorb energy, so use black absorbing stones, like onyx and obsidian, to pull energy out of the field, and then apply healing stones to fill the aura with positive vibrations.

If a stone rolls from where you placed it, let it be. Understand that each stone has a consciousness and is instinctually guided. If a patient wants a stone placed in a specific area, then place it there—she intuitively knows what her body needs.

A Healing Treatment

The following is an example of a healing treatment performed on a patient to speed the recovery of a broken arm. The case study is divided into steps so you can understand the various levels that the treatment progresses through and see how the techniques are applied. We use crystal healing in conjunction with energy healing. Later on, we will add specific chakra crystal healing to this treatment.

A crystal treatment follows the format of a basic energy treatment. We begin the treatment by holding an in-depth consultation with the client. What is the client looking for in a treatment? As a healer, what do you think the client needs? What stones and layouts are you going to use? You and the client should decide on a course of action. Briefly discuss with the client the steps of the procedure, including energy awakening, crystal placement, and guided meditation.

Have the patient recline on his back, unless, of course, the injury or ailment is located on the back of the body. Face him north to align body with magnetic currents, as crystals respond well when placed in natural alignment. As with all my energy work, I like a patient to remove at least his shoes to ensure a good energy connection. Crystals enhance energy levels present in a room, so it can be helpful to have many placed throughout the room to aid in building the healing energy.

It is always best to place the crystals directly on bare skin, but most people will want to remain clothed. The healing can be done directly through the clothes. If you want to you can cover the patient with a thin sheet.

To begin the healing treatment, spend a few moments centering yourself and invoking your protective aura. I like to open my crown chakra and draw universal energy into my body, as I never know when I will apply energy therapy techniques to the crystal healing. Energy therapy can greatly enhance a crystal treatment.

As you use each crystal, spend time becoming attuned to it, then breathe your intent into it. Always first align and squeeze a crystal to start it vibrating before placing it on the client.

I think it is important to tell my partner what I am doing as I perform the treatment. It helps put her at ease and focuses her on the procedure.

I always begin by placing an amethyst on the brow over the third eye chakra. It opens a person's connection to his intuition. For body work I place the termination facing down, drawing universal energy down through the body and attuning the mind to the physical layer.

> *I'm placing a crystal on your third eye center to increase your intuitive*
> *abilities and connect your mind to your body so you can easily read your*
> *body's messages and signals.*

Sometimes I also like to have my partner hold a crystal in the palm of each hand. This can subtly ground the sides of the body and help the person relax, further drawing his attention inward. Clarity improves when connection to the crystals is strengthened.

> *Hold these two crystals in your hands to balance the energy of the body*
> *and complete your connection to crystal consciousness.*

Begin by guiding your partner into a gradual meditation by having her close her eyes and begin a gentle deep breathing exercise to relax the physical body and activate the energy field. As with all meditation work, be sure to speak softly and calmly, with lots of pauses so the person has time to make the necessary mind/body connections.

> *Go deep within your body and envision your aura surrounding you. It is*
> *a bubble of white light, healing and loving.*

At this point I like to scan the body with a scanner crystal to find any problems or blockages in the patient's energy field. Move the scanner over the body in wide circles, very slowly, feeling for any change in the crystal. Open your sensors and pay close attention to the signals from the crystal. I often find that closing my eyes helps me to easily attune to the crystal's changes. You are feeling for heat in the crystal or places of coldness that signifies energy deficiencies in the field. Be sure to tell your partner what you are doing. Some healers prefer to use palm induction rather than a scanner crystal.

> *I am using a crystal to scan your body and feel for any energy blockages or deficiencies. Just lie there and feel safe and warm within your bubble of light. Relax and let the crystal sense what it can.*

Make a silent note of anything you pick up. Use palm induction at this point, along with crystal scanning, in order to double-check your findings.

Check in with the patient. Use mental scanning to find out what the client knows. What does he see in his body? What does he think is the problem?

Then begin to activate and open the field. Starting with the head, use an activator crystal to direct energy over the aura in tight little circles, gently massaging the field, awakening and stimulating the field's sensors. Work from the head down to the feet, and back up to the head.

> *I'm using a projective crystal to stimulate and massage your energy field. This will active and energize your aura and open it to receive healing energy.*

Focus in on the areas that need work. For a region that has a blockage, you want to aim a healing beam directly into the area to amplify the body's transformative energies. Use the crystal's beam to blast away the energy. Physically move the crystal in small sweeps to drive the energy through the system and disperse the blockage. Visualize the energy moving through the system. Take as much time as you need to work with the crystal. It will heat up when the energy is being transferred and the blockage is removed.

If an area needs a specific focal crystal, add it to the area to infuse healing vibrations into the field.

I am placing an amber healing stone on the injury to spread its vibrations into your energy.

You can add transmitters to surround the focal crystal in order to intensify its energy.

I'm adding quartz transmitters to your arm area to increase the energy flow for healing. Does this feel good? Are there any areas that feel tight or hot? (If the patient experiences areas that feel tight or hot, adding a transmitter crystal to those areas will help move the energy along and decrease the concentration.)

Use your hands to project universal healing energy into the crystal for the energy to amplify. Place your hands over the area to be healed, and visualize the energy moving down the arm, through the crystal, and into the field and body of the client. See it healing the tissues, reknitting the bone together. You can also use an activator to increase the energy of the focal crystal.

I'm using my hands to project healing energy through the stone—universal energy that heals and protects the body. This energy increase will feel good, as it will strengthen the tissues of the arm and facilitate new growth of the bone.

If a patient wishes to use affirmations, now is an appropriate time to begin this technique. Remember that all affirmations should be phrased in the present tense and have a positive approach.

As with any type of bodywork, crystal healing can release deep-seated emotions, and it is a good idea to always have a box of tissues handy. Be sure to allow the emotional release and acknowledge it as part of the natural healing process. Remind the person that she is surrounded by a white bubble of love, and that she is safe and should feel comfortable experiencing any emotions that surface. External acceptance from the healer can help a person to come to acceptance with her emotions. Let her know that this release is positive.

In a situation like this, your primary role is not that of a psychologist, but that of a healer. We help our partners remain focused and concentrated on breathing deeply and feeling safe. Remember, this is a time for gathering information, not interpreting it.

For a body unused to crystal vibrations, an intensive treatment should last no more than half an hour. I'm more inclined to treat a person who is new to crystal vibrations for ten-minute periods several times a day rather than performing one long treatment. The body can only take so much intense energy concentration, and we do not want to overload it

The frequencies of crystals can alter perception of time. Have your partner be aware of his body. He will know when the focal area has absorbed all it can take. There is a feeling of completion, and the crystals will often roll off untouched, as they, too, are aware of when the healing is finished.

Your arm should be feeling nice and warm now, concentrated with healing energies. When the focus area starts feeling heavy and full, then we know it has absorbed all the energy it can right now. Let me know if you start to feel fullness or heaviness in the arm.

Remove the crystals at this point. Take off the activators and then the focal crystal. Lastly, remove the quartz crystals from the brow and the palms. Wipe the stones gently with a silk or cotton cloth before putting them aside to be cleansed and charged. Crystals have dulled and even cracked under the extreme pressure of the energy generated in a healing. Be sure to cleanse them after each session, and then give them time to charge and clear their focus.

Slowly return your attention to the present and this room. When you feel ready, open your eyes.

Do not rush a patient to get up. She has just been through an emotionally intensive journey and needs time to relax and adjust to the new vibrations in her system.

Aftercare

Discuss the treatment and the results with the client. See if the client feels different, or picked up on any insights that need to be discussed and explored. Having the client write out the affirmations used in the healing session can help foster a personal connection to the words, and the client will be more inclined to use them in daily meditation.

If I feel that a patient needs it, I like to give him a specific crystal to take home and work with. I remind him to place it on his area of need and say his healing affirmations. The stone can also be placed on the third eye for meditation or held in the hands while the client focuses on healing energies. The crystal can be put in a bag to wear around the neck or kept in a pocket and rubbed periodically throughout the day to infuse the body with positive vibrations and act as a trigger for the mind. Healing crystals can also be permanently held on the inflicted area of the body for healing; advise a client to use gauze tape or tensor bandages to make them stay in place, especially during the nighttime.

Crystals can also be used for psychological healing. Through their healing vibrations they have the power to facilitate the beauty within the heart and bring forth the strength of the inner spirit. They can be used to work through depression and anger apexes. Breathe pain into a crystal and bury it in the ground, giving the upset energy to the earth for the earth to transform. Lie down and hold one in each hand, placing another on the third eye to bring calmness and balance. A client can also place them under a pillow to prevent nightmares and infuse a slumber with soothing vibrations.

Please remember to engage in aftercare for yourself, too. Take a few moments to document everything in your healer's notebook. I like to do this immediately after the healing so I do not forget any aspects of the treatment. Be sure to care for the needs of your crystals, then spend time replenishing your energy. Perform the waterfall grounding exercise to cleanse your aura, and if you have opened your chakras, take the time to close them.

Chakra Work

The chakras respond excellently to crystal vibrations, and much healing work can be done with them. In this section I have included a detailed discussion of the centers and the appropriate crystals that are effective on each chakra. Generally we want to use a stone whose color corresponds with the chakra color in order to infuse the chakra with its needed vibrations. I have given you a description of the stones and the placement patterns that I use in my work. Others may have different uses or placements of the stones, and as you develop your crystal knowledge you will come to formulate your own crystal applications as well.

Root Chakra

Our focus with the root chakra is on grounding the energy of the body. If a patient has problems with addiction, with grounding her emotions, or has issues with stability, then work on the root is appropriate. I like to use either dark grounding stones like onyx, obsidian, or the red stimulating stones of carnelian and bloodstone. Bloodstone is a helpful stone to use on the root and is the stone to use here for blood healing and circulation problems. When treating grounding and stability problems, you can also use onyx or bloodstone on the groin, knees, feet, and ankles to promote grounding.

Sacral Chakra

The second chakra is where we deal with our emotional issues. The sacral needs the soothing, purifying energies of amber and citrine. Amber soothes the emotions and brings joy and healing. It can also be applied to heal sexual dysfunction and sexual repression. Use amber on the sacral chakra for healing the vagina, ovaries, and uterus. Citrine at the second chakra stimulates creative and energetic energies. It activates the center and bestows fertility. It can be used to treat the spleen, allergy problems, kidney disease, and arthritis.

Solar Plexus Chakra

The solar plexus chakra is involved with gut instinct and manifestation. Stones that heal the solar plexus include citrine, tiger's eye, and carnelian. When we cannot manifest results, tiger's eye is the stone to use, while citrine dissolves blockages from unresolved and emotional issues. Carnelian is a cleansing and balancing stone. Surround a carnelian with quartz transmitters pointing into the stone to activate it. It can also be applied to help heal eating disorders and digestive problems.

Heart Chakra

Emotional healing stones like rose quartz and amber are very useful for the heart chakra. Rose quartz teaches self-love, tenderness, forgiveness, and compassion. Amber purifies emotions and helps us through difficulties like sorrow, guilt, and grief. Place amber on the heart chakra for the healing of generalized disorders and immune system strengthening.

Throat Chakra

The throat chakra is concerned with communication and truth. I use turquoise for communication ability, creativity, and speaking the truth. Turquoise can also be placed over the mouth to heal the pain from angry, hurtful words. We all say things we do not mean in moments of anger and frustration, and crystals can help with forgiveness. Working with the throat chakra can help to halt and transform verbal behaviors, providing soothing and comforting words of healing. It is also beneficial to use turquoise on the throat chakra to heal sore throats, inflammation, swelling, and the choking sensation from asthma and allergies.

Third Eye

The two stones of the third eye chakra that I primarily use include a strong terminated amethyst and a large blue tourmaline. Amethyst is an important stone for the mind because of its connection to spiritual energy. It is a meditative, spiritual, and transforming stone. It connects the brow to higher consciousness, bringing inner knowledge to the self. Blue tourmaline is calming and works to relax the mind. It is an all-purpose healing stone, which, when placed on the third eye, infuses the entire system with a beam of healing energy.

Crown Chakra

The primary stone that I use on the crown chakra is a large clear quartz with an ample base and a strong termination. It is used here to stimulate higher consciousness. When a patient is reclined for a treatment, I place the termination so that it touches his head and the base points away. This opens the base up to receive universal energy and filter it down through the termination into the crown. If a client has a problem with a crown chakra that is too tightly closed, apply an amethyst in the same manner to flood the system with spiritually charged vibrations. If the crown is excessively open, I use a quartz with the termination facing up so its balancing properties help bring the chakra back to a normal size.

Adding Chakra Work to a Crystal Healing Treatment

To begin, follow the same format we used for the basic crystal healing treatment. After completing a general scan of the auric field, perform a scan of the chakra points, looking for agitation or areas of blockage. Take note of everything you discover.

You can perform a crystal healing on a specific chakra, or you can perform a general full system healing by placing the appropriate stones on each of the chakras to facilitate balance. If you are going to place stones on all the chakras, be sure to work from the root up to the crown, as the body will need to have an activated root chakra in order to ground the energy stream created by the energy from the stones.

I use an activator to open the chakras before placing the stones on the centers. To do so, begin by touching the termination of the activator crystal to the skin. This activates the lowest level of the chakra. Then pull the crystal back a few inches to work the upper levels of the chakra. Project energy through it and on to the chakra center. Rotate the point of the crystal slowly clockwise to stir and activate the energy of the chakra in a slowly widening spiral pattern.

To infuse a chakra with a stone's energies, place the corresponding chakra stone directly on the chakra center and surround it with activators that point into it. This will bring energy into the chakra and help to open it up. You can then take a large activator crystal and project energy through the focal stone into the chakra. To send a direct stream of energy, you want an activator crystal with a strong termination. Hold the activator crystal and project healing energy into the stone. You can also use your palm to project healing energy through the stone and into the auric field.

If you are working on the upper body or head, either at the crown, brow, or throat chakra, you need to also place a grounding stone on the root chakra to balance the work being done and help ground the energy flow.

If you are performing a full system chakra healing and have stones on all seven of the chakras, you need to watch for excessive energy buildup on one spot. The energy can build up and overload a chakra, especially with a new patient unused to energy vibrations. Sometimes people may need to have some of the stones removed, and they will tell you if this is the case. The energy from stones cannot hurt us, but it can temporarily overload the system. The energy field cannot continually receive vibrations; the individual chakras need time to exhale and project out energy. If there is too much stimulation in the area, simply remove the stone and place a transmitter below the chakra, with its termination pointing down to help the energy flow through the system.

Have the client focus on pulling the healing energies of the stone into her body. On the inhale, she is to pull the energy from crystal into the chakra and down into the entire body, and she is to use the exhale to push the energy down to the root chakra and out through it. Use your hands to project healing energy through the stones and into the field of the client.

After the placement of the crystals, you need to realize that this is a vulnerable and exposed time for the patient. His energy field is infused with foreign energy, and he will be hypersensitive. Have him focus on regulating his breathing and bringing up whatever images come to him. Be sure he is comfortable and feeling safe.

When I feel that the client has absorbed all the energies he can take in, I remove the crystals from the body, from the crown to the root, to ensure a constant grounding flow. Refer to the aftercare section in the general crystal treatment for further information.

Look for a few key pieces to use in your work: you want a straight clear quartz activator, and one stone for each chakra, including a rose quartz, an amethyst, a citrine, a turquoise, a carnelian, a tiger's eye, a bloodstone, a carnelian, an onyx, and a few clear quartz.

Obtain one stone for each chakra, and begin working with them slowly, learning how and where to place them. Remember that if you follow your inner intuition, you will be guided by the wisdom of the stones. Be bold and confident in your choices, but do not be afraid to change your mind. Sometimes I plan to place a crystal on a certain area, but just as I go to do so, I feel a strong urge to place it somewhere else. When you open yourself as the healer, spirit always shows you the way.

Your healing experiences with the stones will be different, intimate, specified by an individual's personal need. Crystal healing is a powerful and creative art form, using crystals to weave spiritual energy into other energy fields. It is a skill that is as ancient and beautiful and rare as the stones themselves. Taking the time to learn it will enhance your healing skills greatly.

II

Color Therapy

Color therapy involves the application of the energy vibrations of color to the energy field in order to balance and align the aura and promote healing.

*M*an holds a deep relationship with color. In our visually dominant world we are constantly surrounded by it, and it permeates and influences every aspect of our lives. We are the only species on earth able to see the full spectrum rainbow. The wondrous phenomena of the rainbow is caused by the refraction and reflection of light in raindrops. The water splits the white light into the separate colors of the visible spectrum. Each color actually has its own energy and is really a physical manifestation of its energy vibration.

The colors of nature are the truest colors, as they are incredibly rich and natural. We innately absorb the hues of nature into the body, taking in the green of the grasses and plants, the blue of the sky and the sea, the red of the sunset and the flowers, the yellow of the sun, the purple of the mountains and the night sky. In our daily lives we mimic the colors of nature, bringing the shades of the outside inside—into our homes, our cooking, and our clothing. When we are unwell we often talk of being off-color, a phrase that testifies to the impact of color on our lives.

Science tells us that the physical body is color receptive; every cell of the body is made up of contracted light, and we know that light responds to color. We also take color vibrations in through our eyes, through our breath, and we absorb them through the pineal gland in the brow. Color and light drastically affects the functioning of the pineal gland. The lower the level of light it receives, the higher the level of the hormone melatonin it is triggered to release; thus, the body receives more of this hormone at night and during the darkest days of the winter. Scientists believe that this is what leads to emotional disorders like SAD (seasonal affective disorder), an ailment that causes some individuals to become depressed and lethargic in lower-light conditions.

Our energy field absorbs color vibrations as well. The power centers of the chakras draw the color's essence into the energy field when a colored substance is placed on or near the body. The vibrations are channeled through the aura and into the tissues and organs of the body. Color also has the ability to affect us on an emotional level. Advertisers have long understood the impact of bright and artistic colors in consumer product choice, and color is carefully chosen in interior environments to influence the emotional response. Yellow is used in hospitals to promote cheerfulness, and blue is always avoided in mental hospitals, as it can increase feelings of depression and sadness. Color management is very important in our visual world.

Color affects us emotionally, but it also can produce physical changes in the mind and body as well. It has the power to speed up the systems of the body or slow them down. It can influence blood pressure and circulation, increase oxygen levels and amounts of red and white blood cells traveling to tissues, thus boosting the immune system, and it can also be used to physically raise or lower the temperature of the body. It further can be applied to soothe inflammation and speed the healing of wounds, to trigger the endocrine glands to release hormones, to break up density deposits in the body, and to stimulate the nervous system. Color also alters our moods, energy levels, can increase or decrease the activity of brain waves, and is effective at reducing pain. Scientific research into the healing powers of color is proving that color therapy is an important tool in promoting health and wellness.

Color has been used for healing for thousands of years. In modern color therapy, we use specific color rays to penetrate into the auric field and gently restore balance to the tissues of the body. Instead of channeling white light to the body for the healing, we channel the specific color that the tissue needs. Applying a specific color is a more direct form of healing, as the body does not have to filter out all the unneeded rays of color from the white light.

Types of color therapy include the application of colored light and colored cloths, the ingestion of colored water, and the channeling of color vibrations into the aura through visualization and hand work. Color healing can easily be incorporated into an energy treatment to increase its effectiveness, or it can simply be applied on its own. It is a safe, effective, and dramatic method of healing.

The Colors

Red

Red is a passionate, primal color. It has the longest wavelengths and travels at the slowest speed. Red is the vibration of the warrior, the force that gets things done with an unstoppable thrust. It is an aggressive color that is associated with the root chakra, the blood, and the flesh of the body. Use red when you want to arouse, stimulate, excite, power up, and create a zest for life. The slow, intense vibrations incite self-expression, confidence, drive, passion, courage, and heat.

Physically, red vibrations have been shown to quicken the heart rate, speed up circulation, and increase the speed and supply of blood to an area. Red also increases the level of hemoglobin in blood, which provides more oxygen to the body, and it raises the amount of white blood cells in the blood, boosting the immune system and speeding the healing of wounds. Red can be physically applied to treat the bones, muscles, and the blood. It further activates the adrenal glands and triggers a release of adrenaline.

This masculine color is used to treat any condition for which you want to rev up the body, including depression, lack of enthusiasm, low energy, low blood pressure, sluggish metabolism and digestion, shock, anemia, iron deficiency, infections, poor circulation, and paralysis, or when you want to speed up the general healing process. Use red on the root chakra for healing of any of the above disorders, and also to strengthen deficient root energy in order to ground the system to the earth. The color red was worn during the Victorian Age at nighttime to keep the body warm, and, indeed, it does help raise the body's temperature. In moderation, red is also used to treat impotence and infertility. It can further be used to burn up the damaging cells of cancer.

But too much red can be dangerous. It is an overwhelming energy; it can seize you and take you along with its primal force without the slightest bit of thought or rationality. We all know how passion can sometimes lead to frenzy. The power of fire can heal, burning through the unnecessary, but it can also harm, burning us up in its greed, lust, pain, and anger. An overexposure to red, be it in the natural coloring of the skin, clothing, or mental state, leads to problems later in life.

A hot temper, emotional intensity, agitation, anxiety, and anger are all increased by red. Do not use red when dealing with these types of circumstances. Red should also be avoided for hot physical conditions of the body, such as fever, asthma, hyperactivity, ulcers, inflammation, heart problems, high blood pressure, bleeding, swelling, or pain. I advise against projecting red and heat energy into the womb or abdomen of a pregnant woman, as it can bring on premature labor. Red is also harsh on the eyes, and the eye area should be avoided. Individuals with excessively red skin should also avoid prolonged exposure to red.

Avoid wearing red clothing when you have a backache or other muscle pains, as it can aggravate the hurt. Too much red can actually burn the energy field and the skin, so use red very sparingly, no more than ten minutes during an intensive treatment.

Pink

Pink is a healthy color. It is a beautiful hue and the most powerful love color. It is a central color often associated with the heart, and, indeed, I often use pink on the heart chakra for strengthening the heart and healing general disorders. It can also be applied on the heart to mend a broken heart and heal emotional trauma.

Pink creates balance in the energy field, as it encourages love to flow through the body. It is composed of the passion of red soothed with the purity of white. The energies of pink are soft; they gently promote health and wellness in the body. Cancer can be treated with pink, as the energy picks the healthy cells and nourishes them with love. Pink is also excellent for skin problems, as it encourages the tissues to heal and repair themselves, and it works well to speed the healing of internal problems.

Orange

Orange is a social color, as it is composed of the physical vibrations of red combined with the intellectual energies of yellow. Orange is a color about connections, friendliness, the ability to relate to others. It represents joy and happiness, healthy sexuality and emotional commitments, fruitfulness. It energizes the body without the overstimulating heat of red, building energy and vitality. Orange is also a creative color, allowing us to express our feelings and manifest substance.

In mental healing, orange is used for any condition in which a person is closed off, like inhibition, repression, autism, depression, and withdrawal. It is associated with the sacral chakra, and helps one release imaginative and creative energies. It stabilizes the emotions and is appropriate for all types of emotional concerns. It can also help heal sexual problems that are rooted in the mind.

In physical healing, it is used to unblock and boost energy levels. It creates a free flow of energy, transforms negative energy to positive vibrations, and creates subtle changes in biochemical structure. It can be applied to help kidney weakness: to help the problems of bedwetting, painful and excessive urination, and to dissolve kidney stones. Orange also increases the oxygen level absorbed by the body, and can be used on the lungs to help clear up phlegm, and alleviate allergies, bronchitis, coughing, influenza, and other breathing problems. It works wonders to strengthen the entire process of digestion, promoting the flow of energy and relieving abdominal gas, constipation, and indigestion. The color orange is also an antispasmodic, bringing relief for muscular cramps and spasms.

Orange can also be used as a general tonic for the body to bring pimples and boils to a head, heal abscesses, dissolve kidney or gallbladder stones, or break up deposits in rheumatism; it can also be applied to help remove excess weight from the body. It heals physical sexual problems as well.

Since orange stimulates, do not use it for excess energy or hyperactivity. It raises the blood pressure and should not be used with those individuals who have high blood pressure or heart problems.

Yellow

Yellow reflects the color of sunlight, with its nourishing, life-supporting vibrations penetrating straight to the soul. Yellow gives us the warmth of our inner sun. It is the color of happiness. It is also a cerebral color that brings analytical energies into the body. It facilitates intellectual stimulation, communication, humor, and clarity of thought. Yellow generates positive magnetic currents that can be applied to heal both the mind and the body.

The healing vibrations of yellow are used to help with mental difficulties like depression, problems retaining knowledge, addictions, low brain power, and the inability to make decisions and judgments. But for mental conditions like paranoia, delusion, anxiety, and mental exhaustion, yellow is not recommended. It brings in too much mental energy for people suffering with these conditions and can lead to mental detachment. Use the soothing colors of blue and green instead.

Yellow is the color of the solar plexus chakra, and can be used to heal problems with organs associated with the center of the body, including the stomach, the spleen, the endocrine gland of the pancreas, the liver, the gallbladder, and the kidneys. Yellow helps soothe liver problems, diabetes, gallstones, stomach concerns, kidney problems, and it can be used to strengthen the lymphatic glands. The energies of yellow also activate the nervous system; its magnetic currents stimulate and strengthen motor nerves, generating energy in the muscles, making yellow a treatment for paralysis. Yellow is recommended for arthritis because it dissolves density deposits in the body. It also improves the texture of the skin and can help heal scarring, rashes, and eczema.

Green

Green is truly the color of life and healing. Nature is green, oxygen-producing trees are green, healing herbs are green, nourishing foods are green. As it is the center of the spectrum, green is a balanced color, with its vibrations being neither hot nor cold. The energies of green bring harmony and balance to the mind, the body, the emotions, and the electromagnetic field. To attune to the energies of green brings abundance, healing, and financial success to one's life.

Green is the color of the heart chakra, and can be used to treat heart problems, high blood pressure, fatigue, and lung and breathing problems. It can also be used to soothe emotional concerns, such as negativity, lack of love in your life, insomnia, anger, and paranoia. It provides stability to the heart and the emotional layer.

Physically, green is a growth color, so its energies can be applied for regrowth of bones and rejuvenation of tissues. It aids the healing of bruises, sores, cuts, and internal damage. It is also useful to help alleviate headaches, fevers, diabetes, and problems of the nervous system. Green is very good for the eyes, as the eyes focus green-colored light almost exactly on the retina, making its vibrations a restful and soothing color for them.

Green is an extensive cleansing color; it clears and stabilizes physical, mental, and emotional levels, eliminating chaos and stagnation. Green is also a color that provides energies of nourishment to these layers.

Blue

Blue is a soothing healing color that promotes restfulness and relaxation. It contains calming energy, like the stillness of the sky and the vastness of the ocean. It is a peaceful, spiritual color. Blue is also a creative color and is good for facilitating strong communicative ability and expressiveness.

On a physical level, blue is related to the throat chakra and helps alleviate all ailments of the throat and mouth, including sore throat, inflammation, tonsillitis, laryngitis, gum infections, stuttering, hoarseness, toothaches, and mouth sores. It also alleviates skin itching and irritation, healing burns, sun exposure, rashes, and eczema. Use blue to treat heated internal problems, such as inflamed tissue, swelling of any kind, stomachaches, ulcers, broken veins, headaches, muscle pains, backaches, yeast infections, ear infections, digestive irritation, fever, high blood pressure, and any situation that needs cooling down. Blue is a good color to use to boost the immune system and strengthen the lymphatic system. It further helps stop diarrhea, vomiting, nausea, and excessive bleeding.

Since blue is a relaxant, it can be used to treat hyperactivity; excitable children can be dressed in blue clothing to calm them down, blue bed sheets can be used to alleviate insomnia, and blue-painted classrooms and common rooms in prisons are used to promote relaxation and calm feelings. It also aids mental concerns such as hysteria, stress, nervousness, tension, and fear.

Blue needs to be used in moderation, as you do not want to slow a person's system down to the point that there ceases to be enthusiasm or drive. Blue is not good for conditions in which the body's systems are already slow; do not use it for colds, poor circulation, low blood pressure, seasonal affective disorder, depression, blocked digestion, perpetual coldness, paralysis, or lethargic behavior. I do not advise using prolonged exposure to blue on individuals with very pale skin that contains strong bluish undertones; they already have too much blue in their systems.

Purple

Purple is a strong color, as it is composed of the feminine energies of blue and the masculine energies of red mixed together. It calms without slowing, stimulates without heating. It is a spiritual color; its energies bestowing inner strength, power, dignity, and calmness. Purple opens the mind and brings us into the realm of spiritual awareness and seeing on other levels.

Physically, purple can be applied as a strong painkiller. It moves energy along, reestablishing rhythm to the system. It clears blockages and helps the body discard that which is unneeded and unhealthy. This makes it a perfect color to apply for the dissolving of cysts and tumors. It further soothes the nerves, alleviates agitation in the intestines, kills internal parasites, and strengthens weak cell structures. Violet can be used instead of red for grounding with individuals who are too nervous or high-strung for the intense energy of red.

Associated with the brow chakra, purple can be used to heal diseases of the eyes, ears, and head. It alleviates black eyes, soreness in the eye, vision concerns, ear problems, baldness, dandruff, and other ailments of the scalp. Purple works wonders at curing headaches. It also has a strong effect on the mind, strengthening intuition, recall, meditation, and the psychic skills.

But because purple can bring the mind inward, it is not for those individuals suffering from depression, solitude, withdrawal, schizophrenia, and other mental illnesses and concerns.

White

White is a protective color. It neutralizes energy, as it contains all colors of the rainbow. It gives strength and vitality. White stands for perfection, purity, light, and truth. In healing, I like to use white to overcome addictions and for general cleansing of the mind and body. It is also a good color to use to promote bone growth. White is the healing color to use when you are unsure of what is causing a problem.

Specific Color Healing Treatments

An intensive color treatment is one that specifically focuses on healing. Color healing treatments include breathing in color, colored light treatment, application of colored sashes and clothing, and colored liquid treatment.

Breathing in Color

One of the best ways to take in color is to breathe it into the body. When we inhale we take in the essence of the color, and when we exhale we push it further into self, anchoring it in the aura. The best way to apply the technique is to sit in the colors of nature and breathe in the natural living vibrations of flowers, trees, and other vegetation. Deeply inhale the needed color, filling the self up with the color's rays. Breathing in color is often used in conjunction with other types of treatments. It can be used to take in the color essence of silk cloths and colored light, and it is a way to absorb the energies from a color visualization.

Healing with Silk Cloths

When we heal with silk cloths, we choose the appropriate color and apply it next to the skin so the body can attune to and absorb the vibrations of the color's power. Lay a silk sheet over the entire body for general healing, or apply small pieces of silk directly on the chakra or the afflicted area. Have the client visualize taking in the energy from the color. She should also breathe in the essence. In this type of treatment, we need to specifically focus on the healing vibrations for the treatment to be completely effective. As we know, after the nerves in the skin are stimulated for a while, they stop firing, which is why we cease to feel clothing on the body soon after we put it on. For a treatment to be intensive, we must constantly be aware of the treatment so the brain is regularly receiving messages. This can be done by slightly shifting the colored cloth every few moments in order to trigger the nerves to send signals to the brain.

Healing with Colored Light

Colored light can be specifically applied on affected parts of the body to promote healing. In hospitals today, blue light is used to treat premature babies suffering from jaundice. I use colored light bulbs to provide the healing color I need, shining them directly on the skin for about five to ten minutes. I have even seen individuals use strands of Christmas lights in the appropriate color. I also recommend using a light box. You can build this box out of wood with a piece of glass on the front face. The box can be powered with a colored light inside, or the bulb can be clear and the glass can be colored. If you make it so the glass side can be removed, then it could be replaced with whatever color you need.

Healing with Colored Liquid

In colored liquid treatment, both water and oil can be charged with colored light and used to promote healing. Pure distilled water can be charged with colored light, or it can be charged with sunlight in a colored glass and consumed to relieve problems and promote healing, while oil is charged with color and then applied directly on the skin to heal the afflicted area. To charge oil or water with light, let the liquid sit in the appropriate colored bottle for about six hours in front of a forty- to sixty-watt bulb or on a sunny windowsill. You can also charge the liquid with colored light in a clear bottle.

A normal dosage of colored water is two ounces taken one hour before meals. Colored water therapy works best to alleviate minor irritating symptoms like constipation, diarrhea, colds, phlegm buildup, headaches, stomachaches, and digestive upsets. It can also be used to help alleviate mental disorders as well as physical problems. Colored water will hold its charge for about four to five days as long as the bottle is properly sealed. For skin, tissue, and muscle aliments, rub colored oil directly on the skin.

Healing with Color Visualization

Color visualization is a healing technique that uses the power of the mind. To apply the technique, relax and visualize yourself surrounded in the color; feel yourself filling with the color's energies. Spend time experiencing the true nature of the color, visualizing what it actually feels like to be in the color. Gather the color's energy into your hands and direct it to specific parts of the body that need healing. The client can visualize being infused with the color as you project it to him.

You can heal only the specific chakra or area that needs healing, or you can perform a full energy system healing using visualization. To do so, project red light into the root chakra, and have the client breathe the red energies into the root chakra until it vibrates in clear color. Work your way up to the crown in same manner, using orange for the sacral, yellow for the solar plexus, green for the heart, blue for the throat, purple for the brow, and white for the crown. The system will be infused with energy that moves up and down the chakras through the spine and strengthens the individual chakras.

You can also use color visualization to push a disease out of the body. Have the client lie down and stand at her feet. Project the appropriate healing color into her feet chakras, and visualize it entering her energy system and pushing the unwanted energy of the sickness up and out of her. The healing energy is a powerful stream of light that directs the unwanted energy through the system and exits it out of the crown chakra. Have the client visualize the healing energy stream clearing her system as well. After performing this technique, I like to administer the full energy system color visualization discussed previously in order to facilitate the natural energy of the chakras flowing.

Adding Color Healing to an Energy Treatment

While I am performing an energy treatment, I like to augment the treatment with color healing techniques. Working with color gives us a system with which we can effectively approach the chakras. In my assessment of the field and chakra, I hold my open palm over the area and use my inner sight to sense the clarity and intensity of the auric and chakra colors. Each chakra contains more than one color, but they all have their own primary color that is dominant in the energy center. The strength of the colors tell you the health and energy needs of the field and chakras. When all the chakras are open and healthy, all colors of rainbow appear in the aura. Individual chakra colors should be bright and clear. They should shimmer and move with life.

Stress, illness, negative lifestyle patterns, poor nutrition, and emotional concerns are all contributors to color problems in the aura and chakras. Blotchy and weak colors in the field and chakras need energy, while muddy, dark colors indicate a buildup of unwanted stagnant energy that needs to be cleared. Assessment of the field and the chakras' color or temperature gives us information on how to treat the problem.

Each color has a complementary color. On the color wheel red and green are complementary hues, as are violet and yellow, and blue and orange. In treatment a color is often used in conjunction with its complementary color. If a chakra is excessively open, then I would use the chakra's complementary color to relax and subdue the center. If the chakra was closed and energy deficient, then I would apply the chakra's primary color to facilitate the chakra's natural flow of energy.

For example, if we were working on a root chakra that was excessively open, it would be channeling too much red energy, as red is the natural color of the root, and so we would apply the complementary color of green in order to subdue the center. After a period of exposure to the green, I like to apply the complementary healing color for about five minutes. I would then expose the root chakra to a brief treatment of red, for about one minute, in order to reestablish the natural color and energy flow of the chakra.

The root chakra, along with its bodily tissues and organs, including the blood, spine, prostate, testes, legs, and feet, have a primary color of red and a complementary color of green. The sacral chakra, along with the bladder, small and large intestine, ovaries, fallopian tubes, and uterus, possess a primary color of orange and a complementary color of blue. The solar plexus chakra and the kidneys, liver, stomach, and pancreas have yellow as their primary color and purple as their complementary color. The heart chakra and its linked body tissues—the heart, lungs, breasts, chest, arms, and hands—have a primary color of green and a complementary color of red. Pink can also be used as a primary healing color for the heart chakra. The throat chakra and its associated organs—the throat, thyroid, and neck—possess a primary color of blue and a complementary color of orange. The brow chakra and the organs associated with it, including the eyes, ears, nose, face, pituitary gland, and sinuses, have a primary color of purple and a complementary color of yellow. The color I use to treat the crown chakra and the problems associated with it is white.

While I am performing the energy healing, I project healing energy into the field or chakra, visualizing the energy in the color that is needed. I also can apply the needed color either by light, oil, or silk cloth to the afflicted area or chakra. For a general healing, the color can also be administered through the soles of feet. The foot chakras have a strong connection to the whole body and can deliver energy throughout the system. While you are applying the color, have the client inhale deeply to take in the color's energies. The energy of the color blends with the chakra's own color, and the strength of the energy coming from the chakra amplifies. This, in turn, facilitates physical healing of the body's tissues.

12

Emergency Healing

The ability to heal in an emergency situation is a very valuable skill, and a healer never knows when it will be necessary.

The primary objectives of emergency first aid are to save lives, to prevent conditions from worsening, and to promote recovery. In many emergency situations, it is best to call 911 and follow the directions of the operator. But there may be times when this cannot be done; in these cases, first-aid skills are extremely valuable and can save lives. I can give you the basics of first-aid training, but to expand your first aid healing skills you should take a certified first-aid course. Be sure to take a course that includes training in CPR.

Basic Information

The most valuable skill that a healer can possess in an emergency situation is the ability to keep calm and think rationally. Breathe deeply and center yourself before performing any actions. If you allow your mind to connect to the healer within, she will show you the correct path. Assume a leadership position and take charge of the situation.

A good healer carries a first-aid kit. It does not have to be a large kit, but it should contain bandages, sterile gauze pads, cotton balls, tape, surgical tweezers, antibiotic cream or spray, a sterile needle, latex gloves, a mouth guard, syrup of ipecac, charcoal, and Tylenol. Carry a cell phone, as you never know when you will need it.

The most important factor in any first-aid treatment is safety—the patient's and yours. Wear gloves when giving first aid and use a mouth shield when administering artificial respiration. Before you approach any situation, it is essential that you ensure the area is safe for you to enter. Check for dangerous conditions like live wires or poisonous gases, and do not attempt to intervene if the area is not safe. Rescue individuals are given specific training in dealing with dangerous situations, and healing under perilous conditions needs to be left to these trained professionals.

Be sure to call emergency services and report the emergency. Remain calm and speak all information clearly and slowly. State the type of emergency and give a precise location. Be sure that the dispatcher has all the necessary information before you hang up the phone. This is very important, as details can often be missed in the franticness of the situation. If someone else is notifying emergency services, have him report back to you to ensure that help is really on the way.

If the area has been deemed safe, then the first objective of an emergency healer is to check for consciousness. If injuries are suspected, never move the person unless absolutely necessary. Gently tap the person's shoulders and call loudly out to her. If there is no response, you need to send for an ambulance. If injuries are suspected, do not move the individual. Check for breathing without moving the patient. Put your head down close to the injured person and listen for her breathing, look for any chest movement, and feel for her breath on your cheek. Try to minimize any neck movement. If neck injuries are not seen or suspected, then you can open the the person's airway and check for breathing. Place one hand on the forehead and tilt it back gently, and use your other hand to lift the chin. Look for chest movement, listen for breathing, and feel for breath on your cheek.

The Recovery Position

The recovery position is used to help the recovery and prevent the injured person from choking to death on his own vomit. Use the recovery position only if the patient is breathing and neck and spine injuries are not suspected. It is to be applied if the breathing is difficult or noisy, the person is vomiting or bleeding from the mouth, or if you must leave him unattended to notify emergency services or help another injured person. To perform the position, lay the person on his side with the top leg bent and the head rested on the top arm.

Artificial Respiration

If a person is not breathing, you need to perform artificial respiration. To perform artificial respiration on an adult, first open the airway. Cover the person's mouth with yours, and pinch the nostrils firmly closed. Blow a steady stream of air into the person to make her chest rise. If the airway is blocked and the air will not enter into the body, perform treatment for a choking adult. After giving one breath, check for a carotid pulse by placing your fingers (not your thumb, since your thumb has its own pulse) on the neck and feeling for the pulse. You need to give yourself up to ten seconds to locate a pulse. If there is a pulse present, begin to give the person one full breath every five seconds.

If the person is a child, then after determining a pulse you want to give one breath for every three seconds. For a nonbreathing infant, cover the infant's mouth and nose with your mouth to administer the breaths. Check for a brachial pulse, and if the infant has a pulse, then you want to give one breath every three seconds. If you cannot locate a pulse on the person, you need to begin cardiopulmonary resuscitation, or CPR, if you are trained to do so.

Heart Attack

There are several warning signs of a heart attack, including heavy, squeezing pressure in the chest, jaw, or arms; shortness of breath; sweating; weakness; nausea and/or vomiting; and abdominal discomfort with indigestion and burping. Assist the person to sit or lie down in a comfortable position. Call an ambulance and reassure the person that help is on the way. Be sure to loosen a tight collar, belt, and other restrictive clothing.

Bleeding

Bleeding can often be very serious, as it can occur with severed blood vessels. Before treating anyone, ensure your own safety. If the bleeding is severe, it is important that you send for an ambulance. Help the person to sit or lie down. Cover the entire cut with a clean cloth dressing and apply firm pressure directly on the injury. If there is no cloth available, then have the person apply pressure with his hand. Elevate the limb if a fracture is not suspected. If the blood soaks through the dressing, do not remove it. Instead, apply another dressing on top and bandage the dressing firmly.

If there are broken bones involved in the injury or objects protruding through the skin, then it is important that you take special steps. Do not remove the embedded object, as this will tear the tissue and create further injury. Cover the wound with clean dressings and apply pressure close to the injury, but be sure that you do not press directly on the broken bone or embedded object. Apply some padding around the object in order to prevent its movement, and then bandage the pads firmly in place.

In the case of a nosebleed, the patient should be seated with her head titled forward. Have her pinch his nostrils firmly for about ten minutes. She should avoid blowing her nose for at least two hours after the nosebleed. If the bleeding cannot be stopped, call for an ambulance.

Bone Injuries

If an injured limb is painful and swollen or shows obvious deformity, then a broken bone is a strong possibility. Try not to move the person unless his safety is threatened. Call for an ambulance immediately. Attend to severe bleeding and apply cold to injuries to relieve pain. Use your hands to support a limb to prevent movement.

If you suspect neck or back injuries, it is important that you ensure that the person does not move, as movement could cause further damage. Keep the injured person still until help arrives.

Eye Injuries

For all serious eye injuries, you need to notify emergency services immediately. Never rub the eye, and try to prevent the person from doing so as well. If there are chemicals in the eye, wash the eye continuously with cool, running water for at least ten minutes. If there is a foreign object embedded in the eye, do not try to remove it. Instead, bandage the eye lightly and try not to move or disturb the eye. Having the patient lie on her back can help her remain calm and still until help arrives.

Burns

First, ensure that *you* are safe before attempting to help. Before treatment, check to see that the person is breathing and has a pulse. An ambulance should be called for severe burns larger than the size of a quarter. In the treatment of burns, it is very important that you do not touch or blow on them, break any blisters, apply any ointments or medications, or peel off any clothing that is adhered to the burn. Burns are treated best with cool, running water. Flood the injured area with water for fifteen to twenty minutes, and then cover the burn with a clean cloth and bandage it lightly. In the case of electrical burns, turn off the electricity before touching the injured person to avoid being electrocuted.

Hypothermia

Hypothermia arises from the loss of body heat. It can be very serious, as it can lead to unconsciousness. If the patient is unconscious, call an ambulance. Ensure that he is breathing and has a pulse. Remove him from the cold environment and prevent him from further exposure. Do not attempt to rewarm him.

If the person is conscious, remove him from the cold environment and take off any wet clothing. Wrap her in warm blankets and clothing and give her warm drinks, but never anything with alcohol.

Poisoning

Ensure your safety. Try to identify the poison and its container. Contact the poison control center for specific instructions. Only induce vomiting on the direction of a poison control dispatcher. If the poison is corrosive or hydrocarbon, do not induce vomiting, as it can burn the inner tissue of the throat.

Use syrup of ipecac to induce vomiting. Place the person's head lower than the rest of the body to avoid inhalation.

If the patient is unconscious, ensure breathing and pulse, and then place him in the recovery position. Do not induce vomiting.

Choking

Ask the person, "Are you choking?" If she can speak or cough, the air passage is open far enough to force out the obstructing object, so encourage coughing and reassure her. Do not hit a person on her back.

If the individual cannot speak or cough, you need to perform abdominal thrusts to force out the obstruction. Stand behind the patient and wrap your arms around his waist. Make one hand into a fist and place it above the person's navel. Grasp your fist with your other hand, and then sharply thrust your hands inward and upward into the abdomen. Repeat the abdominal thrusts until the obstruction clears the airway.

If the person becomes unconscious, attempt to give artificial respiration. If the air will not enter the body, then administer five abdominal thrusts. Straddle the person's legs, and position one hand in the center of the abdomen just above the belly button. Place the heel of the your other hand on top. Give five quick inward and upward thrusts. Then inspect the mouth for foreign material, and, if necessary, insert a finger deep into the mouth to sweep out any obstructing material. Open the airway and give two full breaths. Repeat abdominal thrusts, mouth sweep, and breaths until the obstruction clears.

If an infant is choking on a foreign object, you need to support the infant and administer back blows. Place the infant on her stomach and support her on your arm, keeping her head lower than the trunk of her body. Using the heel of your hand, give five back blows between the shoulder blades. If that does not dislodge the object, then you need to turn the infant over and administer chest thrusts. Cradle the child on your arm, keeping her head supported and lower than the trunk. Place two fingers on the breastbone just below the nipple, and administer five sharp chest thrusts. Continue to give alternating sets of back blows and chest thrusts until the foreign object is removed.

If the child becomes unconscious, attempt to administer artificial respiration. If air does not enter into the body, give five back blows and then five chest thrusts. Inspect the mouth, and if foreign material is seen, insert the little finger of your hand into the infant's mouth and sweep out the material. Give the infant two breaths and continue administering back blows, chest thrusts, and breaths until the child is able to breath on his own.

Appendix

Specific Ailments and Their Treatments

Aches and Pains

Nonspecific aches and pains of the body affect the soft tissue areas, including tendons, muscles, and ligaments. It is important to treat pain at its first onset, as it can often interfere with normal functioning and become chronic.

Diet and Vitamins: Weight control is an issue, as excess weight can be a burden to the body and trigger pain.

Massage Therapy: Gentle deep tissue massage alleviates aches and pains. Ask for feedback so that you are not pressing directly on a painful area and causing more discomfort.

Exercise: Regular exercise strengthens muscles and works to prevent injury. Stretching and yoga promotes pain relief in the body and increases mobility and strength.

Hydrotherapy: Cold compresses are effective for acute sprains, as they minimize swelling and internal bleeding. Warm baths are wonderful for nonspecific aches, pain, and stiffness. Whirlpool baths reduce inflammation, and also stimulate the circulation and detoxification of the tissues.

Energy Work: Pull unwanted energy from painful areas and project healing energy back into the system. Work on the specific chakra that governs the afflicted area.

Crystal Healing: The energies of amber and carnelian help to relieve pain and promote healing. Blue tourmaline soothes inflammation.

Color Therapy: Blue is effective for cooling irritated tissues, and purple is a powerful painkiller.

Acne

A skin condition that can range from mild to severe, acne is caused by the overproduction of oil from glands in the skin. It primarily occurs on the face, chest, and back. The excess sebum clogs pores, and infections develop in the form of pimples, boils, blackheads, and spots. Acne is triggered by hormonal imbalance, improper diet, allergies, or stress, and it can be a devastating condition for young people.

Diet and Vitamins: Eat a healthy diet that is low on sugar and fatty foods to discourage the growth of bacteria, and high in fresh, raw fruits and vegetables. Eat plenty of garlic and onions for their antibacterial properties, and include foods rich in vitamins that enhance the skin, such A, E, and the B vitamins. Drink plenty of water to flush toxins from the body and promote clear skin.

Herbal Treatment: Use a chamomile and rosemary infusion as an astringent to apply all over the face after cleansing. Apply essential oil on the spots; use chamomile, lavender, or tea tree oil. Mix five drops of the desired oil with 25 ml (5 teaspoons) of almond oil, and apply directly on the spots. Tape a wet chamomile tea bag on troubled spots overnight. Drinking dandelion or burdock tea can also be helpful.

Hydrotherapy: Gently cleanse the face three times a day with a medicated soap. Back acne can be exfoliated with a shower brush. Face steaming can help open pores and remove blocked sebum.

Light Therapy: The ultraviolet rays of the sun are very helpful for eliminating acne, so brief, periodic sun exposure is recommended, but always use a sun block.

Energy Work: An infusion of healing energy into the face can be helpful. Focus on grounding and promoting the flow of energy through the body.

Color Therapy: Purple is effective for treating bacteria, and orange brings pimples to a head. Use pink for general skin conditions as well.

Mental Work: Stress relaxation techniques can be very helpful.

Professional Treatment: See a dermatologist. Adults with bothersome acne should be tested for possible allergies.

General Care: Never squeeze spots, as this may leave scars.

AIDS and Immune System Deficiencies

Most experts believe that AIDS is caused by HIV (human immunodeficiency virus). HIV is highly infectious, with symptoms that include heavy night sweats, fatigue, weight loss, mouth ulcers, diarrhea, thrush, and herpes infections. It may take several years before AIDS develops from HIV. But when it does, the immune system is attacked, and the helper T cells are specifically targeted. This leaves the body unable to fight off infection and very susceptible to the development of secondary infections. Most individuals with HIV/AIDS also suffer from fatigue and stress as well.

Diet and Vitamins: Eat a diet high in vitamins, especially C, E, and beta-carotene. Eliminate low-nutrient and processed foods high in sugar and salt. Cut down on alcohol. Eat garlic, as it increases the level of helper T cells. Ensure that a daily supplement program is followed.

Herbal Treatment: Tea tree oil and eucalyptus oil are useful in massage and baths because of their antiviral and immune system enhancing properties, and lavender is helpful for stress relief. St. Johns wort may be effective in fighting the disease, but further testing still needs to be done. Ginseng and garlic boost the immune system.

Massage Therapy: Regular massage provides stress relief and relaxation. It also aids lymphatic drainage, promoting the elimination of waste and toxins from the blood.

Energy Work: Work on the entire energy field to clear and strengthen it. Focusing on the root and heart chakra is appropriate for improvements in immune system functioning.

Crystal Healing: Agate strengthens the immune system and promotes a healthy energy flow. Onyx removes poisons and illness from the system. Amber and amethyst are effective for pain and stress relief.

Color Therapy: Red boosts the immune system and raises the level of white blood cells. Pink soothes the body with love.

Mental Practice: Practice relaxation and meditation techniques for stress reduction. Visualization is particularly effective in encouraging a healthy immune system.

Alopecia

The medical term for hair loss, alopecia can be due to many causes. It can occur as a consequence of illness, malnutrition, stress, thyroid problems, or mistreatment of the hair. Baldness can also be inherited, or it can occur as a side effect of various drug treatments.

Diet and Vitamins: Avoid an excess of stimulants, such as coffee, tea, and alcohol. Eat foods rich in vitamins B and C, as both are good for the hair. A daily supplement of vitamins B and C is recommended.

Herbal Treatment: The essential oil of rosemary stimulates the scalp, and lavender is a balancing oil that can help to prevent further hair loss. Add three drops of each to about 15 ml (1 tablespoon) of water, and use the mixture to massage into the scalp nightly.

Massage Therapy: Gently massage the scalp daily to stimulate the hair follicles.

Energy Work: Energy infusion into the scalp and crown chakra is appropriate to promote hair growth.

Color Therapy: Purple stimulates the hair follicles, while green is an effective color for hair growth.

Mental Practice: Practice relaxation meditation to relieve stress. Visualize hair follicles being stimulated and growing.

General Care: Avoid braiding hair or putting it in ponytails; also, avoid using a curling iron or rollers, or having hair permed, colored, or bleached.

Professional Treatment: See a trichologist (a hair and scalp specialist). Get tested for possible thyroid problems.

Anxiety

Anxiety is a debilitating condition that can be brought on by numerous causes that are specific to each person. Gradations of anxiety include paranoia, nervousness, and panic.

Diet and Vitamins: Avoid the stimulus of caffeine. Ensure a proper nutrient count in daily diet. A daily vitamin B12 supplement can help alleviate anxiety. Vitamin C is also recommended.

Herbal Treatment: Calming oils such as rose, lavender, and sandalwood can be used in a bath, inhalation, or massage treatment. Ginseng alleviates stress.

Massage Therapy: Gentle and relaxing massage can be very effective.

Hydrotherapy: Hot baths relax the body and soothe the mind.

Energy Work: Work on the crown, third eye, and solar plexus chakras to relieve stress and anxiety in mind and body. Energy work on the root chakra promotes security. Focus on removing unwanted energies and projecting soothing, healing energies into the system.

Crystal Healing: Amethyst relieves mental stress, while rose quartz helps with grief, self-love, and personal forgiveness. Bloodstone grants courage in times of stress and conflict.

Color Therapy: Blue calms anxiety and pink fills the body with love.

Mental Practice: Meditation and relaxation techniques can help reduce anxiety. A regular program of meditation can balance emotions and lead to self-discovery.

Professional Treatment: A patient suffering from prolonged, intense cases of anxiety and emotional upset needs to seek professional treatment. There are many beneficial drugs that help rebalance the chemical system of body.

Arthritis and Joint Pain

A condition that causes chronic inflammation of the joints, arthritis can be very painful and can result in restricted movement. Pain can result from a high-acidforming diet, an injury, aging, inflammation, or cold, damp environments.

Diet and Vitamins: Be sure to keep body weight low to reduce stress on the joints. Avoid stimulants like salt, coffee, sugar, and alcohol. Eat detoxifying foods such as fresh vegetables and fruits, foods high in fiber, and calcium foods, as milk helps the body to build synovial fluids to lubricate the joints. Fatty fish oils can help reduce inflammation.

Herbal Treatment: Hot compresses of cider vinegar, juniper, and cypress oils can be laid on the afflicted area to reduce swelling. An oil made of three drops chamomile, three drops eucalyptus, and three drops lavender placed in 25 ml (5 teaspoons) of carrier lotion can be spread on afflicted areas regularly to ease inflammation and pain. Drink dandelion tea and take burdock tablets to help reduce inner irritation. Peppermint tea will bring down internal inflammation.

Exercise: Partake in gentle exercises like swimming or yoga as often as possible to increase mobility of joints. Keep weight down to reduce overall burden on joints.

Hydrotherapy: Hot baths with juniper and cypress oils can help ease inflammation and pain. One-half pound (.5 kg) of Epsom salts can be added to a bath to facilitate elimination of toxins such as uric acid from the body. Stretch thoroughly after bathing to loosen joints and prevent congestion.

Energy Work: Focus on pulling pain and unwanted energy from the afflicted area, and then project healing vibrations back into system.

Crystal Healing: Onyx removes pain, while blue tourmaline soothes inflammation.

Color Therapy: Yellow works to dissolve density deposits in the body. Purple is effective for pain relief.

Mental Practice: Relaxation and pain management visualization techniques are effective.

Professional Treatment: Obtain testing for food allergies.

Asthma

An irritation of the upper respiratory tract, asthma causes the bronchi walls to contract and restrict breathing. Most cases of asthma are allergy related, but attacks can also be triggered by anxiety.

Diet and Vitamins: Avoid stimulants like coffee, tea, and alcohol. If molds trigger attacks, avoid cheese, mushrooms, yeast, and soy sauce. To reduce inflammation, eat foods like fish that are high in omega-3 fatty acids. Soup and fluids help to reduce bronchial mucus.

Exercise: Engage in exercise as frequently as possible. Swimming is recommended, as there are few irritants in the water.

Energy Work: Apply the energy smoothing technique to facilitate clearing of the system and promote a healthy energy flow. Work on the throat and heart chakra is appropriate.

Crystal Healing: Citrine placed on the lungs and solar plexus aids breathing problems. Blue tourmaline and turquoise on the throat facilitates clear breathing passages.

Color Therapy: Orange heals breathing problems and promotes the clearing of passageways.

Mental Practice: Imagery techniques for stress reduction can be helpful, as can relaxing meditations. Visualization helps to open and clear breathing passages.

General Care: Avoid irritants like pollen, dust, smoke, and pet dander. Avoid steam inhalants, as they can trigger choking attacks. Get tested for specific allergies.

Athlete's Foot

Caused by a fungal growth, athlete's foot is a highly contagious condition that results in itchy, cracked, and peeling skin.

Diet and Vitamins: Eat foods rich in vitamin A, like dark green and yellow vegetables. Eat garlic for its antifungal properties. A vitamin B supplement is recommended.

Herbal Treatment: Mix five drops tea tree oil to 15 ml (1 tablespoon) of almond oil, and apply nightly to feet after soaking them.

Hydrotherapy: Soak feet for about fifteen minutes nightly in a basin of warm salted water containing ten drops tea tree oil. Always dry feet thoroughly, especially between the toes.

Energy Work: Focus on pulling out unwanted energy from the feet, and then infusing them with healing energy.

Color Therapy: Purple is an antifungal, and pink heals the skin.

General Care: Wear cotton socks and open sandals as much as possible. Bathe feet daily, and do not sleep in socks.

Backache

A backache is the most common cause of disability in America. Several things can cause back problems, including: lifting heavy objects, pregnancy, shoes or high heels that fit poorly, and even an infection.

Herbal Treatment: A poultice of lavender or pine needles, or a compress of eucalyptus can be applied on the body. Use eucalyptus, lavender, or chamomile essential oils in a base as a massage oil. Add ten drops of lavender, pine, or eucalyptus oil to a bath, as these are anti-inflammatory oils.

Massage Therapy: Gentle, deep massage of the muscles can be beneficial.

Hydrotherapy: Take hot baths to soothe the back.

Exercise: Engage in daily stretching and gentle exercise like swimming or walking.

Energy Work: Apply the techniques of pulling unwanted energy and pain from the system, smoothing to disperse blockages, and projecting healing energy to heal tissues.

Crystal Healing: Amber and carnelian promote the healing of muscles, while onyx can be used to absorb pain.

Color Therapy: Orange is highly effective for muscle spasms and pains, while purple is a strong painkiller.

Mental Practice: Relaxation along with stress and pain removal techniques can be effective.

General Care: Refrain from lifting. Wear a proper back brace to support the back. A new mattress on the bed can also be helpful if the backache is recurring. Weight control may be an issue.

Bites, insect

See *Stings.*

Bronchitis

An infection of the bronchial tubes, bronchitis causes coughing, shallow breathing, chest pains, and upper back irritation. It can be also be caused by smoking, pollution, stress, or an allergy.

Diet and Vitamins: Eat a raw fruit and vegetable diet. Avoid mucus-forming foods, such as dairy and starchy foods. Eat garlic and take vitamin C to build the immune system.

Herbal Treatment: Use steam inhalation with antiseptic oils such as eucalyptus and tea tree. Horehound tea can be beneficial.

Deep Breathing: Practice deep breathing methods to strengthen the respiratory system.

Energy Work: Focus on removing unwanted energy from affected areas. Use smoothing techniques to facilitate the flow of energy through the body. Work on the heart and throat chakras.

Crystal Healing: Citrine placed on the solar plexus chakra helps to unblock breathing, while amethyst soothes and strengthens the respiratory system.

Color Therapy: Orange opens breathing passages, while green heals the lungs.

Mental Practice: Relaxation exercises can be beneficial. Visualize clear unblocked airways.

Professional Treatment: Obtain testing for food allergies, especially if the symptoms are recurring.

Bruises

Bruising occurs when there is injury to the skin tissue, and blood leaks from the broken vessels into the body tissue around the damaged area. The color fades as the blood is absorbed. Bruises can be quite painful.

Diet and Vitamins: Eating foods with a high vitamin C content can help prevent bruises if you bruise easily. Also, try taking a daily vitamin C supplement.

Herbal Treatment: Use a lavender poultice directly on the bruise. The essential oils of lavender and peppermint are beneficial to bring down the bruise. Mix 15 ml (1 tablespoon) of carrier oil with three drops of the desired oil and spread gently over the area. A poultice of comfrey is also effective.

Color Therapy: Blue soothes the bruise and helps it heal faster.

Hydrotherapy: Apply an ice compress to reduce bruising and pain.

Burns

Caused by both dry and moist heat, burns damage the skin and are very painful. All burns, except very minor ones, require professional medical attention immediately.

Emergency Care: Immerse the afflicted area in cold water immediately.

Herbal Treatment: Use a few drops of lavender oil directly on the skin. The juice of aloe vera can also be very soothing and can help prevent scarring. Apply daily for about two weeks.

Color Therapy: Use blue to cool and heal the tissues. Pink helps the skin to rejuvenate.

Cancer

Cancer occurs when certain cells of the body begin to rapidly multiply and form tumors. If left unchecked, tumors can interfere with the functioning of vital organs and cause death. The main causes of cancer include genetic defects, poor diet, industrial pollution, and negative living habits, such as smoking. Complementary therapies do not offer a direct cure for cancer, but they can help alleviate pain and other symptoms and support the immune system.

Diet and Vitamins: Eat fruits (especially citrus fruits) and dark veggies for vitamin C, beta-carotene, and bioflavonoids, as these chemicals protect against cancer. Eat high-fiber foods. Avoid fatty foods, those high in animal fat, and foods that may contain pesticide residues. Ensure a regular system of daily vitamin supplementation.

Herbal Treatment: Echinacea and garlic boosts the immune system. Burdock and dandelion help to fight internal cancers and woman's concerns. Ginseng fights cancer cells and alleviates stress.

Massage Therapy: Gentle massage can be beneficial for cancer patients, but any treatment must be okayed by the patient's physician first.

Energy Work: Apply energy pulling to remove unwanted energies over the afflicted area, and then infuse the system with healing energies. Work on the chakra that is associated with the afflicted area. Work on the root chakra is also appropriate for general cleansing of the system.

Color Therapy: Use green to kill cancer cells. For a pregnant woman, use black to absorb negative energy of this type, and red to burn it up. Red also boosts the immune system. Pink can also be applied to spread love and healthiness to the cells.

Mental Practice: Healing meditations and visualizations can help greatly.

General Care: Stop smoking, as smoking is the main contributor to lung cancer.

Catarrh

Catarrh is the excretion of phlegm of the lungs, nose, and sinuses. It can occur as a result of colds, flu, bronchitis, hay fever, stress, or allergies.

Diet and Vitamins: Drink fluids to loosen and expel phlegm.

Herbal Treatment: Use an expectorant oil such as eucalyptus in steam inhalations and in baths. Chamomile or ginger tea can be effective.

Massage Therapy: Massage on the chest and back with eucalyptus essential oil in a base oil, as this helps to eliminate toxins.

Energy Work: Apply pulling techniques to remove unwanted energy from the nose and throat. Work on the heart and throat chakra is appropriate.

Color Therapy: Orange clears up phlegm.

General Care: Stress-relieving relaxation and meditations are beneficial. Yoga can be relaxing as well.

Professional Treatment: In cases of chronic catarrh, get tested for allergies.

Chest Infections

Infections of the chest can occur with colds or the flu. Symptoms can include catarrh, coughing, and breathing difficulties.

Herbal Treatment: Use steam inhalation with tea tree or eucalyptus oil. Also, put ten drops of oil in a bowl of hot water to use as a room diffuser. A mustard seed poultice can also very effective to bring up phlegm. Mix up mustard seeds into a paste, adding a little bit of hot water. Apply the paste to the chest and leave it on for about ten minutes. It will feel very hot, like the chest is on fire, but it is safe to leave the paste on for up to ten minutes. After removing the paste, wrap the body up warmly. Alternatively, ten drops eucalyptus oil can be mixed with 15 ml (1 tablespoon) of carrier oil and spread on the chest.

General Care: Rest in bed. Stay warm and indoors. Avoid cold, damp air and fog.

Chickenpox

Primarily a childhood disease, chickenpox produces a mild fever and severely itchy blisters. It is highly contagious.

Herbal Treatment: Chamomile, lavender, and eucalyptus oil can be applied to spots. In 200 ml (7 fluid ounces) of water, add three drops of each along with 50 ml (1.5 fluid ounces) of witch hazel. Sponge on the skin as required.

Hydrotherapy: Baths are very helpful to relieve itching. Place one cup of baking soda in the bath water, and bathe; repeat three times a day as necessary.

Color Therapy: Pink heals the skin, while blue lessons itching and irritation.

Cholesterol Levels

Cholesterol is essential to the functioning of the body, but it is widely misunderstood. There are two types of cholesterol: a healthy cholesterol called high-density lipoprotein, or HDL cholesterol, which protects against plaque formulation in blood vessels; and an unhealthy cholesterol, low-density lipoprotein, or LDL cholesterol, that actually stimulates the creation of plaque. So in cholesterol control we aim to have higher amounts of HDL and lower levels of LDL.

Diet and Vitamins: Eat a diet of fresh vegetables and fruits. Vitamin C lowers total cholesterol and raises HDL levels. Vitamin B complex has also been shown to lower LDL cholesterol. Fish oils raise HDL cholesterol.

Herbal Treatment: Garlic lowers the body's total cholesterol count.

Exercise: Physical activity lowers LDL cholesterol and raises the level of HDL cholesterol in the body.

Mental Practice: Meditation and relaxation techniques reduce stress, and this helps the body maintain healthy cholesterol levels.

Circulatory Problems

Circulatory problems of the arteries and veins can be a painful situation that often becomes chronic, so treatment at the first sign of a problem is crucial.

Diet and Vitamins: Eat plenty of garlic, citrus foods, and foods high in vitamin C and E. Fish oils containing omega-3 fatty acids can also be beneficial. Avoid coffee, tea, and alcohol. Control weight to avoid stressing the veins.

Herbal Treatment: Massage with the stimulating essential oils of rose, lemon, and rosemary.

Massage Therapy: Engage in regular sessions of stimulating massage to arouse tissues and rev up circulation.

Exercise: Engage in plenty of exercise on a regular basis to stimulate the system.

Mental Practice: Focus on stimulating blood flow and pain reduction.

Energy Work: Apply the technique of smoothing to establish flow in the system. The infusion of healing energy into the body also increases and strengthens circulation.

Color Therapy: Red speeds up and strengthens circulation.

Colds

The common cold is a highly contagious viral infection of the upper respiratory tract. It can be caused by many different viruses and has no cure. Colds primarily occur in winter, when the body's resistance to infection is lowered, and symptoms can include coughing, sneezing, catarrh, sore throat, and aches. Look under the specific symptoms to find further applicable treatments.

Diet and Vitamins: Eat plenty of foods and juices containing vitamin C, like citrus fruit and orange juice. You can take high dosages of vitamin C, up to 3,000 mg a day, while suffering from a cold. New evidence has found that chicken soup with lots of garlic and onions is indeed beneficial. Take garlic as a natural decongestant and antimicrobial. Drink fluids to loosen and expel phlegm.

Herbal Treatment: Chamomile and peppermint tea can be helpful, as can steam inhalations with eucalyptus and tea tree oils. Sprinkle a few drops of eucalyptus on a tissue and inhale regularly to combat stuffiness. Put a drop on your pillow at night as well. Take echinacea and garlic to boost immune system.

Massage Therapy: Massage with eucalyptus oil can treat aching muscles and work to break up congestion.

Energy Work: Pull out unwanted energy from nose, ears, eyes, and other congested areas. Work on crown, third eye, throat, and heart chakras.

Color Therapy: Red increases the immune system, and orange breaks up phlegm and helps promote healthy breathing. Purple is an antiviral.

Constipation

Constipation is the inability to easily pass food through the colon. It can be the result of a sedentary lifestyle, low fiber in the diet, stress, tension, allergies, or all- around poor health.

Diet and Vitamins: High-fiber foods produce soft, easily eliminated stools. Eat bran, apples, and vegetables. Drink water to add extra fluid to the body, at least eight glasses a day.

Herbal Treatment: Massage or bathe with rose and rosemary oils. Chamomile and mint tea can be effective. Dandelion root and burdock are also helpful.

Massage Therapy: Abdominal massage is effective. Rub the stomach in gentle clockwise strokes, the direction of the large intestine's path in the body.

Breathing: Deep breathing exercises can help promote elimination.

Energy Work: Energy techniques like smoothing will stimulate the system and promote elimination.

Crystal Healing: Carnelian placed on the sacral chakra works to rev up a sluggish system.

Color Therapy: Orange promotes the flow of energy through the body, alleviating gas, bloating, and constipation.

Mental Practice: Meditation and relaxation exercises can be beneficial. Focus on letting go of pain and fear. Think movement, the free flow of energies.

Professional Treatment: Obtain testing for food allergies if constipation is persistent and recurring.

Cough

Coughing is a reflex action that occurs when the nerve receptors that line the respiratory track are stimulated or irritated. It can result from inhaled irritants like smoke or chemicals, from water, respiratory infections, asthma, or from choking on a piece of food.

Diet and Vitamins: Vitamins A and C are effective in helping to alleviate conditions that cause coughing.

Herbal Treatment: Use steam inhalation with eucalyptus oil. A horehound infusion can be helpful.

Hydrotherapy: A hot bath or shower that creates a lot of steam can ease coughing. A room humidifier can also be effective.

Energy Work: Pull excess energy from the throat chakra.

Color Therapy: Blue soothes and relaxes the throat muscles, while orange helps to eliminate phlegm and move energy out of the throat and chest.

General Care: Avoid toxic environmental air, and improve air quality by adding plants and air filters to rooms.

Diabetes

Diabetes is a condition in which the body cannot produce or respond to insulin. It affects every organ. Untreated, it can lead to heart disease, kidney failure, and blindness.

Diet and Vitamins: Eat regularly to stabilize blood sugar levels. Eat a balanced diet of starches, fats, and proteins in each meal. Avoid excess sugar and alcohol. Foods high in cholesterol should be avoided.

Herbal Treatment: Garlic boosts the immune system. Burdock and dandelion stabilize blood sugar levels and act as internal cleansers.

Energy Work: Work on cleansing the entire system. Treatment of the solar plexus and pancreas is appropriate.

Color Therapy: Yellow is a very effective healing color for treating diabetes, as its magnetic currents balance the systems of the body.

Depression

Ongoing depression is often a serious emotional concern that can become chronic. It is extremely debilitating and most often requires professional help.

Diet and Vitamins: Eat high-grade proteins that contain the amino acid tryptophan and the nutrient choline to increase the efficiency of the nervous system. Foods like eggs, meat, fresh fish, and dairy are recommended. Avoid alcohol, as it can be a depressant, and caffeine, as it can hinder sleep and mood.

Herbal Treatment: St. Johns wort is often effective for depression.

Energy Work: Work on the crown, the third eye, and the heart chakra.

Color Therapy: Orange raises moods, increases energy levels, and soothes emotional concerns. Yellow is a very cheery color that is very beneficial for depression.

Crystal Healing: Amber promotes joy, while rose quartz heals the heart and bestows forgiveness and self love.

Professional Treatment: Advise a patient to seek professional help as soon as possible, as depression is a serious problem that can lead to suicide if left untreated.

Diarrhea

Diarrhea is a common symptom of intestinal overstimulation and activity. It is caused by various factors, including infection, food poisoning, diabetes, inappropriate food, allergies, antibiotic use, immune system deficiencies, and emotional concerns.

Diet and Vitamins: Drink water, apple juice, herbal teas, broth, or low-sugar sport drinks such as Gatorade to replace lost minerals, salts, and fluids in the body. Eat bland foods like eggs, toast, and potatoes to avoid irritating bowels. Avoid citrus drinks and fruits until the system returns to normal. Avoid alcohol, as it is dehydrating, and caffeine, as it stimulates the system.

Herbal Treatment: Chamomile tea will ease diarrhea.

Energy Work: Energy infusion into the system works to calm the body. Focus on the solar plexus and sacral chakras.

Color Therapy: Blue slows diarrhea, while purple kills internal parasites.

Mental Practice: Work on calming and relaxing the system.

Professional Treatment: Seek professional treatment if the diarrhea persists for more than one day, if it worsens, if it is accompanied by blood or worms in the feces, or if it occurs with severe pain, vomiting, or fever. For recurring diarrhea, consult an allergist for allergy testing.

Earache

A common infliction in children, earaches are a painful condition that almost always indicates an infection or inflammation of the inner ear. A persistent earache should be examined by a professional.

Diet and Vitamins: Eat vegetables and fruits to boost the immune system. Avoid high-salt foods, as they can cause a buildup of inner ear fluid.

Herbal Treatment: Warm a teaspoon of almond oil and add one drop of rosemary or lavender to it. Put a few drops in the ear and seal with a cotton ball. Peppermint tea can be used as gargle to treat ear problems.

Hydrotherapy: Steam inhalation works to relieve inflammation and blockages, while hot baths can be relaxing and alleviate pain.

Energy Therapy: Work on clearing unwanted energy from the ears.

Color Therapy: Purple is a painkiller, and it also soothes ear problems.

Professional Treatment: Seek professional treatment if the earache persists.

Eczema and Skin Rashes

Also known as dermatitis, eczema is characterized by dry itchy skin that is raw and painful. It is often hereditary and is aggravated by stress and poor diet.

Diet and Vitamins: Eat foods high in vitamin A, B complex, and C, as they are essential to the health of the skin. Vitamin E can be applied directly to the skin to promote healing. A daily dose of fish oil capsules can also be effective.

Herbal Treatment: Use chamomile or lavender oil, and apply a few drops directly over an area. A rinse of chamomile tea in a bath or by itself is also beneficial.

Massage Therapy: Massage can help alleviate stress in the body.

Hydrotherapy: Short warm baths help cleanse the skin.

Energy Work: Energy infusion into the system can break up irritation and promote healing.

Color Therapy: Pink heals the skin while blue soothes itchiness and irritation.

Professional Treatment: Check out possible allergy causes, such as foods, laundry products, or other household substances.

Eye Problems

The first resort in all eye problems is to consult an eye doctor for treatment.

Diet and Vitamins: Carrots and dark green vegetables are rich in beta-carotene, which helps to alleviate vision problems. Vitamins C, B, and E strengthen eyes.

Herbal Treatment: To soothe an irritation, rinse the eye in an infusion of chamomile tea.

Hydrotherapy: Flush eye in cool running water to cleanse it. For stressed eyes, alternate warm and cold compresses.

Color Therapy: Purple is effective for eye problems.

Professional Treatment: Consult an allergist for possible allergies.

Fatigue

Fatigue is a overall feeling of tiredness and weariness that can border on exhaustion. It is a debilitating condition that can become chronic.

Diet and Vitamins: Fish oils have been beneficial in treating fatigue. B vitamin complex is also recommended. A magnesium supplement can be helpful, as chronic fatigue lowers magnesium count in red blood cells. Vitamin C and garlic can also be helpful. Avoid sugar, as it can increase fatigue by robbing nutrients from the body. Alcohol should also be avoided, as it lowers immunity.

Herbal Treatment: Aromatherapy oils help relieve stress and tension. Use lavender for antiviral properties, rosemary for muscular aches, and echinacea to help build the immune system.

Massage Therapy: Relaxing massage helps relieve stress and depression.

Exercise: Gentle exercise can help increase strength and stamina, but it must be accompanied with nutritional treatment as well.

Energy Work: Focus on infusing the system with healing energy. Work on the heart chakra is appropriate.

Crystal Healing: Agate raises and stimulates the energy field.

Color Therapy: Red boosts the immune system. Orange activates personal energy.

Mental Practice: Work on reducing stress and connecting to healing energies. Meditation is useful for conserving energy to overcome fatigue.

General Care: Fatigue can improve with the removal of mercury amalgam fillings in the teeth. Be sure to get enough sleep to help the body recover. Seek professional treatment.

Flatulence

When the stomach and the intestines become distended by gas, flatulence occurs when the gas escapes the body. In some cases it is allergy related and can often be easily controlled through diet and relaxation techniques.

Diet and Vitamins: Eliminate sugary foods that ferment in the intestines, such as cabbage, beans, radishes, green peppers, cucumbers, and fruits. Add fresh herbs such as basil, cloves, mint, nutmeg, and oregano to foods to help facilitate digestion. Yogurt can help alleviate the problem. Avoid bran and high-laxative foods.

Herbal Treatment: Massage essential oils such as anise, basil, and clove into the stomach to facilitate the digestion process. Peppermint tea can also alleviate gas. Basil tea aids digestion.

Energy Work: Apply smoothing techniques to facilitate the clearing of the system. Work on the solar plexus and sacral chakras is appropriate.

Mental Practice: Practice relaxation techniques. Some people swallow air when they are nervous or stressed, which creates gas buildup; calming meditations can help with this problem.

Professional Treatment: Get tested for allergies. Often people lack the enzymes needed to digest certain foods, such as wheat or milk.

General Care: Avoid carbonated drinks, straws, and gum, which all lead to swallowing air.

Hair Loss

See *Alopecia.*

Hay Fever and Other Airborne Allergies

Hay fever is an allergic condition that is normally associated with pollen, but may be caused by any irritants, including dust, mold spores, food, pet dander, and insect bites. Symptoms range from breathing difficulties to swelling and hives. A weakened immune system is a leading contributor to the severity of allergic symptoms.

Diet and Vitamins: Lower fat intake to boost the immune system. Eat garlic. To reduce internal inflammation, take fish oils for their omega-3 fatty acids. Avoid honey and bee pollen capsules. If spores trigger symptoms, avoid cheese, yeast, and other fermented foods.

Exercise: Exercise can help respiratory allergies, especially swimming and walking.

Energy Work: An infusion of energy into the system unblocks passages and promotes free flow.

Color Therapy: Orange clears up breathing problems, while green stimulates the lungs and heart.

Mental Practice: Meditation and visualization is effective in opening the respiratory system and increasing the efficiency of the immune system.

Professional Treatment: See a specialist to test for specific allergy triggers.

Headaches

Headaches are a painful and common symptom that can be created by a myriad of causes. A few of these include tension in the muscles, which produces a pain called a muscular headache, caffeine, allergies, or stress, which creates changes in the arteries of the head region and produces a vascular headache, or they can also be caused by inflammation, pressure, or eye strain. A migraine, which is a severe type of vascular headache, can be accompanied by nausea or dizziness.

Diet and Vitamins: Certain foods are known to trigger headaches, including: bananas; alcohol; caffeine; chocolate; food additives; monosodium glutamate; nitrates found in bacon, hot dogs, and processed meats; artificial sweeteners; and cheese. Keep track of trigger foods and avoid them. Add daily supplements of vitamins C, A, and E.

Herbal Treatment: Chamomile tea can give pain relief. Eucalyptus essential oil in a massage treatment breaks up congestion, while rose oil bestows relaxing energies.

Massage Therapy: Massage head, temples, base of skull, neck, and shoulders for pain and stress relief.

Hydrotherapy: Take warm water baths to relieve stress and pain. Apply an ice pack or cold washcloth to the head and back of neck, or, alternatively, apply cold and heat to the back of the neck. Use steam inhalation to break up sinus headaches.

Energy Work: Work on pulling energy from the crown and third eye chakra.

Crystal Healing: Amethyst relieves headaches when placed on the forehead and neck.

Mental Practice: Focus on relaxing, calming, stress-relieving meditations and visualizations.

General Care: Rest in a dark room while migraines are occurring. Test air in the house for environmental causes.

Professional Treatment: Severe, recurring headaches need professional treatment to rule out serious problems and allergies to prescribed medicines. Test for allergies.

Heart Problems

Pain of the heart should always be checked by a doctor, as it can be an indication of severe problems and disease. Proper treatment and management can often reverse heart problems before coronary disease sets in.

Diet and Vitamins: Eat foods high in fiber, raw fruits and veggies, and whole grains. Take a complete vitamin and mineral supplement. Additional doses of antioxidant substances such as vitamins C and E, beta-carotene, and zinc are also beneficial. Calcium and magnesium have been shown to reduce blood pressure. Eat garlic, as it thins the blood, lowers cholesterol, and reduces blood pressure. Maintain a healthy weight to prevent high blood pressure and stress on the heart. Avoid fatty meats and foods high in cholesterol, such as eggs, organ meats, and whole milk.

Herbal Treatment: Garlic strengthens the heart.

Massage Therapy: Massage stimulates circulation while maintaining muscle tone and flexibility.

Exercise: Physical activity tailored to an individual's specific needs can be very effective at strengthening the heart and protecting against strokes.

Mental Practice: Inner calmness and stress reduction meditation and visualization exercises are important.

General Care: Stop smoking, and drink alcohol in moderation.

Heartburn

A burning pain in the chest, heartburn can be caused by several factors, including eating too fast, problematic foods, excess weight, tight clothing, and acid regurgitation. Stress can also trigger an episode of heartburn.

Diet and Vitamins: Avoid heartburn-triggering foods, such as garlic, onions, hot spices, chocolate, tomato, and citrus fruit. Avoid caffeine, alcohol, and coffee. Eat small meals. Don't drink carbonated beverages or use a straw, as both puts excess air in the body. Drink milk to wash the acid down.

Herbal Treatment: Peppermint tea aids digestion, while chamomile tea soothes the system.

General Care: Lose weight. Mobility can help; don't bend over or lie down directly after eating. Ensure that clothing is not too tight. Do not eat during the two hours before bedtime.

Professional Treatment: If pain persists, seek a doctor to rule out an ulcer or hernia.

Herpes

There are over seventy different viruses in the herpes family. Herpes zoster causes chickenpox and shingles, while the Epstein-Barr virus causes infectious mononucleosis. Herpes simplex I causes blisters on the mouth, commonly referred to as cold sores, while herpes simplex II is sexually transmitted and creates blisters on the genitals. The blisters are highly contagious, and those suffering from herpes should always seek medical treatment.

Diet and Vitamins: Eat garlic to kill bacteria; a normal dosage is one clove every four hours when you first feel the blisters coming on. Avoid caffeine and alcohol.

Herbal Treatment: Apply eucalyptus oil for its antiviral properties, and lavender oil for its antiseptic properties. Mix five drops of each to 10 ml (2 teaspoons) of carrier oil and apply to the area regularly. Apply one drop of tea tree oil neat to the blisters. Herbal tinctures and pills of burdock and dandelion are also effective.

Hydrotherapy: A sitz bath can help ease inflammation.

Energy Work: Work on boosting the immune system through clearing the system and infusing it with healing energy.

Color Therapy: Purple is an effective antiviral color.

General Care: Use precautions when having sex. Avoid having sex when blisters are forming. Avoid touching the eyes, as the blisters can spread to the eyes. Avoid smoking and excessive sun exposure.

Professional Treatment: Seek professional treatment for medications.

Indigestion

Indigestion occurs when the body has difficulty processing food. It can encompass a wide range of symptoms, including stomachache, heartburn, bloated feelings, and flatulence.

Diet and Vitamins: Avoid spicy foods, foods high in fat, and caffeine. Avoid alcohol as well. Be sure to chew foods thoroughly. Eat fresh fruits, vegetables, and whole-grain foods to obtain fiber to speed the digestive process. Drink water and juices; eight glasses daily is recommended to flush the system.

Herbal Treatment: Chamomile tea soothes stomach upsets. Peppermint tea aids digestion, clearing away gas and relieving bloating. Massage or bathe with rose oils for general relaxation. Sandalwood and lavender essential oils relax the stomach.

Massage Therapy: Gentle massage of the stomach and large intestine can help.

Hydrotherapy: Warm baths can alleviate symptoms and promote relaxation.

Energy Work: Focus on promoting flow. Work on the solar plexus and sacral chakras.

Mental Practice: Focus on relaxation and calmness in times of illness and pain.

Insomnia

Sleep is one of the most important functions in daily life, as it works to recharge and rejuvenate the body. The inability to sleep is a very disruptive problem that can last for days or even months.

Diet and Vitamins: Avoid stimulates like caffeine, alcohol, chocolate, and exercise from late afternoon onward. To induce sleepiness, eat foods such as turkey and tuna fish, which are high in L-tryptophan. Do not eat during the three hours before bedtime. Try drinking warm milk to promote sleepiness. Excess weight can be a factor contributing to insomnia, so weight control is an important issue.

Herbal Treatments: Chamomile tea is an excellent sleep-inducing beverage.

Massage Therapy: A soothing massage before going to bed can be beneficial.

Hydrotherapy: A warm bath or soak in a Jacuzzi can bring on the urge to sleep.

Exercise: Regular exercise can promote a consistent sleep pattern.

Color Therapy: Blue promotes restfulness and sleep.

Mental Practice: Relaxing meditations can be very helpful. Try the whole-body relaxation treatment to promote sleep.

General Care: Make the bedroom a place that focuses on sleep; don't eat or work there. Ensure that you have a comfortable mattress and bedding, and try to stick to a regular sleep schedule. Avoid sleeping pills, as they lead to the rebound effect and the body becomes dependent on them in order to sleep. Fresh air and a darkened room are also beneficial. Do not take naps during the day.

Nausea and Vomiting

Nausea and vomiting are warning symptoms that something is wrong internally. Nausea usually precedes vomiting and is produced by a host of possible causes that can be both physical and psychological.

Diet and Vitamins: Do not eat heavy food; toasted bread or dry crackers can be helpful.

Herbal Treatment: Mint tea is very effective at soothing the stomach.

Energy Work: The infusion of healing energy into the system can curb nausea.

Color Therapy: Blue relaxes the body and alleviates nausea.

Mental Practice: Relaxation and stress reduction techniques can be helpful in preventing acute illnesses and physiological issues that can cause nausea and vomiting.

General Care: Get plenty of fresh air and lie down. Nausea caused by motion sickness can be helped by sitting in the front seat of the car and by attaching a grounding strip to the bottom of the car.

Premenstrual Syndrome

Premenstrual syndrome, or PMS, is a collective term for the medley of symptoms that occurs each month before the start of a woman's period. These symptoms can include water retention, cramping, bloating, soreness of the breasts, irritability, mood swings, and sugar cravings.

Diet and Vitamins: Eat plenty of green vegetables and salads. Vitamin B and C supplements can be helpful. Avoid sugar, caffeine, fatty foods, and salt, as all aggravate symptoms.

Herbal Treatment: Lavender oil in a bath can be soothing, as can a massage treatment. Burdock and dandelion soothe painful women's problems and support the ovaries, womb, and breasts.

Mental Practice: Meditation for stress relief can be helpful.

Sore Throat

A sore throat is usually an indication of a bacterial or viral infection. It is often preceded by a feeling of irritation and scratchiness in the throat. At this early stage, the symptoms can often be alleviated completely.

Diet and Vitamins: Drink plenty of liquids, especially fluids containing citrus, such as lemon, orange, and pineapple juice. Eat garlicky foods to boost the immune system. Also, drink hot water with honey and the juice of half a lemon added to it. Extra dosages of vitamin C can be beneficial—up to 3,000 mg a day.

Herbal Treatment: Steam inhalations of tea tree and rosemary oil can be effective. Gargle with two drops each of tea tree and sandalwood oil in warm water five times a day. This can also be used as a preventive measure in winter. Echinacea and garlic can be taken to boost the immune system.

Energy Work: Pull unwanted energy from the throat chakra. Focus on projecting healing energy into the body.

Crystal Healing: Turquoise on the throat chakra heals soreness and promotes clear communication.

Color Therapy: Blue soothes soreness of the throat.

General Care: Stop smoking; avoid cold air and keep warm; gargle with warm saltwater. Get plenty of rest.

Stings

Insects stings and bites are serious and often very painful. Watch for allergic reactions and, if suspected, seek medical attention immediately.

Bee Sting: Remove the stinger with tweezers. Add one drop of tea tree oil to the sting, and use a cold compress to relieve any pain.

Spider or Insect Bite: Squeeze the site to make it bleed in order to wash out any poisons. Add one drop of tea tree oil to the bite, and apply a cold compress to relieve pain.

Sunburn

A sunburn is inflammation of the skin due to excess exposure to the ultraviolet rays of the sun. It is associated with skin redness, irritation, blisters, and peeling. Over long-term exposure, sunbathing causes wrinkles, leathery skin, and can lead to skin cancer.

Herbal Treatment: Be sure to wait at least half an hour before apply anything as the skin needs time to breathe. An effective remedy that I learned from a friend entails mixing five drops lavender and five drops chamomile oil to a tub of plain yogurt. Cover the sunburned area with the mixture, put on an old tee shirt, and go to bed. Repeat the next night if necessary. Vinegar can also be used as a soothing astringent.

Energy Work: The gentle infusion of healing energy into the body promotes healing.

Crystal Therapy: The energies of amber and blue tourmaline work to heal the burn and alleviate pain. Rose quartz soothes the skin.

Color Therapy: Blue soothes irritated tissues and removes heat from the body.

General Care: Do not sunbathe, and wear sunblock when in the sun. Avoid sunlight between the hours of ten and two, when the sun is at its strongest.

Toothache

A painful condition, a toothache occurs when bacteria decays through the enamel of a tooth to the dentine inside. It begins to eat the pulp, affecting the nerve center of the tooth. A visit to the dentist is necessary as soon as you develop a toothache, as left untreated, the bacteria can enter the bone and a dangerous condition known as an abscess is created.

Diet and Vitamins: To stop aggravating the ache, avoid very hot or very cold beverages and foods. To prevent decay, eliminate sugary foods and drinks from the diet.

Herbal Treatment: Put one drop of clove oil on the ache to numb the pain.

Energy Work: Use the pulling technique to remove pain from the area, and then infuse the mouth with healing energy.

General Care: Be sure to clean teeth meticulously. See a dentist as soon as possible if a toothache develops.

Urinary Problems

Urinary problems are usually quite painful and can be caused by a variety of conditions, including irritability of the lining of the bladder, blocked arteries in the kidneys, bacterial infection, prostate enlargement, stones, or tumors.

Diet and Vitamins: Avoid coffee, tea, spicy foods, citrus fruits, and alcohol. Cranberry concentrate in capsules can help alleviate an infection; take 400 mg daily. Take high-calcium foods and low-fat dairy foods to reduce bladder irritability.

Herbal Treatment: Echinacea is effective to treat inflammation and infection. Sandalwood or lavender oil in a massage or bath can help ease pain and discomfort. Dandelion heals the urinary system, and burdock strengthens the kidneys.

Energy Work: Work on the sacral and solar plexus chakra.

Color Therapy: Yellow heals the kidneys, and orange clears the urinary system.

General Care: Drink plenty of water to provide kidneys with needed fluid to flush out the system. If the problem is painful and recurring, seek professional help.

Varicose Veins

Varicose veins are a circulatory problem in which the vein distends and causes redness and unsightly marks.

Diet and Vitamins: Avoid stimulants that can cause capillaries to dilate, such as coffee, tea, chocolate, and alcohol. Drink citrus drinks, rose hip tea, and eat foods high in vitamin C. A daily supplement of vitamin C can be helpful.

Herbal Treatment: Massage gently with rose oil and chamomile oil; mix two drops of each with 10 ml (2 teaspoons) of carrier oil, and rub on legs, working from the feet toward the heart.

Hydrotherapy: Avoid excessively hot water baths, saunas, and facial steams, as very hot water can cause further damage.

Exercise: Try to exercise frequently to increase circulation.

General Care: Avoid wind and excess sunlight, as both contribute to veins. Use sunblock. With varicose veins, avoid standing for long periods of time, keep the feet elevated, and do not cross the legs, as this inhibits blood flow.

Yeast Infection

A yeast infection occurs when there is a fungal overgrowth of the *Candida albicans* organism in the stomach and, for women, in the vagina. The bacteria level in the body is normally regulated by other "friendly" bacteria, but conditions such as stress, illness, poor nutrition, and antibiotic use can cause an overgrowth of yeast. Symptoms of the infection include white discharge and itching.

Diet and Vitamins: Live yogurt helps replace levels of friendly bacteria in the body. Eliminate foods that promote yeast growth, such as sugar, sweet fruits, refined carbohydrates, mushrooms, breads, cheese, and alcohol. Eat vegetables and whole grains. Garlic should be eaten daily to kill yeast and boost the immune system. Lactobacillus acidophilus capsules resemble the natural "friendly" bacteria in the body and can be taken daily as well. Increase intake of vitamins C and B.

Herbal Therapy: Lavender or eucalyptus douches can be used. Tea tree oil can be applied topically as an antifungal agent. A peeled garlic clove can be wrapped in a thin layer of gauze and inserted into the vagina for a few hours to promote healing.

Color Therapy: Purple fights infection.

General Care: Avoid perfumes in the bath; dip a tampon in natural yogurt and insert into vagina for an hour to alleviate itching; avoid intercourse during an infection to prevent passing it on to your partner.

References and Resources

Bach, Edward. *The Twelve Healers and Other Remedies*. England: C. W. Daniel Co, Ltd., 1933.

Bagnell, Oscar. *The Origin and Properties of the Human Aura*. New York: University Books, 1970.

Becker, Robert O. *Cross Currents: The Perils of Electropollution, The Promise of Electromedicine*. Los Angeles: Jeremy Tarcher, 1991.

Brennan, Barbara A. *Hands Of Light*. New York: Bantam, 1988

Bricklin, Mark. *Rodale's Encyclopedia of Natural Home Remedies*. Pa.: Rodale Press, 1982.

Campbell. Neil A. *Biology: Third Edition*. Calif.: Benjamin/Cummings Publishing Company, Inc., 1993.

Erichsen-Brown, Charlotte. *Use of Plants for the Past 500 Years*. Ontario: Breezy Creek Press, 1979.

Gallert, Mark L. *New Light on Therapeutic Energies*. London: James Clarke & Co. Ltd., 1966.

Grad, Bernard. "Some Biological Effects of the 'Laying on of Hands': A Review of Experiments with Animals and Plants." *Journal of the American Society for Psychological Research*. Vol. 59, no. 2, 1965.

Haas, E. M., M.D. *Staying Healthy With Nutrition*. Calif.: Celestial Arts, 1992.

Hahnemann, Samuel. *The Chronic Diseases, Their Specific Nature and Homeopathic Treatment.* New York: W. Radde, 1845.

Hay, Louise, L. *You Can Heal Your Life.* Calif.: Hay House, Inc., 1984.

Hyman, J. W. *The Light Book.* New York: Ballantine Books, 1991.

Kabat-Zinn, J. *Full Catastrophe Living: Using the Wisdom of your Body and Mind to Face Stress, Pain, and Illness.* New York: Delacorte Press, 1990.

Krieger, Dolores. *Therapeutic Touch: How to Use Your Hands to Help Heal.* New York: Simon & Schuster, 1979.

Krochmal, Connie. *Guide to Medicinal Plants of the U.S.* New York: New York Times, 1973.

Louria, Donald B. *Your Healthy Body, Your Healthy Life.* New York: MasterMedia Limited, 1989.

Moyers, Bill. *Healing and the Mind.* New York: Doubleday, 1993.

Pao, E. M., and S. Mickel. "Problem Nutrients in the United States." *Food Technology.* Sept. 1981.

Palaiseul, Jean. *Grandmother's Secrets.* New York: G. P. Putnam's Sons, 1974.

Roos, P. A. "Light and Electromagnetic Waves: The Health Implications." *Journal of the Bio-Electric-Magnetics Institute.* Vol. 3, no. 2, Summer, 1991.

Voisin, Andre. *Soil, Grass and Cancer.* New York: Philosophical Library, Inc., 1959.

Weed, Susan S. *Healing Wise.* New York: Ash Tree Publishing, 1989.

Westlake, Aubrey T. *The Pattern of Health: A Search for a Greater Understanding of the Life Force in Health and Disease.* London: V. Stuart, 1961.

Wrench, G. T. *The Wheel of Health.* New York: Schocken Books, 1972.

Index